Continuing Cooperative Development

Continuing Cooperative Development

A Discourse Framework for
Individuals as Colleagues

Julian Edge

Ann Arbor

THE UNIVERSITY OF MICHIGAN PRESS

Copyright © by the University of Michigan 2002
All rights reserved
Published in the United States of America by
The University of Michigan Press
Manufactured in the United States of America
♾ Printed on acid-free paper

2005   2004   2003   2002   4   3   2   1

A CIP catalog record for this book is available from the British Library.

U.S. CIP applied for.

ISBN 0-472-08823-8

To the four edges of my world:
Cyril, Vera, Ingrid, and Karolina

Acknowledgments

I wrote most of this book during the months of October, November, and December 2000, a period of sabbatical leave for which I thank my colleagues in Aston University's Language Studies Unit. The work reported in chapter 10 was supported by a travel grant from the Aston Modern Languages Research Foundation, for which I am grateful.

My thanks to Earl Stevick for putting me in touch with the late Dick Evans, and to Dick for suggesting the possibility of contacting the University of Michigan Press with regard to this project. At UMP, my thanks to Kelly Sippell for her immediate, unwavering, and constructively critical enthusiasm for the book, also to the editorial team for their tireless and sensitive work with my version of our shared language. Thanks to Bill Johnston for his comments on the manuscript and to Ingrid Edge for the photographs. Faults that remain after so much good help are truly my own.

Much of the text was written to the music of Keith Jarrett, evoking in me thoughts of the individual spirit pushing on, and of the Mingus Big Band, declaiming the joyful strength of the cooperative. My gratitude to all those who make the music.

The cover photograph is of a Chinese flask given to me by my friend and colleague, Keith Richards. The tiny paintings on the different sides are similar but not identical, and the incidence of shadow and light also affects exactly what one can see. This image has become a working metaphor for our efforts in cooperative development. The aim of Understanding is to put aside all thoughts of what you can see on your side of the flask, the better to become aware of what the Speaker can see. The aim of the Speaker is to work to see more. Thanks again, Keith.

Finally, in a larger scenario, my sincere gratitude to all those who have joined in with this work and made it their own. We continue.

Contents

Introduction

The title of this book, *Continuing Cooperative Development,* has three resonances for me. First, it emphasizes the fact that the type of professional development that the book seeks to enable will always remain an ongoing proposition. There is no destination as such; the goal is to continue developing. Second, developments in the style of nonjudgmental discourse that the book introduces are currently continuing in various countries and contexts, some of which are represented here by guest authors. Third, the book continues my own professional development, drawing as it does on my earlier book, *Cooperative Development* (1992).

One thing is surely clear: the intervening ten years have seen a shift in the field of TESOL away from the idea of the teacher "using a method," or "applying a theory." The idea of teachers responsively and responsibly investigating their professional contexts in order to develop personal understandings and shared theorizations of their work has become much more accessible and mainstream than it was, even if it remains just as demanding for those who want to pursue these goals. *Continuing Cooperative Development* aims to mitigate these demands and to support such a creative, exploratory approach.

I have completely revised the earlier text and made some adjustments to the design of cooperative development itself, working in ideas that I have learned along the way. In addition, there are many more examples here of authentic exchanges set in situations in which this style of work has been used on specific projects. I have also introduced a range of new tasks that have proved successful over the years. Anyone who would like to access the old activities, which remain equally valid and useful, can download them from: <**www.les.aston.ac.uk/lsu/staff/je/CD/**>.

In addition, I have found that my earlier ideas have transcended their initial teacher-to-teacher, pairwork mode and have opened up a style of group development that can both support individual development and have a powerfully positive effect on the level of collegiality available in the workplace. This group strength can, in turn, be used to invite in visitors to share at least an outsider's experience of what such collegiality can mean in terms of potential for individual and institutional development. I believe that we can see here the bases of yet more beginnings.

In terms of presentation, I have once again relied on the intelligence of the reader to recognize that one can be serious without expressing that seriousness in a formally academic style. The main body of the book, therefore, proceeds with a minimum of references and acknowledgment, while chapter 12 picks up these obligations and takes some of the argumentation further.

I have looked for a quotation to open this book more inspirational than the one I used before. On reflection, I am quite happy to say that I have failed to find one. It's still Bob Marley, 1980:

None but ourselves can free our minds.

Part 1
In Preparation

I set out in chapter 1 to identify the readership I hope to address, to introduce myself, and to express the common purposes that I hope have been instrumental in bringing us together in the first place.

Chapter 2 then lays out a set of basic values and attitudes that underpin the overall approach to professional self-development presented in the book, before closing with an overview of how the rest of the book is organized.

Chapter 1 People, Perspectives, and Purposes

Who Is This Book For?

I have written this book for people who teach. Whether you teach young children or doctoral students, somewhere in-between or somewhere else altogether, is not for me the issue. This book contains data from all these scenarios. I want to link up with what it is that some of us have in common: *a readiness to invest a little more of our time and energy than we are paid for.* We do so in an effort to develop a style of teaching, and, more than that, of being a teacher, that is coherent with our sense of who we are and that is satisfying for our students and for ourselves.

My own professional field is Teaching English to Speakers of Other Languages (TESOL). Although the kind of work introduced in this book is not specific to TESOL, it is from TESOL and allied fields that my examples are taken and with which I expect most of my readers to be engaged. I hope you will allow me to address you directly.

I expect that you are probably not a committed disciple of a specific "one-method-fits-all" approach to language teaching, because you have noticed, both from your experience and from your reading, that learners develop their language abilities in different ways. You recognize that these differences are influenced by a host of features, including age, prior knowledge of other languages, national and educational culture, social context, various forms of motivation and aspiration, individual styles of perception and evaluation beyond conscious control, as well as the conscious deployment of natural aptitudes and learned strategies.

You have probably also made the connection between these frequently noted facts about the individuality of learners and the less frequently made point that teachers are also individuals-in-context. Just as it makes no sense to expect all learners to be at their best when following an imposed set of prearranged steps, it is equally unconvincing to suggest that teachers will each be at their best if they all follow the same routines. It would be inconsistent to the point of incoherence to insist on respect for the contextualized, individual processes of the learner if one were not prepared to show equal respect for the contextualized, individual processes of the teacher.

You probably do not want me to exaggerate this point. Of course there are common factors involved, general principles arising from the nature of language and human learning, that will underpin all our efforts. On that basis, you will find it reasonable to say that the best language learner that I can be will behave in some ways similarly to and in some ways differently from the best language learner that you can be. And the best language teacher that I can be will behave in some ways similarly to and in some ways differently from the best language teacher that you can be.

I would like to say that it is the space between our common humanity and our individual, contextualized differences that constitutes the territory of our potential development as teachers. It is exactly this space that I want to explore. It's a big country.

If you agree with me that the discourse of individualization that we hear is often rather one-sided, then we may also agree on a parallel between this and the frequently voiced requirement that teachers be engaged in continuing professional development. That is to say, you will have noticed, with some sense of irony, the contradictions between this demand and others: the way, for example, in which society insists that teachers should all be using the "best methods"; the way in which everyone has an opinion about what these best methods are; the way in which employers like to pay teachers only for hours spent teaching; and the way in which politicians are much more sympathetic toward teachers' needs when they are in opposition than when they are in power.

Despite these ironic observations, however, you are not really attracted by the easy pleasures of cynicism. You are sympathetic to the idea of working on your own professional development, and if you discovered an appropriate kind of satisfaction in such work, you probably would find the extra time and energy to make the effort required. You do not want to become involved in abstract theorizing, but nor are you (any longer) totally satisfied with "*it works*" as the ultimate motivation for and justification of the way in which you spend your professional life.

And beyond a desire to increase the effectiveness of your teaching in technical or procedural terms, you are probably also attracted by the idea that there is a potential for connection between professional development and personal development. If you can become more aware of your own aptitudes, preferences, and strengths and use them in your teaching, you might not only develop your own best style of teaching you might also develop as the type of person that you want to be.

You may feel a little nervous about that last proposition, but your mind is not closed to it. You would probably want to agree that teaching has a basis in certain values (again with a potential to differ in different circumstances) and that teachers who embody these values in the way they teach, like anyone else who embodies their values in the way they treat other people, have a kind of coherence about their lives that is admirable as well as effective.

You may have an intuition—and you may know some examples of this phenomenon or be familiar with the research exploring it (e.g., Huberman 1993)—that some people move along through a career in teaching with more overall satisfaction than others and also come to retirement with a very different attitude about how they spent their lives. Was it more or less a waste of time, battling with ungrateful people who never realized how hard you worked? Or was it a pretty interesting way to spend a working life, leaving you with the feeling that you had made some kind of a contribution? The difference can be decisive in a person's life, and the clearest single indicator of which outcome is more likely is the extent to which teachers, after initial training and with competence achieved through experience, continue to develop their teaching in small-scale ways that respond to features of their own context.

If you're still reading, and if you recognize a person here that you can relate to, then I believe we may have interesting work to do together.

I have addressed most of my comments so far to experienced ESOL teachers. But if you are just starting out in TESOL or are taking an initial training course, I believe that this work can also be of use to you, because an involvement with continuing self-development is something to begin as soon as possible. There are skills here to be learned that will stand you in a good stead during your course of study, as well as in your workplace thereafter.

I sincerely hope and believe that this work will speak to teacher-educators, for two different reasons: first, because teacher-educators are also teachers and need to be demonstrating, through their own example, a commitment to ongoing professional development; second, because if teacher-educators find the approach taken in this book useful for themselves, they might want to show their course participants how it works, as I do mine. But please note here: the approach taken in this book depends on equal-to-equal, peer relationships. It does not offer an approach to teacher training or education, any more than it offers an approach to TESOL methodology.

Is this book relevant to researchers? It is if you are interested in the processes and the facilitation of teacher development or in the relationship between thought and language or in the analysis of genuine discourse data that makes claims about how we can influence both our thinking and the collegiality of our relationships via the conscious choices we make in our use of language. But one warning here, too: this is meant not so much as a book *about* teacher development as a book *for* teacher development. To say this is already to begin an argument about what we mean by educational research and what we see as its appropriate outcomes, but I'm not going to pursue that argument here. Well, not in detail, but let me say two things. First, although you can certainly comprehend what is in this book by reading it, you cannot properly understand what I have to tell you without involving yourself in at least some aspect of the experience that the book frames for you. Second, and as the other side of the same coin, this work is of particular use to action researchers.

What about people in managerial positions? If you see it as a part of your mission to facilitate the continuing professional development of your workforce, but you are not sure what to do apart from organizing occasional visiting speakers, this book offers a disciplined framework that teachers (and administrators) can be invited to try out and report back on. It has a clear program of tasks toward the acquisition of specified skills that can, in turn, be used to pursue locally specified goals. In-house evaluation will tell you to what extent the desired outcomes are being achieved.

That is my wide angle on the readership I seek. Let me now finish this section by saying that, no matter how much I might wish it to be otherwise, this book is not for everyone, not even inside my intended core audience. I have been working in this area for too long to want to kid myself now. How could it be for everyone? I want to introduce you to a particular way of working on your own development. So much of what I have said so far turns around the idea that no single way of being a teacher can be right for everyone. That same stricture must apply to my work and to this book.

Is this particular way of use or interest to you? So far, I have described some aspects of the readers for whom I have written. Do you feel addressed? If you are still undecided, I hope you can take the time to read the next brief section, in which I sketch a couple of my perceptions regarding our professional situation in these interesting times.

Where We Are Now

This section is important to me because I think that we have suffered quite a lot in TESOL from the stream of new directions that have been pointed out to us over the years as general themes. I offer a personal selection since 1969:

*There's no point in teaching **about** language. Teach the sentence patterns; never mind about vocabulary in the early* *stages. Don't let people make mistakes. Never use L1. Language form is sterile; teach through situations. Situations are not transferable; teach functions. Functions are not systematic enough; use tasks. Teachers should talk less. Only natural acquisition counts in communication. Teacher talk is useful input. Making mistakes is necessary and helpful. Correction serves no purpose. Teach discourse organizers. Encourage self- and peer-correction. Use of L1 and translation can be positive. Teach lots of vocabulary; never mind about grammar in the early stages. Introduce longer lexical chunks. Focus on form. Raise learners' awareness* **about** *language.*

What these items have in common is that they all started not from an appreciation but from a rejection of what and how we actually were teaching—as we were, where we were, at any given time. These external models of how we should behave have not only frequently been mutually contradictory but have also invariably appeared to indicate that good teaching was somewhere else and that we needed to move toward it from whatever we were doing at that moment.

I question this attitude. Of course we want to hear about new ideas and practices, so let them keep coming, but we also need a way to proceed that is based on a recognition of where we are. We cannot sensibly set off in any direction without an awareness of where we are; even if we agree on common goals, the nature of individual next steps toward these goals must depend on our current positions. So my counterbalancing perspective on good teaching is that it is not somewhere else at all. It is right here and right there. I would say to every reader of this book that the best way for you to teach is exactly the way that you do teach, provided only that you are committed to the development of your teaching in ways that you believe to be sensitive to the needs of your students and yourself.

I realize that this is not a universally held position. The eminent teacher-educators Zeichner and Tabachnich, for example, write (1991, 2):

We do not accept the implication that exists throughout much of the literature, that teachers' actions are necessarily better just because they are more deliberate or intentional.

Well, I guess I do accept that implication. Or, at least, that must be my default expectation unless there is evidence to the contrary. As I start from the position that I can work sensitively with my colleagues and students on my own self-development, I find that I also need to extend that same respect to my peers. It may be possible to identify a case of a teacher who is deliberately and intentionally acting in ways that are demonstrably harmful to his or her students, although I personally have not come across such a teacher. If the person concerned refused to respond to compelling evidence at hand, then we would probably be looking at disciplinary procedures, but we have now come a long way from what I see as the point of my perspective, which is this:

> As well as an *external model* approach to the continuing professional development of teachers, we need an *internal growth* approach. This approach extends trust and respect to those fellow professionals who are working on their own development as educators, in context-sensitive directions that they judge to be appropriate, whether or not these directions mirror the fluctuating fashions of TESOL orthodoxy.

A complementary perception of mine in this area is that we in TESOL have learned a lot through "whole-person" approaches, in which we regard our students not simply as classroom-bound language learners but as whole people. A similar concern for teachers as whole people has not always been so apparent, but it promises to be equally fruitful and possibly quite refreshing. By definition, our main criterion for success as teachers is the achievement of our students. I do not intend to repeat this statement of the obvious throughout the book. Let me state again here that I take this to be a matter of definition: *a teacher is a person who helps others to learn.* But we should also pay attention to the stress and burnout that we see around us and insist that another major criterion for judging success in the provision of teaching is the continuing human growth of those committed to the profession.

I want to teach in ways that are coherent with the ways that I believe I should deal with people in general, allowing for the specific extra responsibilities that I have as a teacher to provide structure and evaluation. I want that sense of coherence to grow. I want to go out bigger and better than I came in.

It is because of these feelings that I began this chapter by talking about *people who teach,* rather than simply teachers. It is my way of building in a reminder that teachers are not just bundles of teaching functions to be employed in classrooms, to be assessed as more or less efficient according to politically or financially motivated criteria, and to be developed—in passive voice—as technical delivery units. I do not mean this as a naïve attack on employers and governments. I do believe that people who teach understand very well the financial and political agendas that necessarily cut across our best pedagogic efforts. My request, I suppose, is for a little more respect. My purpose is to help formulate a way of working that demands that respect and, in the worst case, enables people who teach to construct and promote their own self-respect, even in the absence of what we think of as our due from others.

I want to develop this idea of purpose a little further in the next section. I will keep it short.

What's to Be Done?

My large-scale, overall purpose is ambitious, and there is no point in being embarrassed about it. To begin with, I am interested in my development as a human being, most specifically in the terms of this book, in my identities as teacher and as colleague. I am motivated by the purpose of making a sense of growth, of *becoming,* a part of the way in which I work. I am further motivated by the idea of building collegiality on this basis, both for its own sake and because individual self-development is itself a social phenomenon.

Beyond immediate group collegiality, I have a vision of influencing the institutions in which we work to become more engaged in the processes of open, continuing development—to become *learning institutions* in the sense of institutions that learn, not only institutions where learning takes place. And I have a vision of creating an environment of openness, collaboration, and growth that will influence everyone who comes into contact with it—students, parents, politicians, and society at large.

You may have turned off at some stage along this progression. You may have come to a point at which you found the goals either unattractive in general principle or not feasible in a particular context. These are matters of individual perception and evaluation that I am content to leave to the insiders concerned. In more than thirty years of TESOL around the world, I have regularly been humbled by the space for development found by colleagues in contexts that I had thought to be intimidatingly repressive. I have, equally, been saddened occasionally by the refusal of colleagues to extend their sphere of responsibility into areas that had more or less been cleared for them.

But the issue for me now is less one of how far we can get and more one of the direction in which we want to be moving. If we know our context and we are working to embody the values that we find worthwhile, then we will be making our contribution toward the developments that we would like to see. We will also be preparing ourselves to respond to the further opportunities that present themselves should we be successful in influencing the constraints around us to move in sympathy with our direction.

If you share any part of this sense of a direction in which to move—from the individual to the societal—then you could use this book to formalize some cooperative work with colleagues toward the immediately specific enabling goals of increasing your:

- awareness of your own strengths and skills;
- appreciation of the strengths and skills of others;
- willingness to listen carefully to others;
- ability to interact positively with changes in your teaching environment;
- capacity to identify directions for your own continuing development;
- potential to facilitate the self-development of others.

My immediate purpose in writing this book is to involve as many people as I can. This is not a book of hypotheses or of theories for teachers to apply. I am reporting from experience. The experience has been interpreted and in part theorized so that I can tell it. But I am not writing only to be understood. The value of the telling has to be judged by its success in motivating more people to get involved in the experience.

I hope that you now have a view of where I stand, of the landscape that I see around me, of my intended readership, and of my purposes. If you perceive similar constraints and opportunities and share these purposes, then you may be wanting me to get on to the *so what?* of it all. What are we going to *do?* Or perhaps that notion is just a sign of my own impatient nature. I hope so, because just right now, I am convinced that our next move needs to be to clarify the concepts, values, and attitudes on which future action is to be based. I do this in chapter 2, where I also provide an overview of the rest of the book as a whole.

Welcome. We have made a start.

Chapter 2 Concepts, Values, and Attitudes

What I want to do at this point is to lay out as straightforwardly as I can the basic concepts, values, and attitudes that underlie the action that follows. There is further discussion and proper acknowledgment of sources in chapter 12.

Individuals and Colleagues

At the heart of *professional development* as I am using the term is the idea of self-development. This works on at least two levels.

First, as an individual, my development is in my own hands. In at least some important aspects of my teaching, only I can really understand what I am trying to achieve, how my efforts work out, and what I learn from them. If I follow up this opportunity for insight, I can find a sense of personal satisfaction in my work that goes beyond the occasional feeling of having had a really good lesson. Any lesson can be a part of finding out more about teaching, about learning, and about myself. And in just the same way that I say to students that their learning depends at least as much on what they do between lessons as on what we do in them, what I learn from my professional experience depends centrally on the quality of my thinking about that experience and my planning for subsequent experience. Everyone *has* experience. Not everyone *learns* very much from it. I want to take on the responsibility of doing so.

Second, as member of different schools or societies or cultures, only we have the insights of insiders into what is happening with our learners in our classrooms, how our exams influence our syllabuses, how our traditions inform our styles of learning and teaching. If we follow up this potential, it may free us from the frustration of seeing our teaching future defined by the latest method, the latest guru, or the latest coursebook.

At both levels, of course, we can go on learning from others—from in-service training courses, from visiting speakers, and from new (and old) publications. But the idea that we should go on taking ideas from others and applying them to our own situations allows us to meet only a part of our potential. To serve our own *development,* we need a way of working that encourages us to look more closely at ourselves and to work on what we find.

At the same time, this emphasis on the self doesn't mean that we should work in isolation. The isolation of the teacher is frequently what holds us back. We all too regularly limit teaching to an individual, subjective experience shared with no one. As a direct result of this, we restrict our ability to develop and we hand over to outsiders important questions about what good teaching is and how it might be assessed.

I want to investigate and assess my own teaching. I can't do that without understanding it better, and I can't understand it on my own. Here, we are close to the heart of a paradox. When I use the word *development* in this book, I always mean *self-development.* But that can't be done in isolation. Self-development requires other people: colleagues and students, in the first instance, but also possibly parents, administrators, employers, employees, and others, where appropriate. By cooperating with others, we can come to understand better our own experiences and opinions. We can also enrich them with the understandings and experiences of others. Through cooperation, we have a chance to escape from simple, egocentric subjectivity without chasing after an illusory notion of objectivity.

That last point is an important one in all areas of human endeavor, and it bears a moment's reflection, not to say a little repetition. We are used to hearing the word *objectivity* in a positive sense. In its meaning of *fairness* and *lack of prejudice,* we shall want to hold on to its positive connotations. But the word is also used to evoke a sense of *truth* and *reality*—what *really* happened—and it is this usage that sometimes gets in our way. Let us explore this claim a little.

If I have a one-to-one conference with a student about a piece of writing and we both come away dissatisfied, it is likely that we will tell different stories about what happened. She might say that I was insensitive and made no real effort to appreciate the work she had done. I might say that she was inflexible and made no real effort to learn from what I was trying to tell her. I don't believe that I was insensitive. She doesn't believe that she was inflexible. If we had a tape recording of the meeting, we would have something very like an objective (if incomplete) record of the things that were said, and this could indeed be helpful to us in our efforts to improve our communication with each other. But it would not provide objective evidence of (in)sensitivity or (in)flexibility. We might both be able to listen to the tape and say, "You see!?!" as though we had proved something, but all we would be doing is reinforcing our original, subjective responses. And these subjective responses are what is important in any exchange. There is no important meaning other than the meanings that the people involved in an exchange construct with each other. There is no *objective* truth that we could get to if only our unfortunate humanity did not get in the way.

So the best that we can do in terms of understanding our various situations is to realize that we have a subjective understanding—that other people's understandings may well differ from ours—and then to try to bring these different understandings out into the open. When we collaborate with other people, then our goal should be *intersubjectivity.*

All that we have said so far locates this work somewhere in the broad tradition of the responsive teacher, the reflective practitioner, the teacher-researcher, or the teacher as action researcher. And this *is* the broad tradition with which this work is allied.

At this point, however, I want to invite you to take up a very unusual stance inside that tradition. This stance is what makes this work different and as exciting as it is to some of us.

I need people to work with, but I don't need people who want to change me and make me more like the way they think I ought to be. I need people who will help me see myself clearly so that I can make my own evaluations. To make this possible, I need a distinct style of working together with other people so that each person's development remains in that person's own hands. This type of interaction will involve learning some new rules for speaking, for listening, and for responding in order to cooperate in a disciplined way.

This mixture of awareness raising and disciplined discourse is what I call *cooperative development.* Cooperative development (CD) is a way of working together with one or more colleagues in order to develop as a person who teaches in your own terms.

Here then, no teacher-training or teacher-education element is involved, in the sense that these imply a difference in status among people working together. CD is a way of cooperation among equals. Teachers cooperate in order to work on individual (self-)development. That is what this is all about.

Think about the people you work with. Who do you trust, or who could you come to trust, enough to want to share your thoughts and ideas with them? Who would you be prepared to invite into your class now and again to watch you teach? Not so that they could evaluate your teaching, but so that they would understand more of what you mean when you talk about your teaching.

Work together with the ideas here, and see if they can work with you. After a while, you may find that you develop a cooperative style of your own. If you find a way to cooperate and develop that suits you, whatever the details of that cooperation are, this book will have achieved its purpose.

Please make sure that you at least talk to one or two people about these ideas. Of course you'll want to read the book before you commit yourself to anything, but you can't get the most out of the book only by reading it. You need to think about becoming involved in active cooperation with at least one colleague. And now would be a good time to think about putting in some preparation for that.

Learning and Knowing

In the previous section, I refer to how we can learn from books and experts and to how we can learn from our experience. These are two different ways of learning, and I believe that they produce different types of knowledge.

The former type of learning is a mainly cognitive process that produces *intellectual comprehension.* I have this kind of knowledge of how a lightbulb works, of why millions must starve every year on our rich planet, of arguments in favor of neurolinguistic programming techniques.

The latter type of learning involves at least as much of an emotional process that produces *experiential understanding.* I have this kind of knowledge of how to help mature students get involved in action research, of how it feels to be called "Daddy," of making decisions when being threatened at gunpoint.

I do not want to get too tied up in giving new technical meanings to everyday words, so I am not going to continue to use *comprehension* and *understanding* in this differential way. But I hope that this distinction between intellectual learning and experiential learning, between intellectual knowing and experiential knowing, is an acceptable one.

If you think about teacher-education programs in general and about in-service programs in particular, you might agree that one of their major problems is incompatibility between intellectual learning and experiential knowledge. That is to say, it sometimes seems that what we are told by a teacher-educator or learn from a book just does not gel with what we know to be true from our own experience. It is very difficult to bring the two forms of learning and knowledge together.

To make progress on this front, we need to turn to a third dimension of learning and knowing, a dimension that is not sufficiently recognized in educational systems. It is easy to accept the idea that we learn from experience and from other people. It is now time to remind ourselves of a converse and equally true principle:

> We learn by speaking, by working to put our own thoughts together so that someone else can understand them.

A lot of what we think we know is a jumble of unexamined information and feelings. When I try to put my thoughts into a coherent shape, as I have to do if I am going to communicate them to someone else, I often find that my ideas are less clear than I thought they were. And I find that my opinions are not always as solidly founded as I might wish they were. I find, then, that my ideas need developing, that my plans need sharpening up.

There is another, more positive angle on this experience. Sometimes it is exactly when I am trying to formulate my ideas that I see properly for the first time just exactly how they do fit together. By exploring my thoughts, I discover something new. That *something new* may well be the basis for a new plan of action that will move me along in an interesting direction.

Finally, it is in my attempts to express myself—to express my *self*—that I bring together my intellectual knowledge and my experiential knowledge in a way that obliges me to fuse the two into one person's integrated statement: mine. This is an enormously empowering move, for reasons that I find strikingly captured by the Canadian philosopher Charles Taylor (1985, 36):

> *Articulations are not simply descriptions. On the contrary, articulations are attempts to formulate what is initially inchoate, or confused, or badly formulated. But this kind of formulation, or reformulation does not leave its object unchanged. To give a certain articulation is to shape our sense of what we desire or what we hold important in a certain way.*

Experience and book learning can drift along in their separate ways indefinitely, but a serious attempt to articulate an individual opinion or position will bring the two together. And when I have made the statement that brings together my intellectual comprehension and my experiential understanding, I shall also have a much clearer idea of what I need to do next, whether that means acting in the world of experience or reading another book. Even more than that, by making myself aware of that next step, I have created an obligation to take it. I have taken responsibility.

On a lighter note, there is an old joke in which someone says, *"How do I know what I think until I hear what I say?"* What I mean by cooperative development obliges us to smile and take that joke seriously.

You can probably see from the emphasis I have put on the importance of expressing oneself to someone else that the role of the cooperating colleague, or colleagues, comes in here. So at this stage let us think of one teacher as the Speaker and a colleague as the Understander. By making every effort to Understand the Speaker, the Understander assists the Speaker's development. The role of the colleague in cooperative development is to help the Speaker develop the Speaker's own ideas by clarifying those ideas and following where they lead.

Let us be quite clear about this: I have nothing against a healthy exchange of opinions, nothing against passing on a bit of advice, and nothing against someone showing me how to do something. All these have a role to play in being a teacher and being a colleague. But these are not the processes that we are involved in here. I am suggesting a deliberately different way of behaving, of speaking, and of listening. This way of behaving requires a lot of discipline, because it is different from our usual ways of interacting. Cooperative development is carried out in the roles of Speaker and Understander for agreed-upon periods of time or until participants agree to stop. The roles can then, of course, be exchanged.

This form of cooperation will not be what we think of as a *natural* interaction, but that's because *natural* is a misleading word. In the next section, we shall spend a little time thinking about usual forms of interaction and then go on to suggest some changes toward the purposes we have in mind.

What we have established in this section is the importance of three ways of learning:

- through our intellect;
- through our experience;
- through articulation.

Cooperative development focuses on the power of learning through articulation.

As you think over what you have just read, it would be useful to take a little time to supply your own examples of what you have learned intellectually; what you have learned through experience; and perhaps also what you have learned by articulating your ideas and emotions, possibly to a friend or a journal. As you think of these examples, you will note that it is not possible to keep the categories separate. There are differences operating, but they affect each other. I do not mean to suggest that we have watertight categories here, just that it is useful to note that different weightings do make a difference. So try to formulate for yourself learning experiences that you have had in these different dimensions. Does this differentiation ring true for you?

Ways of Interacting

When two people sit and talk together, certain norms are followed. This isn't usually a conscious matter. Nor is it natural. It is social. The norms are learned as a part of growing up in a particular speech community. In conversations and discussions in any culture, there are subconsciously operating rules about individual contributions and about how one is going to fit one's own contributions into the interaction. There is plenty of room for individual variation inside these norms, and such variation is part of the basis for some people being referred to as dour, hesitant, talkative, pushy, bossy, or downright rude.

If we think of a conversation in terms of space for ideas and talk, two people will usually share the space between them on a roughly equal basis. How equal will depend on such individual differences as we have mentioned above, on differences in knowledge, and on a shared idea of what is polite. Roughly speaking, we might think of a **conversation** as being like the first illustration on page 23.

In a more competitive interaction, such as a **discussion**—to say nothing of an argument—the point is usually not so much to understand what the other person has to say as to win. And here, of course, the stronger ideas, or those put forward most successfully, will tend to take up more space. See the second illustration.

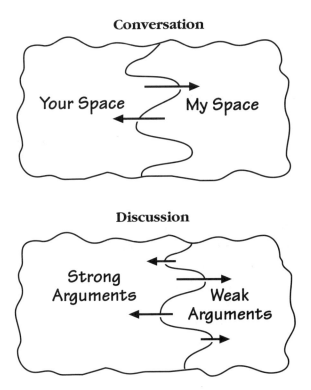

Such competitive behavior is highly prized and praised in the educational culture in which I grew up, being seen as indicative of the desired critical thinking. We might want to call this *competitive development,* in the sense that it is undeniably the case that one's mental processes can be sharpened and one's ideas developed in this kind of exchange, through an intellectual version of the survival of the fittest.

There is a downside, however, as there usually is when we stop noticing something, when we come to think of it as natural. Tannen 1998 has documented the pervasive extent of this *argument culture* in the United States and Britain, at least. Tannen draws our attention to the way in which news programs on radio or television will, as a matter of course, investigate a topic by inviting proponents of opposing views to battle it out. We have legal systems committed not to the discovery of what actually happened in a case but to the adversarial clash of lawyers on a win/lose basis. A great deal of domestic falling out is caused by a desire to come out on top, to have the last word, to be the one who was right all along, even if that involves concealing one's mistakes.

Let me risk an analogy here. When you are driving a car, you have to give a certain amount of attention to your rearview mirror. If you should ever get yourself into a situation where someone is trying to overtake you and you do not want them to overtake you, you have to give even more attention to that mirror. That seems natural. Let us hope you make a success of staying in front. But with the best will in the world, we would not be likely to describe this situation as ideal in terms of your ability to pay maximum attention to where you are going or of your being alert to the possibility of preferable alternative routes, certainly not routes that might even lead you to reconsider your destination.

By the same token, when you are engaged in a discussion, if some of your attention is devoted to shoring up your argument, some to predicting where the next attack will come from, some to implementing your own offensive strategy, some to watching out for tactical opportunities, some to ensuring a safe retreat if necessary, and some to making sure that you don't make any social blunders while you are engaged in this exchange, then your brain is awash with all the chemicals essential to those processes. But with the best will in the world, we would not describe this situation as ideal in terms of your ability to pay maximum attention to where you are going or of your being alert to the possibility of preferable alternative routes, certainly not routes that might even lead you to reconsider your destination.

Nor would we want to say that you are best placed to pay maximum attention to the potential of where your interlocutors want to go. You are certainly not helping them stay alert to the possibility of preferable alternative routes that might lead them to reconsider their destination.

The central idea of cooperative development is that we should set aside some time, just a little time, on a regular basis, in which we consciously change the rules of engagement. Whatever rules you are used to, I am asking you to try suspending them. What I want to introduce is a new set of norms for face-to-face interaction—not a complete set of rules, of course, but enough to shape a way of interacting with a colleague that seems particularly useful when the aim is to encourage independent self-development. One person Speaks in order to develop. The other person Understands—which is a lot more than just listening—in order to support that development.

In cooperative development, the Understander deliberately sets out to make as much space as possible for the Speaker while at the same time actively working to help the Speaker use that space creatively. In the terms of our previous illustrations, we might present an image of cooperative development something like this:

Cooperative Development

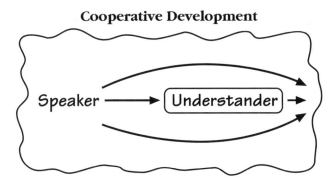

The collaborating colleague's entire purpose is to Understand, in a deep and rich sense that we shall investigate further, because of the growth that can arise from the experience of being Understood. Cooperative development depends totally on the idea of an agreement between two people to work together for a certain period of time according to rules that they both understand and agree on. As their work together continues, they may want to renegotiate the rules, but common understanding and agreement remain essential.

We shall soon look at the details of this new style of discourse, but we need to begin with some underlying attitudes on which the rules of exchange are based. Without the underlying attitudes, the forms would be meaningless. The three principles that I list below entail qualities that the interaction between Speaker and Understander must have for cooperative development to take place.

These, too, have to be talked about by the colleagues concerned until they agree on how these principles function for them.

Underlying Attitudes

In this section, I want to describe the attitudinal foundation of co-operative development as a form of discourse designed to further a certain style of inquiry and growth. These ideas are taken directly from the work of Carl Rogers, and I would like to begin with a fundamental proposition of his (Rogers 1992, 28):

> *I would like to propose, as a hypothesis for consideration, that the major barrier to mutual interpersonal communication is our very natural tendency to judge, to evaluate, to approve or disapprove, the statement of the other person, or the other group.*

The most important characteristic of the discourse of cooperative development is that the Understander makes every effort to avoid this natural tendency to judge, and the Speaker knows that.

The nonjudgmental nature of this discourse is built, in turn, on three underlying principles that I am going to characterize under the headings of **respect, empathy,** and **sincerity.** I have to make this point about definition, because we are once again in the realm of giving unusual meanings to everyday words. In this work, respect, empathy, and sincerity form a mutually defining set of terms, in the sense that each one draws a part of its meaning from the totality of what they all mean together.

Colleagues have to agree on the meaning of this set of terms in order to be able to work together as Speakers and Understanders. On the basis of this agreement, they can each take on their different responsibilities.

Respect

First, the Understander accepts the Speaker's decision as to what should be talked about and worked on. You may see a class of mine and think that I really need to work on the way I use pair-work. But if I want to work on how I correct pronunciation, you accept that decision out of respect for my judgment about where I can best develop right now.

Second, the Understander accepts what the Speaker has to say and accepts the Speaker's evaluations, opinions, and intentions without judging them according to the Understander's knowledge or values. As Speaker, you may want to talk about a better way than you now have of allowing class time for student correction of written work. I may have already tried letting students correct written work in class and may be quite convinced that it is a complete waste of time. But as Understander, I must put my experiences aside and accept the validity of your hopes and aims. We are working for the development of the Speaker's ideas. The Speaker needs to feel that these ideas can be pursued safely as they start to flow, without their being attacked because they show some weakness to someone else or because someone else has other views.

By the same token, my respect for your ideas also excludes my approving of them. I may be firmly convinced of the importance of having students correct written work in class. This conviction I also put aside. I may be considered by some to be rather an expert on the organization of student correction of written work in class, but I must sincerely attempt to see what the Speaker articulates from the perspective of the Speaker, who might not—in fact, probably cannot—be meaning quite what I would and might have come to a particular position for reasons very different from mine.

When I work as an Understander, I am called on to extend respect for the development of the Speaker on a different plane from agreement or disagreement. My *agreement* is not requested; my positively meant *acceptance* is.

This is not easy. Let us be clear: this book is not about doing something easy. It is about doing something exciting. Development of the type we are seeking takes place when Speakers recognize their own real views and then see something in those views that they wish to investigate or to take further or to change.

This is not easy, either. As Speaker, I shall be trying to push my own thinking further by the power of its own momentum, by an act of will and motivation, by public intellectual endeavor at the cutting edge of my own current capacity, affectively supported by the knowledge that it is acceptable for me to get things wrong while I try things out because I have been given an evaluation-free zone to work in. In this zone, I not only am *able* but am *obliged* by our agreement to explore beyond what I know in search of my next-step discovery. This is very hard. One cannot do it for too long, but then most people never *ever* get the chance.

Furthermore, it is in the Speaker's sincere commitment to do this work, and in the Speaker's acceptance that the Understander cannot offer evaluation, agreement or disagreement, approval or disapproval, suggestions, opinions, or advice, that the Speaker's respect for the Understander is expressed, thus making the nonevaluative respect that we are describing mutual and reciprocal between both participants.

Empathy

It is not enough for the Understander to respect the Speaker's right to hold different views on teaching or to teach classes in different ways than the Understander would. In order to assist the Speaker's development, the Understander has to try to see things as if through the Speaker's eyes, to understand the classroom, the learning, and the teaching according to the Speaker's frames of reference. Moreover, although I have just emphasized difference, when the Speaker's views appear to coincide with the Understander's, it demands at least as much effort to achieve empathy rather than to fall back into the comfort of one's own positions.

Empathy is a very difficult concept. I find one helpful perspective in the following comment from George Miller (in Elbow 1986, 154):

> *In order to understand what another person is saying, you must assume it is true and try to imagine what it might be true of.*

So, this is not sympathy, which I take to mean my feeling emotion for and about someone else. Nor is it identification—my vicariously sharing someone else's experience and emotion as if I were them. I have come to think that empathy is best described in terms of what one does and to what purpose. When I successful empathize with someone, it is me, remaining me, recognizing what they see the way they see it and recognizing what they feel the way they feel it so well that I, as myself, can show it to them so well that they recognize it in turn.

Through an act of acceptance and imagination, the Understander enters the world of the Speaker. As the Understander attempts to empathize with the Speaker, the Understander may have to ask for more and more clarification, and the Speaker will work to make what is said as clear as possible. The more the Speaker feels able to reveal, the greater the sense of trust and empathy that can be established by a sensitive Understander. And so the process feeds itself. As Speaker, it is when I can see and hear my own position clearly in a supportive environment that I am best placed to evaluate whether or not I like what I see and best placed to judge where I want to go next. This is the force of Rogers and Freiberg's observation (1994, 288)

One way of assisting individuals to move toward openness to experience is through a relationship in which we are prized as a separate person, in which the experiencing going on within is empathically understood and valued.

As well as working to grasp the content of what is said, the Understander works to be sensitive to attitudinal and emotional tone. For example, it may be important that you understand that I do not get involved in team-teaching. But if you Understand from what I tell you that I actively dislike team-teaching, we might have something more interesting to talk about.

For example, is it true that I feel this way? Is *active dislike* the best expression to describe my feelings? Why is that so? What exactly do other people think they get from team-teaching? Do I get that from something else in my teaching? Are my students missing out? Is it time I tried team-teaching a class (again)?

The quality of empathy, then, is one that the Understander tries to develop in cooperation with the Speaker. It is something we aim to get better at, rather than something we expect to achieve totally. It is also something easier to experience than to explain.

Sincerity

The quality of sincerity in this mutually defining set of terms refers to the genuineness of the respect and empathy that the Understander offers. According to the previous two subsections, the Understander aims to accept what the Speaker says without evaluating or judging it in the Understander's terms; this is a matter of respect as we have defined it. Furthermore, the Understander aims to empathize with the Speaker and to apprehend as fully as possible the Speaker's perception and evaluation of whatever is being worked on.

So if I am telling you about how and why I make students memorize lists of words each night, and you do not think that this is a useful activity at all, it is your task to accept my evaluation of word lists and see their use from my perspective. I can only develop from where I am; it is your role as Understander to help me see where I am in my own light. If using word lists is such a bad idea, this will become apparent to me when I work on it. If this does not become apparent to me, you have to accept that it is not a bad idea for me or my students.

Where does sincerity come into this? Are you not being insincere, fundamentally dishonest, by not pointing out to me what you *really* think about word lists?

No. We are both consciously operating here according to a different set of rules, understood by both of us. For the agreed-upon period of the CD exchange, your role is to respect my ideas and empathize with my position.

What would be insincere would be if you only appeared to be respecting my ideas and empathizing with me in order to manipulate me. Insincerity is when you are stringing me along in order to bring me around to your way of thinking in the end, perhaps with a few well-chosen questions that will help me see the error of my ways—from your perspective.

Sincerity is when you are genuine about your respect and empathy. Sincerity involves a transparent fit between your overt actions, your statements, and your deeper motivations.

But what if, to pursue this point further, you simply cannot respect what I have to say? What if you are convinced that I am doing my students actual harm? Then we cannot work together in this mode, and that has to be made clear. It is not the case that an agreement to work with someone in CD mode means that from then on you have to accept any vile, abusive nonsense that a person might produce. What it means is that you do not pretend. It means that the extent to which you can work with a person is measured by the extent of the respect and empathy that you can sincerely offer.

So we have two polar situations to consider. In the first, the Understander has no difficulty in sincerely respecting and empathizing with the Speaker. In the second, the Understander cannot manage to offer sincere respect and empathy, which makes the type of cooperative development that we are describing here impossible. Between these two poles, the space for cooperative development is quite considerable. Here lies the Understander's struggle: to respect, to empathize, and to do both with sincerity.

> Perhaps the touchstone of the Understander's sincerity is to be found in the danger of being changed. When I sincerely offer respect and achieve empathy, I run the risk of being changed by what I Understand. It is when, and perhaps only when, I am open to that possibility that I am properly working as an Understander.

Recap

I have tried to lay out the necessary conditions of respect, empathy, and sincerity that underlie all the work reported in—and I hope enabled by—this book. Until you have experienced this work, you cannot know the amount of energy involved in it, as the Speaker works to articulate a particular future and a colleague works to Understand it into being. This energy is not lost.

To recap the central proposal: for regular, agreed-upon periods, working with a colleague or colleagues who also understand the new rules according to which we are operating, we deliberately abandon the elements of argument and exchange that make a discussion so useful. What we gain is a new experience of a space into which one person's ideas can expand in the search for a discovery that might otherwise not be made in the cut and thrust of argument.

Let me just pick up that last point again; experience has taught me that it bears some repetition. Everyone knows that ideas can be worked out through discussion. Bad ideas can be identified and improved or jettisoned; good ideas can be made even better. I am not disputing this. I argue a lot. I am even quite good at it. What I am suggesting here is that there is also another way forward, a way that does not replace discussion but that adds to our possibilities. We can, by conscious acts of discipline, enhance our discourse of exploration and discovery and add complementary avenues of growth to our repertoire of developmental opportunity.

As you are thinking about this proposal, you might also focus some attention on your everyday experience of interaction. When you are in a conversation, try to notice at what stage of listening to someone else you decide what it is you are going to say next. How long do you then spend just waiting for that other person to finish? What is the purpose of your contribution? To help that other person develop what they are saying? To add your knowledge, your experience, your opinion? To shift the focus of attention onto yourself? To score a point? To win an argument? To change the topic? To prepare the ground for something else you want to say later? To make space for someone else to speak? We are constantly speaking to achieve certain ends. Awareness offers us choice. Choice brings responsibility and also empowerment.

Overview of the Rest of the Book

We are now ready to move into action. The next part of the book introduces the scheme of self-directed professional growth called cooperative development (CD). It explains and exemplifies how the principles outlined here come to procedural life. The reading is supported by tasks, requiring the participation along with yourself or at least one, and preferably two, colleagues. I hope that you will want to do the tasks and work on the acquisition of the skills introduced. This is the experiential crux of the whole book. From that point on, if you find the work satisfying, you can take it in various directions. The book itself pursues a range of such developments.

Part 3 deals with extensions of the original one-to-one mode of cooperative development. I begin in chapter 9 with a case-study treatment of a group development (GD) approach that has evolved in my own teaching context. My colleagues and I then wanted to know if the group that worked so well for us as insiders could be put at the disposal of outsiders on a one-off basis. Chapter 10 is devoted to this work. I am subsequently joined in chapter 11 by colleagues from other contexts who report on work being done in related modes.

Part 4 is first concerned with paying dues. In the interests of a straightforwardly readable style, I have written the rest of this book without making all the acknowledgments that honesty and courtesy require. While making up for that omission in chapter 12, I also set out to situate the work we have been doing in the professional and academic context of professional development, as well as action research, in these new-millennium times.

In the final chapter, I risk taking my own thoughts out to their crumbling edge, the way a Speaker must. I then show one track that leads ahead, before pushing this text off into a possibly unfriendly, but I believe needful, environment.

Part 2
A New Discourse of Development

This is the most explicitly instructional part of the book.

An important element of what you are being invited to do is very much like learning a new language—not in the sense of new grammar and vocabulary but in the functional and communal senses of learning to do new things with language toward new ends. Some of the work is intellectual, some is emotional, but it is all social. It is all about being yourself in a different dialect, so to speak, among people who don't behave in exactly the same ways that you are used to.

Following that language-learning parallel, you won't be surprised to find that this part of the book is a mixture of concepts to understand; rules, skills, and lexical chunks to learn; and tasks to carry out.

Chapter 3 concentrates on introducing the tasks and commenting on how you might use them. The subsequent chapters take you through this introductory course in a new discourse of development. I am focusing here on cooperative development as a one-to-one style of working together because this is the way in which most people use it and because it is easier to explain for introductory purposes.

The examples of CD in use are taken from the work of TESOL professionals in various countries. I have kept individual instances anonymous, but all contributing colleagues are acknowledged in chapter 12. As many of the transcriptions throughout the book are not mine, you will notice some differences in style. I have standardized presentation to a certain extent. Also, so long as communicative authenticity is not impaired, I have favored readability over technical detail.

Chapter 3   About the Tasks

Using the Tasks

The tasks in this book are meant to provide an experiential dimension to the learning that I hope will take place. In each chapter, there are some activities that focus specifically on classroom issues and others that have a broader reference. All the tasks are meant to function in the two areas of self-awareness and cooperative interaction, which make up cooperative development.

The self-awareness work will not tell you about yourself, but it will bring you to a place in which you can start thinking about yourself. In cooperative interaction, you will be able to develop these thoughts. The interactive techniques that you learn will add up to a coherent approach for the continuation of your own professional development.

I have added comments on some tasks in chapter 12. Please do not take what I say as presuming to pronounce on what you made of the tasks, as they are all open-ended. The comments are there to acknowledge sources where appropriate and to add thoughts arising from my own experience of this work in varied contexts since 1987. I hope that these reports can serve as reference points for your own experience, interpretation, and understanding, but I strongly advise you to carry out the tasks before reading more about them.

I say in chapter 2 that cooperative development is generally carried out in the roles of Speaker and Understander, the Speaker being the person who is going to work on his or her development during any given session. I am going to continue this introduction to cooperative development essentially in this mode. For some tasks, I have also added a third (optional) role, that of Observer. The Observer is there to help with the learning, not as a part of

CD proper. The specific duties of the Observer are outlined with each task, but the general function of the Observer is to give the Speaker and Understander feedback on what has happened from a third perspective. In turn, the Observer will also be learning to become analytical in this area and to listen especially for the ways in which the Understander expresses the different moves that are being practiced. Rotating the three roles should help everyone concerned.

Whether or not you work with an Observer, but especially if you do not, it would be very helpful to record your sessions. Establishing a record of what is said is worth rubies in terms of later thinking, discussion, and consequent learning. But remember, you do have to listen to the tapes! I recommend that you do so quickly. A growing pile of cassette boxes can take on a certain threatening quality. Yes, I do speak from experience.

If there is a larger group of you who want to work together, then you might decide to read individually, move into pairs (or threes) for the tasks, and all come together for discussion. Alternatively, you might want to take turns leading the group, the leader being the person who reads the next chapter and sets up the activities, after which there is group discussion, followed by individual reading. I shall leave that to you. I am not going to make such methodological suggestions in each case.

All this talk of procedure, however, does highlight one further issue that deserves more discussion: the *artificiality* of the activities.

Artificiality

First, the activities are fundamentally artificial, because cooperative development is meant to serve the internal motivation of Speakers to work on something important to themselves. As soon as I set a task for the Speaker, I have usurped the Speaker's essential independence. And yet, without some content, how can I present my ideas to you?

What I have done is to provide initial tasks that have consistently proved to be of interest to Speakers and to be reliable vehicles for practice. I also indicate the outline of further tasks for which Speakers must provide their own content. I hope to engage what I take to be a shared belief among teachers that one can experience authentic learning via tasks that are themselves initially artificially constructed.

Second, the tasks are artificial because the Understander is asked to practice certain techniques from an initially very restricted repertoire. I see no way around this—the activities are meant to constitute a learning experience of which conscious practice is an important part. I urge you to take deliberate advantage of these tasks for the practice of the specific skills at issue. Again, I appeal to your experience as language learners and teachers. There is usually a way of carrying out a language-learning task without practicing the specific item that you have been looking at, but if the point of the exercise is to practice the present perfect tense, why not practice the present perfect tense? Probably I protest too much. You will anyway use the book exactly as you wish.

Third, the activities are artificial because they are observed. As I have already said, the purpose of using an Observer is to receive feedback and thus enhance the learning process. Although there is undoubtedly a feeling of self-consciousness connected with being observed, most people usually become accustomed and then quite oblivious to the presence of the third person after a very short period of time. Furthermore, one group of teachers in Pakistan has reported that they maintained the role of the Observer in their ongoing work, as they found that the richness of feedback enhanced their learning and development.

The effectiveness of the Observer role can be helped by sensitive positioning. The Speaker and Understander should sit so that they feel comfortable and natural when speaking to each other. This position is unlikely to be eyeball-to-eyeball. The best idea is to experiment and to talk about how different positions feel. When the Speaker and the Understander are comfortable, the Observer should take up a position that is clearly separate from them but from which the Observer can hear what is said and keep a good eye on the Understander, as this role is usually more difficult to take on in the early stages of cooperative development.

While the role of the Observer is to comment on the interaction that takes place and to elicit retrospective comments from the Speaker and the Understander, these last two should also be engaged in ongoing commentary. This feature of cooperative development is worth introducing in its own right.

Commentaries

A running commentary on the interaction that is taking place between Speaker and Understander can frequently enhance that interaction. If one participant puts something particularly well, it is encouraging if the other points this out. Thus a Speaker might say, on hearing an Understander paraphrase the Speaker's idea, "*I really like the way you put that. That's exactly what I was trying to say.*" Conversely, if one participant thinks that the interaction is going badly, it can also be helpful to say so. An Understander might say, "*I don't think that I'm getting this very clearly. I don't feel that I really Understand what you're saying this morning at all.*" Or if, as Speaker, I feel that the Understander is not letting me follow my own ideas in my own way but is more interested in introducing other ideas, I might say, "*That's interesting, but I feel that it's coming more from you than me,*" or I might just lift my hand slightly in an agreed-upon way in order to say, "*Hold off a little.*"

The quality of interaction may then become the topic of the interaction. This may appear self-defeating in the short term, but it is also a long-term investment in better communication. Such comments frequently make the particular interaction work more efficiently, and they can certainly add to the overall development of empathy in continuing cooperation.

Open Questions

Another useful generalization that we can make at this stage concerns the questions that an Understander will want to ask in order to clarify what the Speaker is saying. Except in very clear-cut cases, open questions that invite the Speaker to say more are usually more effective than closed questions between fixed options or questions that ask for a yes/no response. Closed questions tend to confront the Speaker with a choice between alternatives framed in the Understander's terms. So if I ask, "*Could you tell me a bit more about why you use translation techniques in your classes?*" I am more likely to hear what the Speaker really wants to say than if I ask, "*Do you use translation because the students find it easier?*"

It is also worth noting that while a question such as the former of this pair gives the Speaker the opportunity to expand and clarify, it does not give the Speaker confirmation of having been Understood. That is the particular strength of the response described in chapter 5 in the section entitled "Reflecting."

Silence

Finally, before we begin these activities in language toward action, it is worthwhile to think about the importance of silence in interaction between two people working together. Nothing in this area is natural; everything is social and must be thought of in its own cultural context.

The cultural background in which I grew up has little time for silence. Silence is more or less by definition a waste of time. It is also very embarrassing, and my culture has therefore developed a use of language called "small talk," which is languagelike behavior meant not to communicate but to fill up any silence that may occur when people are together.

Silence in CD interaction, however, is often where creative work is being done. We shall see clear examples of this in the data. It is usually Speakers who feel the strain as they struggle to move forward. One Speaker who has commented on this phenomenon went so far as to describe the feeling as a self-imposed threat, demanding but eventually facilitative:

If the silence could be displayed, it would be more illustrative to describe how much tension I felt....

... It was my own effort that made me come up with something concrete, even taking into consideration that there was a lot of silence and patience of the Understander required. I argue this is mainly attributed to the feeling of threat imposed on me by myself but nobody else. This feeling is the key to get me or any Speaker somewhere desired by the Speaker. It is an absolutely necessary element for the Speaker's development. Without it, you cannot get a sense of achievement.

A more gentle perspective comes in a story about the jazz musician Miles Davis, who was supposedly once criticized for not playing enough notes in his solos. He is said to have replied, "The music is the space between the notes."

I have argued that articulation is important to development, but I also believe that articulation sometimes needs silence in order to find itself. Readers who, for individual or cultural reasons, do not feel threatened by silence may have an advantage here. In the activities that follow, and in cooperative development generally, I encourage you to allow for silence, to leave others and yourself the space to sit and think—sometimes, perhaps, even the space just to sit.

Toward Action

Of course, readers can do whatever they wish with a book. I know that. And one good option is certainly to read the book through and then see if you want to get involved in the tasks.

However, writers also have certain freedoms, so please excuse me if I remind you again that while the book's intellect is in the chapters, its heart is in the tasks.

A rich and developmental understanding is brought about by articulating one's comprehension and experience to a sincerely respectful and empathic listener. I do hope that you have found a colleague or two to work with. Getting the most out of cooperative development depends on having colleagues you can rely on and trust. At the same time, cooperative development can help colleagues develop mutual trust and reliability. Start from where you are, and see where you go.

Chapter 4   Attending

The Power of the Listener

I always start a cooperative development workshop with a variant on one particular activity, and perhaps this introduction will work better if I can persuade you to try it before you read on, because then you will have your own experience to put into the mix. If I can't persuade you, then read on and imagine! (And maybe try the task with a colleague later to see to what extent your experience matches up with the report that I'm giving you.) This is a task for two or three people.

✓ Task 4.1

Individual preparation. Each of you should think back into your experience of being taught at some point in your lives. Identify a teacher of whom you have strong memories, for better or worse. Think briefly about that person, and ask yourself:

- What was it was about them that made them so memorable to me?
- Leaving aside the subject that they taught, what did I learn from them—about teaching and learning or about people?
- How did my learning come about?

Interaction. When you are ready, decide on the initial roles of Speaker and Understander (and Observer). If you are three people, one person acts as Observer and timekeeper. If not, the Speaker should put his or her watch someplace where it can be easily seen.

> *Speaker:* Tell the Understander who this teacher was that you remember, and explore your answers to the above questions. However far you get, you must stop after one minute.

> *Understander:* Don't say anything. Listen positively to the Speaker. Clear your mind of your own memories, and put your energy into making the Speaker feel well listened to for the minute that you have. You can nod, you can smile, you can "Mmm" whenever you wish, but do not actually speak. Pay full, careful, caring attention to the Speaker. This is what I mean by **Attending.**

After one minute, wherever the Speaker has gotten to, the activity has to stop.

Please carry out this part of the task now.

Speaker and Understander now exchange roles.

> *Speaker 2:* Carry out the same task that Speaker 1 did.

> *Understander 2:* Once again, say nothing. But this time, make no effort to make the Speaker feel well listened to. As Understander, do just the opposite: lean back, cross your arms, look at the ceiling. Think of impatience; think of boredom; think of frustration; check your watch. Stop the Speaker as soon as a minute is up.

Now compare notes on what each experience of being the Speaker was like.

Workshop participants have made the following comments:

Speaker 1

1. It was a very positive experience just to be listened to so carefully.
2. The time went so quickly—I had lots more to say.
3. It made me feel that what I had to say was worth listening to.
4. I started to remember other things that I wanted to say.
5. I felt awkward because I wasn't getting any feedback.

Speaker 2

1. It was horrible—I wanted to hit him!
2. I stopped because it wasn't worth carrying on.
3. My brain seized up. I couldn't think of what I wanted to say.
4. I just focused my eyes somewhere else and kept on talking.
5. It all seemed a bit artificial because I knew she was playing a part.

Even though this is, of course, a very brief and highly artificial activity, it regularly inspires a great deal of involvement and real emotion. The main point that arises for me—and it is basic to everything that follows—is the astonishing power of the listener over the speaker. Speakers who are well listened to consistently report that this listening has a positive effect on both the *quality* and *quantity* of what they have to say, in combination with a facilitating effect on their thinking and an enhancement of their feeling of self-worth. Speakers who are badly listened to regularly report just the opposite on all fronts.

Let me now pick up the other points raised. The fifth comment made by Speaker 1 draws our attention to an important initial difficulty of this work. Although the Understander has a lot to say as the role develops, it remains true that the Speaker will never receive the sort of participatory feedback that we are all socialized to expect. It is in adjusting to this change and challenge that Speakers learn to articulate their thinking into the space that the Understander helps to structure for them. The fourth comment made by Speaker 2 reminds us that we do have coping strategies; in terms of this activity, Speakers can find a way through, but it is not a way that is going to lead us far in terms of self-development. The most chilling (and only half-ironic) version of this comment that I have heard was, "Oh, I'm used to this sort of thing; I am a teacher after all." The fifth comment made by Speaker 2 relates to my earlier assertion that one can have genuine learning experiences from artificial activities. I concede that this is not always true for all people with all activities. If you didn't get much out of this one, there are some more at the end of the chapter.

Nonlinguistic Communication

Having reflected for a while on the *power* of positive listening—or Attending, as I am calling it—let us now spend some time thinking about the *style* of it. As language teachers, we know that listening is not a passive process. We also know that we send out lots of messages to the people we are with, even when we are not actually speaking. We communicate by the way in which we sit or stand, by what we do with our hands, by the expression on our face, by the way we keep or break eye contact, by the little noises or exclamations we make while someone else is talking, and in a variety of other ways of which we are not usually conscious.

This unconscious process has been likened to having another self inside us who also communicates whether we speak or not. When these two selves contradict each other, it is usually the "other" who is telling the truth. I can pretend to agree with you, and I can control my face well enough to smile at you, but I may not notice that I have clenched my fists and that my ankles are locked under the chair. The clenched fists are typically a sign of suppressed tension and the locked ankles similarly indicate that I am holding back some information or emotion. These signals may give you a truer indication of my feelings than my smile or my words.

I do not want to go too far down this road in terms of the specifics of what means what. Simplistic rules and generalizations are not what this is about. Nor do I want to suggest that we should put on some sort of pantomime of exaggerated interest, full of "Oohs!" and "Aahs!" Given that the ability we want to develop is the ability to make someone feel well listened to, my actual suggestion is twofold. First, I am suggesting that we can each improve in this area if we inform ourselves of what people have written about body language (see chap. 12). That is, we should become more aware of how qualities such as interest, negative evaluation, and impatience are signaled. Second, we should work on our awareness of how we ourselves behave (see the tasks at the end of this chapter). That is, we should learn to appear as what we are and what we wish to be. If our aim is to encourage the Speaker, but we are sending out signals of aggression or boredom, we are unlikely to succeed.

If we are sending out such signals, we need to ask whether or not they are genuine. If we are feeling aggressive, this is something we can think about and talk about with the person we are working with. Making this aggressive attitude the topic of the cooperation is more likely to help future cooperation than trying to continue with something else when the Understander is in no shape to Understand. In this case, we may need to move out of CD and discuss the situation. If sufficient trust exists between Speaker and Understander, they may want to swap roles for a while at least; the Understander may become the Speaker and explore the question, *"Why am I feeling this way at this point?"* If negativity is a recurring feature, we have to face up to the fact that none of us is compatible with everyone; we may be trying to cooperate with the wrong person.

If, on the other hand, we are unconsciously sending out signals that the Speaker interprets as signals of, say, boredom, we need to be more aware of these signals in order to remedy the situation. During one cooperative development workshop, I noticed that an Understander was staring intently at the floor while the Speaker, as far as I could tell, was becoming less and less sure of herself. I asked the Understander if she usually looked at someone who was speaking to her. *"No,"* she said, *"but I was listening very carefully."* I then asked the Speaker if she had felt well listened to. *"No!"* said the Speaker with some feeling. *"It was very difficult to keep going.*" The point of the story is that the Understander was genuinely surprised to discover that her style of attending to what the Speaker had to say was having a negative effect on the Speaker's ability to express herself. This issue becomes particularly important in cross-cultural exchanges.

While it is relatively easy to see the danger of sending out negative signals, the danger of being too positive about what we hear also has to be countered. If the Understander sometimes nods and smiles and leans forward enthusiastically in approval, this is also evaluative behavior that may well influence the Speaker. Furthermore, the withdrawal of this behavior then takes on negative overtones of its own. One can see the same effect in any class in which the teacher is reacting to student responses. If the first three responses are, "Right!" "Very good!" and "Great!" then silence after the fourth response means that it is not acceptable.

Attending relates particularly closely to the quality of nonjudgmental respect that we have already talked about. We want to let the Speaker know that we are interested; that we are not making judgments, either positive or negative; and that we are making every effort to Understand as fully as we can. Let me pick up a possible difficulty with the word *positive* here. We want to be positive in our commitment to Understand, but we are not making positive/negative value judgments of what the Speaker has to say.

Nonjudgmental acceptance means exactly what it says: equal respect for what the Speaker has to say, regardless of the opinions of the Understander.

In my own work as Understander, I like to start out sitting comfortably, with both feet on the floor, my hands in my lap, and an expression on my face that looks (I hope!) relaxed, alert, and open. As the work goes on, I let my body move, and I monitor it—as though listening to that "other person" inside me. If I notice a move such as crossing arms taking place, I take it as useful feedback. I ask myself, "*Why am I putting up this barrier? Is this significant, or am I merely randomly rearranging my body?*" I work hard to maintain my Attending throughout this process, and I move as naturally as I can back into an open position.

All this comes with experience of working in this way, of

course. The starting point for each of us is to think about how we make a Speaker feel actively and supportively listened to. Then, as we cooperate with a colleague, we can develop this ability in individual terms by talking about the quality of rapport that is building up. The following tasks aim to help you start to think about your own body and its language.

Tasks

The following activities involve silent but active listening. Please note that I am *not* suggesting that the Understander in cooperative development proper should remain silent. Simply, in these particular activities, we are focusing on nonlinguistic responses.

✓ Task 4.2

Most importantly, make an effort to observe consciously the way that people sit, stand, and move their hands, arms, and legs. Stereotypically, it is said that crossed arms and legs represent barriers that we put up when we want to block something out. This does not rule out the possibility that the person concerned is actually just cold, or waiting desperately for a chance to go to the bathroom, but still it is worth keeping the first possibility in mind.

Depending on the circles you move in, you may get the chance to notice how the complexity of both conscious and unconscious nonlinguistic communication increases dramatically when people from different social and cultural backgrounds are involved. Very little of the behavior that we are brought up with is natural; it is essentially social and acquired: what is polite in one culture may be offensive in another. In my culture, for example, it is customary for a listener to maintain eye contact with a speaker. If I am talking to you, I am perfectly free to look away for a while. But if, when I look back, you are also looking somewhere else, I assume that you are not interested in what I am saying. In other cultures, however, I know that relationships of age, gender, and status play decisive roles in establishing the appropriateness of eye contact between speakers and listeners.

So observe yourself and others. My aim is to be myself and to be as aware of myself as I can.

✓ Task 4.3

Perhaps the most important elements of body language in CD terms are what we do with our head, hands, and arms. If you were observing the Understander in these photographs, what might you infer from what you see? My comments are included in chapter 12.

✓ Task 4.4

Collect pictures of people talking to each other in which you think there are obvious comments to be made about some aspect of the body language involved. Invite colleagues to comment first, and see if your assumptions agree with theirs.

✓ Task 4.5

What do you think makes a person feel well listened to or not properly listened to? Make a list, and compare yours with a colleague's.

✓ Task 4.6

One of the surest signs of fellow feeling or affinity between two people is when they unconsciously "mirror" each other's physical position, so that one looks like a reflection of the other. Watch out for this between people who get on well together or who feel attracted to each other. We can also use mirroring in a conscious activity.

Person A leads by sitting with eyes closed and thinking in detail about some meaningful past event that evokes memories of strong feelings and/or of physical activity. **A** does not say what this event was. As with all such exercises, it is safer to concentrate on positive experiences. My examples might be:

- recalling the ups and downs of a tennis match I have recently played;
- recalling conducting a group of EFL beginners at an end-of-term party who are singing a song they learned in my class.

These are my own examples. The point is that the more involved **A** becomes, the better for the activity.

Person B sits opposite **A** and mirrors **A**'s facial expression, posture, and body movement as closely and exactly as possible. **A** keeps eyes closed so as to spare both **A** and **B** any embarrassment.

When **A** has finished, both **A** and **B** comment on what happened. **B** might like to guess at what was going on or at the emotions recalled. A third person, acting as Observer, can also be useful here in adding an external perspective on the mirroring.

In the above exercises, we have focused on nonlinguistic responses. We now want to carry the lessons we have learned into types of exchange where the Understander takes an increasingly active role.

Chapter 5   Reflecting

The Active Understander

Some of your discussion regarding the activities at the end of the last chapter might have raised the issue of whether the Understander is active or passive. Is the Understander supposed simply to sit and listen?

Certainly not. The purpose of the last chapter was to highlight the importance of making a Speaker feel well listened to. This chapter and subsequent ones will give the Understander an ever more active role. But we need to be sure we do not confuse this active role with involvement in a conversation or a discussion.

In a conversation or a discussion, you intervene in order to make space for yourself. You take part by putting forward your own opinion, referring to your own experience, arguing your own case. Or you may ask a question, based on a shared interest in your conversational partner's topic. This is a social responsibility, and if you do not fulfill it, you are not taking part. You may have felt a desire to fulfill this responsibility during the tasks at the end of chapter 4. If you kept to the rules as Understander, you may have felt a little frustration that you were not supposed to add your own contributions. After the tasks, in fact, you may have gone back to some of the things that were said by the Speaker and taken part in a more usual conversational exchange about them by making your own comments and recalling experiences of your own. In this way, you released the frustration built up by your having taken on the role of Understander.

This frustration at not being able to make your usual conversational contribution is, however, at the heart of being an Understander. As conversation, cooperative development is a disaster! In one sense, I even hope that your feeling of frustration will grow as you get involved in more activities as Understander. I hope that you will start to gain satisfaction from not releasing this frustration in a flow of your own opinions and interpretations. And as you gain this satisfaction at your increased skill level, I hope that you will begin to feel that what was frustration is starting to feel more like a form of positive, transferable energy.

This energy can be put at the service of Speakers in order to help them develop their own opinions, interpretations, and plans. Exactly how this can be done is the business of this book, as the Understander takes on an ever more active role that at the same time does not take up the developmental space of the Speaker.

The next step in the building of that role is a crucial one. If, as Understander, you can develop the ability to **Reflect,** then everything else follows.

Reflecting

As should now be clear, the central idea of cooperative development is that it is self-development. I take responsibility for deciding which aspect of my teaching, or my professional life more generally, I want to extend, revise, or move on from. In order to make the necessary evaluation of my present position, I need help in seeing it clearly.

One way in which a colleague can help me is by Attending, by listening supportively to what I have to say. A further method of helping me is when my colleague acts as some kind of a mirror in order to Reflect back my ideas in such a way that I can get a clear view of them. This sounds easy. It is not. In the same way that Attending makes demands on the Understander's respect, as we have used that term, Reflecting requires the Understander's best efforts in terms of empathy. Let us look at some examples of what I mean by Reflecting, taken from different CD sessions, in order to bring out the three main, overt, and overlapping purposes of this central Understander move: to check Understanding, to encourage progress, and to facilitate insight.

To Check Understanding

It may be that what you Reflect back to me is not exactly what I believe I said. What you thus give me is a chance to repair the faults in my communication. It may well be that it is in the area of these corrections that I will discover something more that I wish to go into. Perhaps it is exactly in this area that I was not clear in the first place, either to you or to myself.

Extract 5.1 is taken from the beginning of a session. The Understander's Reflection (11–19) seems to be a reasonable representation of what the Speaker has said (01–09), but it has in fact shifted the emphasis from the teacher's desire to develop her teaching to a need to deal with a particular class. The Reflection makes possible the Speaker's correction (20–26), which is the key to establishing the common ground (27–35) from which the Speaker can continue (36–37).

Extract 5.1

01	SPEAKER	Okay. Well, this is a bit awkward! Er, I have this class
02		on Tuesday afternoon for reading. It's not an exam
03		class, but they will have exams next year. I think
04		that there's more that I could be doing with them,
05		you know? (Understander: Mmm) I don't mean that
06		I've got a problem with them or anything like that,
07		but things are a bit flat (Understander: Uh-huh) and
08		I know that there are things in reading comprehen-
09		sion that I've never really tried, you know?
10		(Understander: Yeah) Erm . . .
11	UNDERSTANDER	Yeah, okay, just let me check that with you, where
12		we're starting from (Speaker: Yeah, sure). So, what
13		you want to work on today is the reading classes you
14		have with your Tuesday afternoon group. You feel a
15		bit hesitant about it, because you don't want to give
16		the impression that there is any big problem here,
17		but you do want to go through how you teach the
18		class and maybe work on trying out some changes.
19		Is that about right?
20	SPEAKER	Yeah. Yeah, sort of. Though as I hear you say it, it
21		still sort of sounds like they are a "problem class,"

22		you know? And I don't mean to say that at all.
23		(Understander: Oh, Okay!) I guess it's the way I
24		teach reading that I want to talk about, and they
25		make a useful example—there's no exams looming
26		and that's where I can try out new stuff.
27	UNDERSTANDER	Okay, got it! Sorry!
28	SPEAKER	No, no! I think if I sounded hesitant, it's because I'm
29		a bit nervous about opening my ideas up like this.
30	UNDERSTANDER	Yeah, right! So, you want to look at the way you
31		teach reading comprehension. The Tuesday class
32		seems like a good place to try stuff out, and you
33		said you said, I think, that there are some ideas out
34		there (Speaker: Mmm) that you've got it in mind to
35		try (Speaker: Yes). Is that right?
36	SPEAKER	Yes. Yeah. That's it. That's what I'm thinking about.
37		You see, I've got this idea . . .

To Encourage Progress

If you can Reflect back to me what I have said in such a way that
I recognize it as mine, then I feel highly valued. I know that you
have indeed been listening carefully in a way that communicates
your respect for, and ability to empathize with, my position. I am
encouraged to continue, perhaps to take more risks with the ideas
that I explore.

We have just seen this at the end of Extract 5.1 (36–37). In Extract 5.2, the Speaker's enthusiasm (08, 17–18) for the Understander's Reflections (01–07, 09–16) is very clearly signaled, and
this establishes a springboard for the way ahead (20–22).

Extract 5.2

01	UNDERSTANDER	Okay, let's see. You've got a new situation to work in
02		that you say is, ah, frightening, but more than that it
03		excites you, I think, and you're, well, you're pleased
04		about it in a way, I think, aren't you? (Speaker: Uh
05		huh!) Because you had to make a couple of hard
06		decisions to get there and things could have worked
07		out differently.

08	SPEAKER	Oh very! But you're right, I *am* pleased *and* excited.
09	UNDERSTANDER	But the main, I think, the really specific point right
10		now is that you have to make, or somebody has to
11		make, and you want to have a say in it, a decision on
12		a coursebook (Speaker: Right). And you feel that if
13		you get this right, then a whole kind of stretch of
14		enjoyable work could be there for you to get into.
15		And, well, you'd really be moving along then and
16		doing what you've wanted to do for quite a while.
17	SPEAKER	That's exactly it! That's exactly where I am! Hey,
18		you're very good at this! (laughs)
19	UNDERSTANDER	Thank you! (laugh) Thank you! You're good at it too!
20		(Both laugh.) Do you want to talk about this
21		coursebook, then? Is that where we're going?
22	SPEAKER:	You bet! This is what I see . . .

To Facilitate Insight

I may find myself in the position of having to acknowledge that
what you reflect is exactly what I said and that now that you have
shown me the image of it, I am not too happy with it. Perhaps it
is here that I shall discover what I need to be working on.

In Extract 5.3, we can recognize not only the Speaker's enthusiasm (06) about the Understander's Reflection (01–05) but
also the moment of insight that occurs as the Speaker considers
the image before her ("putting it like that makes me realize"). She
recognizes an important paradox in her stated feelings about the
class (06–13) and also identifies a longer-term goal for the development of her teaching style (13–17). Both of these might provide
useful focuses for further work.

Extract 5.3

01	UNDERSTANDER	If I've understood you properly, then, you're pretty
02		satisfied with the work that's done in class (Speaker:
03		Mmm), but not everyone does the preparation that
04		you want them to, which means that not everyone is
05		involved in the way that you want them to be?
06	SPEAKER	Yes, that's exactly it! And putting it like that makes
07		me realize two things. One is that . . . well, it's

08	contradictory. I mean, you know, on the one hand, if
09	people don't do the preparation, why should I take
10	responsibility for them? On the other hand, what is
11	the point in saying that I am pretty satisfied with my
12	teaching, if there are students sitting there not doing
13	any learning? And the other is that this is more and
14	more the way that I want to teach, you know, where
15	the learning takes place *between* classes and the
16	classes are the place where I set things up and get
17	responses and give feedback.

A similar insight can arise when the Speaker realizes that the un-satisfactory nature of the Reflection has actually been caused by his or her own original statement. Prior to Extract 5.4, the Speaker had been working on his perception that there are some children in his primary English class who do not fully participate in the lessons. In his original presentation of himself (01-04), he chooses the word *serious*. This is the adjective that he has so far used to describe himself to himself. But when the Understander presents this image for him to look at (05-06), the Speaker immediately recognizes it as unsatisfactory (07). At this moment, obliged to sat-isfy himself as to what is going on, the Speaker opts for a much less flattering description of himself (07-12), which the Under-stander again Reflects (13-17) and the Speaker emphatically con-firms (18-23). Lines 24-25 single out for reconfirmation the cen-tral point that the Speaker has made. This recognition proves to be the key to the Speaker's successful development in this area (Boshell, in press).

Extract 5.4

01	SPEAKER	Yeah, I'm really serious in the classroom, and that's
02		why they might participate in a limited way. I never
03		smile, and I reckon that could make them a bit wary
04		of me.
05	UNDERSTANDER	Let me see. You're saying that it's because you're
06		serious they don't participate in any great detail.
07	SPEAKER	Hang on, perhaps it's not because I'm serious. After
08		all, you can be serious, but still organize them into

09		pairs whereby they are more likely to participate in
10		greater depth, just that you do this in a serious way!
11		No, I think it's because I'm a dominant type of
12		teacher.
13	UNDERSTANDER	So you're saying, that despite being a serious teacher,
14		that's not important. You could provide them with
15		pairwork, just that you would go about organizing
16		this in a serious way. It's you being dominant that
17		puts them off.
18	SPEAKER	Yeah that's right. Being in pairs would probably
19		make them feel more comfortable, and more likely
20		to participate. No, it's definitely me being dominant
21		that puts them off. I try to control absolutely
22		everything in class, and what's more I rarely allow
23		them to do pairwork.
24	UNDERSTANDER	So it's your dominance that puts them off from
25		contributing more.
26	SPEAKER	Yeah I think it must be.

Whichever of the above possibilities occurs, or whichever mixture or combination of them—for the point here is not to establish analytical categories—and even if nothing quite so explicit can be recognized in the interaction, the Reflection that an Understander offers has other reliable effects.

- Very simply, it gives the Speaker a break from Speaking, a chance to review the point that they have reached in their work. This, in turn, often provides a platform for an enthusiastic next step.
- It keeps the Speaker's ideas available for being worked on for much longer than usual. The ideas are held in a state of unfinished perturbation, as it were—not yet finalized, not yet demanding the Speaker's full commitment. They can be taken back, revised, and improved, rather like a spoken version of a draft.
- It at least partly equalizes the sense of vulnerability inherent in the situation. Speakers inevitably make themselves vulnerable by trying to work beyond what they know that they know. If the Understander only asks questions, this keeps

the pressure on the Speaker. But if the Understander says, *"This is what I have Understood,"* then this invitation to have the Reflection accepted, rejected, amended, or taken up as a springboard for the next thought puts the Understander also at risk, in the sense of risking an involvement.

From the Understander's point of view, acquiring the skills of Reflection is vital because:

- Reflection is necessary when you approach memory overload. Interrupt as necessary in order to be sure that you are in touch with what the Speaker has said so far.
- Reflection is the clearest and most effective way to check that you have understood what the Speaker has to say.
- You may think that you have understood when you have not.
- Even if you have understood perfectly, your Reflection may prove to be helpful to the Speaker, for the reasons outlined earlier.

One final point on timing: it is important to get the first Reflection in early in the session, because it establishes immediately the style of the exchange, as well as the Understander's role in it. It thus takes a little pressure off the Speaker to put on some kind of performance and helps the Speaker to settle down.

Having read these notes, it would be useful if you would now look back through the data presented earlier and think some more about what is going on in these exchanges. The data extracts throughout the book are endlessly rich, and I have found it very difficult to know at what level of detail to stop commenting on them! I provide here some more detailed commentary on Extract 5.1. You might like to talk about the data with a colleague either before or after you read my comments.

Now that I have made this suggestion once, I do not intend to go on repeating myself throughout the book. I shall use many extracts from data, and I suggest that you always read

> them carefully yourself, compare your thoughts with mine,
> and where possible discuss the data with at least one col-
> league. How could I not suggest that? Over to you.

The most important points for me in Extract 5.1 are these.
First, the Speaker has the courage to get started and includes an
implicit reference to her nervousness (01). As she addresses her
issue of concern (01-09), we can guess from the occasional
"Mmm" and "Uh-huh" that the transcript picks up that the Understander is attending well. The Understander gets in early with her
first Reflection (11). This takes the pressure off the Speaker, who
then wants to make some corrections (20-26) to the picture offered by the Understander. The Understander Reflects these corrections (30-35), which establishes a clear basis for the coming
work (36-37). Also, the hesitation that the Understander picks up
on (14-16) is reinterpreted by the Speaker in a way that helps the
Speaker bring her nervousness out into the open and acknowledge it (28-29). Speakers regularly report that being able to refer
to initial nervousness is a big help in getting beyond it. Finally, it is
well worth noting explicitly here how the teacher has chosen not
to identify her students as presenting some kind of problem but
identifies her teaching as something that she wants to develop
(20-26). This insistence on taking responsibility is a core issue in
all kinds of self-development work, and it is always worthwhile to
check for evidence of it in the data extracts that I present.

So an accurate Reflection feeds directly into the empathic relationship, and an inaccurate Reflection allows the Speaker to fine-
tune what is being Understood. In either case, the Reflection gives
Speakers a chance to review how far they have gotten in terms
both of their thinking and of its communication. Another effect of
the Reflection is then often to help the Speaker take the next
steps with renewed energy, as all the exchanges demonstrate in
their different ways.

Although I use the metaphor of a mirror to describe Reflecting, I hope that I have made it clear that reflecting also has to
catch the attitude and emotion of the Speaker, because the unspoken emotion might turn out to be more important that the
plain facts. If you can tell me that I sound dismissive of a certain

opinion or enthusiastic about a certain idea, you might help me see a part of the picture that had not been well lit before.

By the same token, Reflecting has some of the characteristics of a tape recorder, at least in the sense that what the Understander says must be a representation of something that can be found in the record of what the Speaker has already said. But Reflection has to be a thoughtful, selective tape recorder. Much of the power of Reflection arises from the fact that what I say comes back to me via the sensitive intelligence of another human being who is trying to show me to myself as I am seen.

In some cases, this might involve using the same words that the Speaker has used. In other cases, a paraphrase might be the most natural and effective way of showing the meanings that have been Understood. In this latter case, it's important to use words and expressions that are appropriate to the Speaker's perspective and ways of expression. The Understander, then, tries to use technical terminology or slang to the same extent that the Speaker does; otherwise the use of language might appear to move the exchange out of the Speaker's frame of reference and into the Understander's. A fictional and intentionally exaggerated example of this might be as follows.

Extract 5.5

01	SPEAKER	I get this feeling that at least some of the students
02		have got a lot more English in them than I'm getting
03		out.
04	UNDERSTANDER	So, if I'm understanding you properly, you sense a
05		latent tendency in a proportion of the participants
06		to underperform their actual communicative
07		competence.

In this exchange, the Understander is taking the Speaker's experience and expressing it in terms far removed from the Speaker's own. It is unlikely that the Speaker will recognize the original statement in this paraphrase.

Also unwanted is any element of interpretation or explanation by the Understander.

Extract 5.6

01	SPEAKER	I find correction a bit of a bother with this class.
02		There are some very competitive students in there
03		who hate to be corrected.
04	UNDERSTANDER	When you say they hate to be corrected, do you
05		mean corrected by you, or are you including self
06		correction and peer-correction in that?

Here, the Understander has supplied an analytical framework for the Speaker to fit his or her experience into. It may be a good analytical framework, but that is not the point. No one will ever know the direction that the Speaker's articulation of experience might have taken if the Understander had said something such as in Extract 5.7.

Extract 5.7

01	UNDERSTANDER	So, there's a negative reaction to correction from
02		some of the students. And this is getting to you a bit.
03		Is that what you want to work on?

In other words, the Understander needs to say, "*This is what I am hearing. This is what I have understood. Have I got it right? Am I representing your views and feelings accurately?*"

What the Understander must not do—because it would be insincere in our terms—is Reflect an idea with the thought or implication that this is what the Speaker should concentrate on or reconsider. The Understander is not there to ask questions that are designed to be helpful or to Reflect in a way that is deliberately formative of the Speaker. The Understander is there to Understand. Evaluation must come from the Speaker. At this point, exploration begins to develop a potential for discovery.

The actual worth of a Reflection then, in any particular instance, turns on the Speaker's response to it. The Speaker in Extract 5.3, for instance, may come to think that there are better places to expend energy than in thinking of ways to make students read texts between classes. Conversely, the Speaker may want to extend her newly realized organizing principle of class-work and learning to structure other areas of her teaching. When the Speaker starts to think like this, in whichever direction she chooses, there is the possibility of development as we have been using the term—creative growth coming out of the self.

In the early stages, Understanders are sometimes embarrassed by the act of Reflecting. They feel silly repeating what someone has just said, or they think that it is insulting to the Speaker. In part, this feeling is unavoidable. Nothing has significance if it is done me-chanically, and the early stages of practicing a new skill do regu-larly feel uncomfortably mechanical in some way. However, I hope that the data presented in this chapter, along with the points listed in justification of Reflection, will help you get past that embarrass-ment, initially in the context of the practice activities.

After some experience as an Understander and as a Speaker, most people come to realize that Reflection is not a trivial act. It is difficult to Reflect accurately and empathically, but Reflection is of great help to the Speaker and to the relationship on which co-operative development is based.

Another difficulty occurs with the use of the early Reflection. While it is simple to understand and accept this idea, it takes some practice before one feels comfortable as an Understander actually Reflecting, perhaps especially so at the beginning of the Speaker's work. Because the move is so useful, I urge you to use the tasks provided to gain exactly that practice. Listen for potential points at which you can intervene to reflect without breaking up a flow of ideas. And as Speaker, when you feel that it could be useful for you to take a break or to hear again what you have said, then you might make a point of signaling this to your Understander.

The Developing Speaker

Let me close this brief presentation of Reflecting by returning to the topic of Understander frustration with which we began this chapter. Here is a comment from one Understander looking back on a session:

My feeling was one of frustration as Understander—I understood her problems so well I didn't need or want to simply Reflect (having been through similar conflicts myself). I interpreted her speaking on this as a cri de coeur and desperately wanted to take an active role as sympathizer and a suggester of solutions. We did discuss these things in a separate chat later on, but somehow it was not the same. Maybe, having acted as Speaker, she had got it off her chest publicly and was slowly coming to her own solutions. Hope so—though I can't be sure.

For the reasons outlined above, I want to say that the Understander here badly underestimates what the Speaker had been helped to achieve and misrepresents the level of difficulty involved. It is not Reflecting that is "simple." Sympathizing and suggesting solutions—these are simple; we do these things all the time.

The Speaker in the session referred to had no doubt as to the value of what had taken place. She said later:

That session really did help me to clear my thinking on the point I discussed and it has helped me shape my priorities and feel less conflict afterward. This I find interesting because I don't think it was a session where "outcomes" were particularly salient at the time.

The following exercises are intended to help you continue to build the skills of the Understander by learning to Reflect.

Tasks

✓ Task 5.1

How might you Reflect the following statements? Read each statement carefully, look up from the page, and Reflect. Even if you are alone, it's important that you actually speak and

not just think about what you would say. Check your attempts with a colleague, and talk carefully about the words
that you choose, especially those that refer to emotions. If
you have a tape recorder, recording your Reflections might
help the discussion.

1. The ESL students that come to me are drawn out of
   five different classes, see? Sometimes it seems like by
   the time the last ones have turned up the first ones
   are itching to go. Everybody is very sympathetic, but
   it isn't anyone else's problem and it isn't going to
   change.
2. We've been getting the most amazing results since we
   stopped trying to stuff them with information about
   what life's like over here and started asking them
   about life over there. They're like different people.
   Plus which, once they've done their talking, they then
   often have questions about this country that they really do want the answers to. This is the most important thing I've learned in years, and I'm sure that
   there's a lot more mileage in it yet.
3. We're getting access to some new computer facilities,
   and we think that specific time is going to be allo-
   cated to it. I don't know. Some colleagues are really
   enthusiastic, and some say it's just another fad that
   will take up learning time. I just don't know. I mean, I
   never use a computer, or very rarely, anyway. I get
   good results the way I teach now. What am I supposed to do?
4. I've been asked if I want to have two post-grad students
   in my class to do some action research. I said, "Sure, so
   long as I'm involved in the research." I think they were
   a bit surprised, but I'm really excited about this. You
   know, I don't want to be, like, the warden at the zoo
   while these people come in and study us. If it starts
   going that way, I'll have to ask them to leave. But if it
   means that we get to look together at what's going on

in my classes and I get a say in what we investigate, and we turn up something useful, well that's cool.

5. We have a failure rate of 10 to 20 percent. I am not saying that that is acceptable, simply that a success rate of 80 to 90 percent is distinctly higher than any comparable institution achieves. Parents want to send their children here, and teachers want to teach here. Next year, the new wing will open with its own sports facilities, and although the details are still confidential, I can say that we have recently completed negotiations for the sponsorship of a new IT center.

✓ Task 5.2

The Understander will frequently have to interrupt the Speaker in order to Reflect. You may find it useful to think about the kind of phrase that you could use in order to make this interruption. How might you extend this list with expressions that you feel comfortable with?

- Just a minute, let me see if I've got this right . . .
- Okay, what I hear you saying is this: . . .
- All right! That's a lot to remember! Let me be sure that I'm with you here . . .
- Can I just check something with you? . . .
- So, if I'm understanding you properly . . .
- Okay then, this is the message I'm getting . . .
- Right, so it looks like this: . . .

Feedback

In the following activities, it would be useful, but is not essential, to work with an Observer. If you do, then the Observer should pay particular attention to the Understander, noting any nonlinguistic communication. Also pay special attention to the Understander's attempts to Reflect, noting anything that seems particularly successful or unsuccessful. Remember, it should not be possible for you to tell what the Understander thinks or feels about what the Speaker has to say.

When the Speaker and Understander have finished, lead a feed-back session, contributing information about what you have observed and asking for the reactions and contributions of the Speaker and the Understander. The following questions are central.

- Did the Speaker feel well Understood? What was this feeling like?
- Did the Speaker understand his or her own ideas better after having expressed them?
- Did the Speaker's ideas develop at all as they were being expressed?
- How did the Understander feel while trying to Reflect without revealing his or her own opinions?
- How does the Speaker feel about not having heard the opinions of the Understander and Observer?

If you do not work with an Observer, discuss your responses after the task, outside your Speaker/Understander roles.

✓ Task 5.3

Individual preparation. Think of a personal anecdote from your own history, either as learner or teacher, that allows you to complete one of these sentences.

- There was one time in class when I felt truly . . .
- There was one time in class when I felt as though I . . .

Interaction. Work as a Speaker/Understander pair or with the additional role of the Observer.

Take turns being the Speaker, and tell the story behind your sentence very briefly to your Understander. The Understander should Attend and Reflect, trying to capture the important elements of the story as well as the attitudes and emotions involved. The Speaker should correct or augment as necessary. See the earlier notes on feedback discussion.

✓ Task 5.4

Individual preparation. Read the following story. Do not talk about it to anyone else.

> In another country, at another time, there was a girl called Lima. Lima's mother died soon after Lima was born. Her father, a very poor man and himself uneducated, made it his main aim in life to make sure that Lima got a good education and so could live a better life than he and her mother had. To this end, he made every sacrifice, and when Lima graduated from school and won a place at a teachers' college, he was a very proud and happy man.
>
> Lima had lots of fun at college but did very little work. When the time came for the final examinations, it was clearly going to be impossible for her to pass. Without her teaching certificate, she would not be able to get any kind of job.
>
> The college had a system of personal tutors, to whom students could go if they had a problem. Lima asked her tutor what she should do. This woman said, "Lima, I have been telling you for three years that you needed to work harder. It's too late now. There's nothing to be done."
>
> Lima then went to see one of her lecturers and told him the problem. He said that he would show her the examination papers before the exam if she would go to bed with him. She did so and passed the examinations.
>
> However, Lima also became pregnant. When her father found out, he threw her out of the house and refused to have anything more to do with her. He said that as far as he was concerned, he did not have a daughter anymore.
>
> Now homeless, penniless, and expecting a baby, Lima met a much older man who was a widower with three children. He said that he would be prepared to marry her as long as she stayed at home and looked after his house and the children.
>
> I never heard what happened next.

Now, without talking to anyone else, number the characters from 1 to 5 according to how easy you find it to sympathize with their actions. Number 1 will be the character with whom you can most easily sympathize. *Do not let anyone else see your sequence.*

Lima   Father   Tutor   Lecturer   Widower

Interaction. Sit in a group of three. Read through the instructions, and decide who will be Speaker, Understander, and Observer. Then carry out the task. If there are just two of you, or if pairwork is more convenient, then work without the Observer.

Speaker: Tell the Understander what sequence you put the characters in, and explain why. Do not speak for more than five minutes. When the Understander repeats your sequence and your reasons back to you, listen carefully to see if you have been properly and fully understood. Make additions or corrections when necessary.

Understander: Put out of your mind your own sequencing of the characters in the story. Attend carefully to the Speaker. Don't make notes. Concentrate on making the Speaker feel well listened to. Do not show any signs of agreement or disagreement with the Speaker. To show that you have Understood what the Speaker has told you, Reflect back to the Speaker his or her sequencing of the characters and the reasoning behind it. You do not have to try to use exactly the same words as the Speaker, but you must do your best to capture the exact meanings that you have understood, including the Speaker's attitudes or emotions. You can either wait until the Speaker has finished before Reflecting or, if you can't remember that much, come in while the Speaker is talking.

When the Speaker feels that he or she has been well Understood, come out of the Speaker and Understander roles and discuss what happened along the lines indicated earlier, in the section on feedback.

✓ Task 5.5

Individual preparation. Make some notes in response to the following questions.

1. How did you get into the field of TESOL?
2. Why did you move to each new job?
3. Do you have, or have you had, other jobs outside your teaching?
4. Have you ever thought about leaving English-language teaching? If so, why did you stay?
5. What ambitions or plans do you have for the future?

Interaction

Speaker: Your aim is to pursue the question, "To what extent do I see TEFL/TESOL as a genuine *career*?" From your responses, choose the ones that you find most interesting. Tell your story, and explain your thoughts to your Understander. When he or she Reflects your ideas back to you, correct them if necessary and expand on them if you wish.

Understander: Attend and Reflect as carefully and empathically as you can.

When the Speaker feels that he or she has been well Understood, come out of the Speaker and Understander roles and discuss what happened along the lines indicated earlier, in the section on feedback.

Chapter 6   Making Connections

In this chapter, we are going to take the use of Reflecting a step further by looking at two ways in which the linked Reflection of separate points can be offered as potentially useful to the Speaker's explorations.

Thematizing

What do you see going on in the following extract from a CD session? The Speaker is working on changes that she is trying to make in her presentation of English to her learners.

Extract 6.1

01	UNDERSTANDER	Excuse me. Let me just check something here.
02	SPEAKER:	Sure.
03	UNDERSTANDER	You said a while back, erm, that when you were
04		teaching students who'd had a lot of grammar
05		teaching in their background, you enjoyed
06		deliberately introducing functional teaching to them
07		(Speaker: Mmm). Yeah? You said, I think, that you'd
08		take a functional label such as request, and ask them
09		to think of as many ways as they could of making a
10		request.
11	SPEAKER:	Yeah, and they found that so hard at the
12		beginning . . .
13	UNDERSTANDER	Difficult to think of language in those terms . . .
14	SPEAKER	Yes, because they hadn't thought about it like that
15		before.
16	UNDERSTANDER	Right, but you thought it was a useful process for
17		them to go through . . .
18	SPEAKER	Yes, I did. I still do. I think it helps you to see things
19		you know in another way . . .

20	UNDERSTANDER	Well, you know how, er, you were just now talking
21		about wanting to show students how some words
22		group together in "lexical chunks"—more or less
23		fixed, depending on ...
24	SPEAKER	Yeah, yeah.
25	UNDERSTANDER	...and how useful these chunks can be.
26	SPEAKER	Oh yes, definitely.
27	UNDERSTANDER	Well, I was wondering if those two—I don't know
28		what to call them—issues, ideas, techniques, are in
29		any way connected for you: the functional and the
30		chunking?

Both of the issues that the Understander Reflects here (3–17, 20–25) are taken from what the Speaker has already said; the Understander is not introducing new ideas to the discourse. In both cases, the Understander is careful to check that the Speaker confirms the validity of the reflection (18–19, 26).

What the Understander then does is to introduce (27–30) the possibility that there might be a common theme linking the two items explicitly mentioned by the Speaker. This move by the active Understander is what we call **Thematizing.** On what basis does the Understander do this? Well, it might be that the Understander simply thinks he or she sees some superficial similarity; it might be that he or she has an intuition regarding a possible connection; it might be that he or she believes that the two issues are very obviously linked. Whatever the case, the Understander simply offers the possibility, leaving the evaluation of that possibility to the Speaker. As I hope you will by now expect me to say, what the Understander does not do is seek to hint at specific connections or manipulate the Speaker in a certain direction, even if that direction seems as plain as day from the Understander's perspective.

What's the point of this? Well, notice again the need to Reflect accurately what it was that the Speaker said on both issues; this has its own worth. The further purpose of the Thematizing move, however, is to help the Speaker establish in his or her thinking connections (and perhaps even larger-scale coherence) of which he or she had not previously been aware or, conversely, to separate out distinctions that he or she had previously not made. Each will assist the Speaker's self-development in terms of the exploration of ideas and the discovery of the next step forward.

How may the Speaker respond? Well, there are several explicit possibilities. The Speaker might acknowledge a connection he or she has already seen but not found interesting and then move on; the Speaker might acknowledge this previously seen connection and choose to pursue what it means; the idea of a connection might be quite new to the Speaker, and he or she might want to explore the possibility of a common theme; the suggestion of a connection might provoke an elaboration of the actual difference between the two issues as far as the Speaker is concerned. All of these are possible, to say nothing of what actually does happen in each instance. The pressure on the Speaker is to know that the Thematization was done out of sincere respect and an effort at empathy. The pressure on the Understander is to be in the moment with the Speaker, ready to go where he or she goes. In Extract 6.2, I have included along with the Speaker's actual response a couple of alternative responses that the Speaker might have come up with. Out of respect for your developing abilities as an Understander, I shall not tell you which is which.

Extract 6.2

01	UNDERSTANDER	Well, I was wondering if those two—I don't know
02		what to call them—issues, ideas, techniques, are in
03		any way connected for you: the functional and the
04		chunking?
05	SPEAKER	Er, dunno. You could see them that way. I mean,
06		there's the idea of seeing language from a different
07		perspective, there's the idea of learning something
08		you can use in your English, not just something that
09		you know. And there's the very definite connection
10		that they both motivate me as a teacher.
11		(Understander: Mmm) . . . Yeah, yeah, there might be
12		something in that. I don't know where it gets us! But
13		it might be worth looking at.
	or	
14	SPEAKER	Mmm. Interesting. But actually not! (laughs) No, no, I
15		don't think so. The functional thing was more or less

16		given, you know? (Understander: Mmm) Here is a list
17		of functions that we have to deal with. It was fun, all
18		right, but it soon became pretty standard stuff. But
19		here, this is much more open-ended: I'm learning
20		along with the students and that makes for a very
21		different sort of teaching. Maybe it's the open
22		endedness of this I enjoy. You know, *that* could be
23		something to check out.
	or	
24	SPEAKER	Maybe. Maybe. What's important to me right now,
25		though, is to concentrate on ways of getting students
26		to use these more or less fixed word groups that we
27		find.

However this goes, the Speaker knows that the Understander's Thematizing move is not meant to suggest a specific connection or even to suggest that the Understander believes that there is a connection; it is another way of opening up possibilities for the Speaker's self-development. Just as the Understander does not come forward with suggestions, the Speaker does not ask for them—they are not what the Understander is there to provide. If there is no way forward on a particular topic at a particular time, the interaction can continue in a different direction. And finally, there is also the possibility that the Speaker may return to this point later and then see a connection or a distinction that becomes important. The Speaker may see this later development as an original idea, which is just what it will be.

Challenging

This idea of bringing together points that the Speaker has raised separately can work in another way, too. In the following extract (Extract 6.3), the Speaker is working on his proposal for doctoral research. Immediately before we join the session, he has said that he moved away from his first research focus because he came to feel that he had taken it up more as a topic that everyone approved of and supported than because he had a real enthusiasm for it. He saw a danger in this that he recognized more generally in his life—an unwillingness to take risks and a preference for acting in ways that others applauded. He had taken some psychometric tests that supported this view, he said, the results categorizing him as a *hub-person,* someone who tends to merge into the group in terms of language and ideas.

He then went on to describe his new topic and to explain why he thought it to be well placed in the department where he hoped to study. As we join the exchange, the Understander has just Reflected the content of the new topic and had this Reflection confirmed. He then moves on to Reflect what the Speaker has said about the place of the proposed research in the department (01–07).

Extract 6.3

01	UNDERSTANDER	Another point I wanted to check with you, on
02		another plane, is you said that you, you saw that as a
03		potentially fruitful place to position the research
04		because you saw it as drawing on Barry's established
05		research and my research interests, and it would be
06		possible to move between the two and sound ideas
07		out. Yeah?
08	SPEAKER	Yeah.
09	UNDERSTANDER	Earlier, when you were talking about the other topic
10		that you took up in the first place (Speaker: Mmm),
11		you raised this doubt about it, where you said you
12		thought that perhaps you'd got yourself into a
13		situation which, lined up with psychometric tests,
14		that suggested that maybe what you do is to try to
15		get yourself into the center of a situation (Speaker:
16		Mmm), as opposed to hold on to things on the
17		outside (Speaker: Mmm), and you described that as a
18		danger (Speaker: Mmm). Is there any sort of . . .
19	SPEAKER	Well, I think . . .
20	UNDERSTANDER	. . . connection there?

Once the Speaker has confirmed the accuracy of this Reflection (08), the Understander brings together (09–18) the Speaker's positive evaluation of the positioning of his research between two established research positions (02–07) and his negative evaluation of the danger of being a so-called hub-person (11–18).

To put the same kind of move into a teaching context, my Understander once challenged me by bringing together two views that I had expressed:

- that students were wasting their time learning word lists;
- that learners learn in different ways and that people should do what works best for them.

So, she asked, how do these two statements fit together, Julian?

In the cooperative development framework, this move is called **Challenging.** The first thing to notice is that there is no question of the Understander challenging the Speaker with the Understander's own ideas or opinions. The Challenge lies in bringing together two statements acknowledged and affirmed by the Speaker that the Understander finds difficult to reconcile.

The underlying attitude is critical to this move. As Speaker, I know that the Understander is not trying to catch me out or prove a point. He or she is sincerely asking me to make my position clear so that he or she can Understand it and empathize with it. As Understander, I have to make sure that this is my motivation; I should not assume that my Challenge is anything other than an opportunity for the Speaker to show that his or her position is actually coherent, so long as I see things the way that the Speaker does. The above Speaker, for example, responded in this way:

Extract 6.4

01	UNDERSTANDER	Is there any sort of . . .
02	SPEAKER	Well, I think . . .
03	UNDERSTANDER	. . . connection there?
04	SPEAKER	I think, I mean, when I talked before about this
05		balance between being in a context and having
06		access to data, if you, if you, position yourself . . . I
07		mean, I must admit, faced with, hearing that back
08		(laughs), it sounds like a clear-cut case of here's me

09		trying to position myself in the hub again! But I
10		think that the chemistry between your teacher
11		development and the kind of conversation analysis
12		that Barry does (Speaker: Mmm), I think it's an area
13		that neither of you have really looked at.
		[He talks briefly about the effects of restricted research time.]
14	SPEAKER	So, I don't think that that crossover has come about.
15		So yes, on the face of it, it would seem as if I am
16		positioning myself, but I think it's an inevitable part
17		of choosing a research interest which you feel that
18		there are others around you who can contribute
19		to it.

So long as the Speaker is satisfied with the resolution of the challenge, that is enough. He or she may return to the issue later, but it is not the Understander's role to get pulled into evaluation, agreement, or disagreement. It is the Understander's role to respect and empathize.

Of course, the Speaker may be confronted with a Challenge that cannot be immediately resolved, which itself becomes an opportunity for work and development.

This is where I found myself. What do I believe about word lists? Are they really such a waste of time? Always? For everyone? I suppose that what I really wanted to say was that I saw students putting a lot of effort into this way, and only this way, of vocabulary learning, while I thought that they could do themselves a favor by trying out some different strategies. That sounds a bit long-winded, perhaps, but it was a good reminder to me of how (too) easily I fall into exaggeration and generalization. It also helped me focus my thinking toward action, because I saw that I had now put myself into a position where I could not back away from having to be more explicit about exactly what I mean by that expression, "different strategies." As we shall see later, it is articulating the practical implications of expressions such as this that so often contains the key to a shift from talk to action.

Challenging is the most threatening move that we have looked at. It would be all too easy to score points by implying that a

Speaker is being illogical or incoherent. To do this would be to behave as if in a discussion, where we take the other person's utterances to be finished products that are sent out into the conversational arena to look after themselves. In cooperative development, the Understander is trying to support the Speaker's process of developing ideas; there is as yet no logical or illogical, no coherent or incoherent. The Speaker's thoughts and feelings are out in the open, emergent in a safe environment, seeking their best form.

Connections and Relationships

It is, of course, possible to make connections between more than two points at any one time, and there is no reason why an Understander should not do so in the sense of Thematizing and Challenging. Similarly, many more relationships are possible than *same* and *contradictory.* Working out the detail of these relationships is the responsibility of the Speaker; offering possibilities is the role of the Understander in his or her continuingly sincere attempts to respect and empathize with the Speaker's explorations and discoveries and, by so doing, to make them possible. As I write this, I am reminded of a line from Boris Pasternak: "Everything must exceed itself to be itself." Well, it's coherent for me.

Tasks

Feedback

In the following activities, it would be useful, but is not essential, to work with an Observer. If you do, then the Observer should pay particular attention to the Understander, noting any nonlinguistic communication. Also pay special attention to the Understander's attempts to Reflect, Thematize, and Challenge, noting anything that seems particularly successful or unsuccessful. Remember, it should not be possible for you to tell what the Understander thinks or feels about what the Speaker has to say.

When the Speaker and Understander have finished, lead a feedback session, contributing information about what you have observed and asking for the reactions and contributions of the Speaker and the Understander. The following questions are central.

- Did the Speaker feel well Understood? What was this feeling like?
- Did the Speaker understand his or her own ideas better after having expressed them?
- Did the Speaker's ideas develop at all as they were being expressed?
- Did the Speaker find the attempts at Thematizing or Challenging useful?
- How did the Understander feel while trying to Reflect, Thematize, and Challenge without revealing his or her own opinions?
- How does the Speaker feel about not having heard the opinions of the Understander and Observer?

If you do not work with an Observer, discuss your responses after the task, outside your Speaker/Understander roles.

✓ Task 6.1

(Please note that you can renew this task very easily by replacing the given statements with others of more specific relevance to your situation.)

Individual preparation. Think about the following statements, and make a few notes to indicate the extent to which you agree or disagree with them.

1. In order to maintain a reasonable atmosphere at work, it is necessary to put up with things from colleagues that one doesn't actually approve of.
2. One essential for a successful language-learning group

is that the learners feel secure, that they feel that the teacher cares about their progress and that there is some purpose to their work.

3. The most common problem faced by teachers has nothing to do with methods, materials, or learners; it is their hopelessly low pay.

4. We look to schools and universities and teachers' colleges to provide trainee teachers not only with theories but also with the fundamental techniques of language teaching: the ability to analyze, present, and practice language.

5. If someone I work with is unhappy about something I have said or done, I like them to come and tell me about it openly.

6. It is unfair to expect teachers to behave as if they are the friends, parents, or guardians of their students. One tries to treat students as well as one would treat anyone that one works with, but that is as far as it goes.

Interaction. Decide who will be Speaker, Understander, and Observer (if available).

Carry out the following task:

Speaker: Articulate briefly your position on these six points.

Understander: Listen actively. Make the Speaker feel well listened to. Reflect the Speaker's ideas and feelings. Listen particularly for opportunities to Thematize and Challenge.

When the Speaker feels that he or she has been well Understood, come out of the Speaker and Understander roles and discuss what happened along the lines indicated earlier, in the section on feedback.

✓ Task 6.2

Individual preparation. Take a sheet of paper, and draw a line down the middle. On the left-hand side, make a list of activities *outside teaching* that you are good at or that you enjoy or both. What are the activities that give you the feeling:"This is me at my best"? What have you been doing when you find that you have been so absorbed that time has slipped away? What kind of tasks do you find worth doing simply for their own sake? Include them in the list. This is private information. You will have the opportunity to tell someone about these things if you want to, but you will be able to choose what you mention and what you don't. Please make the list before you read on.

Look down the list again. Ask yourself, in each case, "What are the skills or qualities or abilities that I bring to each of these activities? What is it that gives me the sense of enjoyment or of satisfaction that I find in them?"

Now, on the right-hand side of the paper, opposite the relevant activities, make a list of these qualities, abilities, and skills and of the sources of enjoyment and satisfaction that you experience outside teaching.

Interaction. Decide who will be Speaker, Understander, and Observer (if available).

Carry out the following task:

> *Speaker:* Your aim is to increase your awareness of the strengths and abilities that you have, to recognize how you use them in your teaching, and perhaps to discover a greater potential for enjoyment and for feeling at your best in your work. Talk briefly about a selection of the nonteaching activities that you have listed and the skills that they entail. Try to discover possible connections

among them. Where and how do you use these abilities in your teaching? When, in your teaching, do you enjoy yourself? When do you feel, "This is me at my best"? Could you use your strengths more often? Could you get more enjoyment and feel at your best more often?

Understander: Listen actively. Make the Speaker feel well listened to. Reflect the Speaker's ideas and feelings. Listen particularly for opportunities to Thematize and Challenge.

When the Speaker feels that he or she has been well Understood, come out of the Speaker and Understander roles and discuss what happened along the lines indicated earlier, in the section on feedback.

✓ Task 6.3

Individual preparation. Make some notes in response to the following questions.

1. What does continuing professional development (CPD) mean to you?
2. What are the most important elements of CPD for you?
3. What was a really important event in your own CPD?
4. What gets in the way of your CPD?
5. What is most facilitative of your CPD?
6. What would be the single most useful change that could be made in your situation with regard to facilitating your CPD?
7. Can TESOL learn from CPD in other fields? How?
8. Is your work in any way useful to the CPD of others?

Interaction

Speaker: From your responses, choose the ones that you find most interesting and explain your thoughts to your Understander. When he or she Reflects your ideas back to you, correct them if necessary and expand on them if you wish. When you are offered connections, pursue them if they are interesting.

Understander: Attend and Reflect as carefully and empathically as you can. Look for chances to Thematize and Challenge.

When the Speaker feels that he or she has been well Understood, come out of the Speaker and Understander roles and discuss what happened along the lines indicated earlier, in the section on feedback.

✓ Task 6.4

Individual preparation. Think about your teaching or about any other aspect of your professional life, and see if you can identify something that you do, perhaps something that your position obliges you to do, that makes you feel a certain discomfort because it is somehow not in line with beliefs or values that you find important.

Interaction

Speaker: Explore this incongruence that you think you have identified between some of your actions and some element of your beliefs or values. See if you can resolve your feeling of discomfort or at least clarify what it is based on.

Understander: Attend and Reflect as carefully and empathically as you can. Look for chances to Thematize and Challenge.

When the Speaker feels that he or she has been well Understood, come out of the Speaker and Understander roles and discuss what happened along the lines indicated earlier, in the section on feedback.

✓ Task 6.5

Individual preparation. This exercise comes out of left field, and you may hate it. I stick with it because some people find it so useful. It comes in three clear stages. You have to complete each stage as instructed, or you will really be wasting your time. If you are working with a group leader, they can talk you through the exercise. If not, read all the instructions first and have everything prepared.

You need two blank sheets of paper and something to write with. You also need about twenty minutes during which you're not going to be disturbed. When you're ready (and not before!) read on.

1. As quickly as you can, without giving too much thought to it, write down at least twenty words that describe you. This is private. You won't be asked to show this list to anyone or to share information that you don't want to. Please make this list now. When you've finished, put it away and out of sight.
2. On the next page, you'll find an image, a pattern, a drawing—call it what you will. When you have finished reading these instructions, please look at this pattern. Try to take in the whole image and concentrate your gaze on it for about eight minutes. There is more to say about this, but read the rest of these instructions first.
3. When the time is up, take the second sheet of paper and write on it as quickly as you can, without giving too much thought to it, writing down at least twenty words that describe you. But this time write with the hand that you don't usually write with. That is to say, if you are right-handed, hold the pen in your left hand. Yes, I am serious. Don't worry about the quality of the writing; only you have to read it.

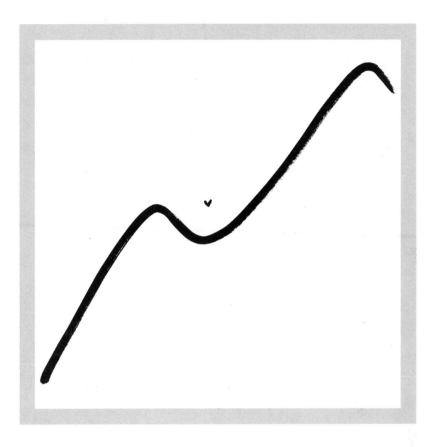

Okay? Now, back to number 2. Make sure you are sitting comfortably, by which I mean preferably on a straight-backed chair with both feet flat on the floor. Straighten your back so that your shoulders are above your hips. Take a deep breath. And let it out. And another. And let it out. And another. And let it out. From now on, try to keep your breathing deep and regular.

While you look at the picture, try to clear your mind of thoughts. The clearing is more or less impossible, but the trying is not. When you realize you are thinking about something, quietly acknowledge the fact and ease that thought out of your mind. Think about your breathing, and concentrate your vision on the pattern. When next you realize you are thinking about something, try again to clear your mind.

Check the time now, and put your watch somewhere out of your direct vision but where you can check it easily. You want to do this exercise for at least five and not more than ten minutes.

- Clear your mind.
- Concentrate on the image.
- Keep your breathing deep and regular.
- Sit in a relaxed, open, upright posture.
- Fold your hands together in your lap.
- Keep your breathing deep and regular.
- Concentrate on the pattern.
- Clear your mind.

When the time is up, carry out number 3, and write your second list.

Interaction

> *Speaker:* You have a choice between two aims, or you can attempt both. One possibility is to explore the experi-

ence of concentrating on the pattern itself. What was it like? What happened? How did you feel? How do you feel now? Would you like to try it again? The other possibility is to look at the two lists of words that you have written about yourself. Do you notice any overall similarities or differences in the items on the lists? Are there any interesting individual items or general contrasts? Does this exploration lead you to any possible insights about yourself?

Understander: Attend and Reflect as carefully and empathically as you can. Listen especially for chances to Thematize and Challenge.

When the Speaker feels that he or she has been well Understood, come out of the Speaker and Understander roles and discuss what happened along the lines indicated earlier, in the section on feedback.

Chapter 7   Focusing

Speaking to Some Purpose

For many of us, once we start "talking shop" we can talk for a long time without necessarily getting anywhere. Endless staff meetings and discussions across the generations bear international witness to this. None of us has time to spare; we are here because we want to use some time in a productive and satisfying way. The undiluted purpose of cooperative development is to move through increased awareness toward action, toward doing something. While one can talk generally, one can only act specifically, and so one of the necessary goals of the Speaker is to focus his or her thoughts and talk toward the specific.

It is worth acknowledging straightaway that this issue of identifying in detail exactly what it is that one is going to work on, to explore, to investigate, to research—whatever one decides to call the process—is well recognized as one of the most difficult aspects of the whole business. So let us acknowledge that fact and then get on with doing something about it. No matter how problematic it is, this narrowing down to something specific remains essential. It is all very well for me to decide that I need to improve the way I teach pronunciation, but I cannot walk into class tomorrow and say, "Okay, guys, today I am going to improve the way I teach pronunciation." It always comes back around to what I am actually going to *do*.

In the light of that last acknowledgment, this is probably also a good time for an admission. Personally, I have never had any difficulty identifying focuses for action. They have always seemed to identify me and to do so rather more frequently than I care for. So, armed and burdened with both acknowledgment and admission, let us get back on track to deal with **Focusing.**

This Focusing process is one with which an Understander can assist. The assistance will be based on respect, empathy, and sincerity, but it will also be persistent: the Understander is not only a good listener. The Understander insists on Understanding toward whatever purpose the Speaker pursues, but there needs to be, if only eventually, a purpose.

Understanding a Focus

In our first example (Extract 7.1), the Speaker is an English language teacher who also teaches on a teacher education course that leads to the award of a teaching diploma. She herself is very clear and specific about what she wants to work on, and she Focuses down to it in a few lines (01-02, 05-06, 08-10). The Understander's role is to show that she is attending (03-04, 07) and then to Reflect the Focus back to the Speaker (please note that I did not say *simply*!), to hold it up for quality control, as it were, before the work proceeds (11-15).

Extract 7.1

01	SPEAKER	You know I do some [teacher] training sessions for
02		the Diploma.
03	UNDERSTANDER	Yeah, is it that, what you want to, er, what we're
04		doing now?
05	SPEAKER	Mmm. They're starting teaching practice next week
06		and I want to go through the way I handle feedback.
07	UNDERSTANDER	After you've observed them?
08	SPEAKER	Yeah. I've got a sort of an idea for a shape to how
09		I'm going to handle it and I'd like to get it really
10		clear in my head.
11	UNDERSTANDER	So, the focus is that, for starters anyway (Speaker:
12		Uh-huh): you want to set out a . . . a sort of outline
13		standard procedure? (Speaker: Yes) For how you're
14		going to handle giving the Dip trainees feedback
15		after you've observed them on TP.
16	SPEAKER	Yep. That's it.
17	UNDERSTANDER	Fire away!

In the next example, the Speaker's interest is in the use of computer-generated concordances. Just before Extract 7.2, she has Spoken about her own excitement at finding new meanings and patterns in the language and about the problems that occur when her students are sometimes overwhelmed by the richness of the real-language complexities that arise. The Understander makes himself some space (01) and then Reflects these two aspects of the topic (03–07, 09–12, 14–17). When the Speaker has confirmed them, the Understander checks again that two topics are available (21–25) and offers a chance to Focus (27–28).

Extract 7.2		
01	UNDERSTANDER	Okay, can I just recap where we are right now?
02	SPEAKER	Yeah, please do.
03	UNDERSTANDER	I hear you saying how much you enjoy this, this kind
04		of work—looking up concordances and that
05		(Speaker: Mmm). You get a buzz off identifying
06		meanings in them that you wouldn't have thought of,
07		or you wouldn't expect to find in a dictionary ...
08	SPEAKER	Yes, that's right.
09	UNDERSTANDER	... and also spotting certain grammatical patterns, or
10		lexical groups, that seem to line up with particular
11		uses of words—you can get really quite excited
12		about that.
13	SPEAKER	Yes! It *is* exciting sometimes!
14	UNDERSTANDER	And then as well, when you use data-driven materials
15		like these with the students, problems sometimes
16		turn up, because they get caught up in the wealth of
17		detail that's there ...
18	SPEAKER	That's right, instead of concentrating on the relevant
19		bits, they get worried about all the other words they
20		don't understand.
21	UNDERSTANDER	Okay, so is it fair to say that you've spoken so far
22		about two things? I mean there's you as a person
23		working with the language, and then there's you as a
24		teacher working with the students. Like two roles
25		there?
26	SPEAKER	Yeah, sure.
27	UNDERSTANDER	Would it be of any use to you to Focus on just one
28		of those roles for a while?

I've left a space for the Speaker's next move, in case you get a feel yourself for what the response might be. In some senses, of course, it doesn't matter. It doesn't matter what your response might be, or my response. Nor does it matter, in one sense, which of these the Speaker actually said:

Extract 7.3

01	SPEAKER	Yeah, yeah, Okay, let me stay with why I think this
02		work is so interesting—what I get from it. Let me get
03		that really clear.
	or	
04	SPEAKER	Well, it's the use of this stuff in my teaching that I
05		want to concentrate on, so let's focus on that.
	or	
06	SPEAKER	No, no. I think I'd like to keep both those together. If
07		I separate them out, I lose something.

What matters here is that the Understander, acting out of respect, empathy, and sincerity, has reflected back to the Speaker what he or she has heard, has given the Speaker a chance to see it and think about it, and has given the Speaker a chance to choose whether or not to make a specific Focusing move. What matters is that the Speaker knows that this is what is happening, that this is not a manipulative move by the Understander, who really means, "Can't we get on to the teaching?" or who really *really* means, "Aren't you mixing things up here?" Finally, what matters is that the Speaker takes her own next step forward.

Both participants know that the point of Focusing is to achieve depth of understanding (strange how we talk about depth of understanding but also about raising awareness!) as a prelude to conscious action. The Understander works to make Focuses available but does so without evaluating them. The Speaker searches for an appropriate Focus, both by Speaking and by evaluating the opportunities that the Understander points out.

In Extract 7.3, there is a choice between two possibilities, but an opportunity for Focusing may occur without any such either/or choice being necessary. Take this example (Extract 7.4) from a CD session in which the Speaker had begun by talking about a mixed ability class and had become enthusiastic about a certain group of students in that class.

Extract 7.4

01	UNDERSTANDER	Okay, so if I'm getting this last part right, there's a
02		pretty distinct group of students in the class who
03		have got the hang of what you expect of them
04		(Speaker: Oh yes) and they're kind of, what?—
05		steaming along happily?
06	SPEAKER	Yes, they've got their own kind of "lift-off." It's
07		amazing.
08	UNDERSTANDER	And is that something that you want to stay with, to
09		dig into a bit more? (Speaker: Mmm) That "lift-off"?
10	SPEAKER	Yes. Yes. I think so. I think there's all sorts of stuff to
11		learn here, about how this happened.

This offering of a Focus has to be guided in great part by the Speaker's initial statement of what they want to work on and by the Understander's sensitivity to what is happening in the moment. We saw another example of this in Extract 5.2 (20–21). What the Understander must not do is try to hijack the Speaker's development in the direction of the Understander's interests and purposes. Nor must the Understander lead the Speaker to Focus on what the Understander believes the Speaker would be well advised to Focus on. As well as depending on respect and empathy, therefore, the ability to Focus the Speaker's discourse thus makes direct demands on the Understander's sincerity in the interaction. You may be sick of my saying this, but experience leads me to believe that it bears an (almost sickening) amount of repetition.

I have stressed the link between finding a Focus and deciding on action. Because of this strong connection, we shall return to the area of Focusing in chapter 8, when we work on setting action goals. Before moving on, however, I have to reemphasize that *when* to Focus is just as much in the Speaker's hands as is *what* to focus on. Offering a Focus is a perfectly valid Understanding move. Turning it down is a perfectly valid Speaking move. I had a vivid reminder of this relatively recently in one of the group development sessions that I describe in chapter 9. Immediately prior to Extract 7.5, I had Reflected back to the Speaker in terms that he accepted the issues he had raised so far. I then offered him a chance to Focus (01–02). He declined (06), affirmed the usefulness of the Reflection that preceded the invitation to Focus (06–08), and then firmly put me in my place with a smile (08–13):

Extract 7.5

01	UNDERSTANDER	. . . so, is there a specific point in there that you want
02		to focus on?
03	SPEAKER	Do you mean in the work generally, or for the
04		purposes of this session?
05	UNDERSTANDER	Yeah, yeah, I meant for our work together now.
06	SPEAKER	Mmm. No, I don't want to do that, not yet, though
07		listening to you has helped me see the choices I
08		have. I think it's because I'm not a linear thinker. I
09		tend to have a lot of balls up in the air, and I don't
10		think any of them get to hit the ground, but I know
11		it's difficult to process, especially for someone like
12		you, Julian, because you want me to Focus on one
13		thing! (general laughter)

So I'm not trying to say that one style fits all. When and where to Focus is always the Speaker's choice, and the more people work together as Speaker and Understander, the more sensitively and productively they can learn to make cooperative development work for them.

In ways coherent with their individual styles, Speakers have to achieve some kind of specificity in their exploratory thinking if their work is to lead to the kind of discovery that can be the basis for action from which further learning can arise. Having described and exemplified the process, let us now take this issue of Focusing forward in a task-based way that also attempts to allow to some extent for individual style.

Tasks

✓ Task 7.1

As Understander, it might be useful for you to think of some phrases that you can use when you want to help someone find a focus. How could you extend this list?

- Is there anything we've covered so far that you'd like to go back to?
- Is there anything in what you've said that you'd like to Focus on?
- Okay, do you want to work a bit deeper into any of this?
- Right, do you want to stop and go further into that?
- You've Spoken about X, Y, and Z, is that right? Do you want to Focus in on any of those?

Feedback

Where the following activities have sections on interaction, it would be useful, but is not essential, to work with an Observer. If you do, then the Observer should pay particular attention to the Understander, noting any nonlinguistic communication. Also pay special attention to the Understander's attempts to Reflect, Thematize, Challenge, and assist Focusing, noting anything that seems particularly successful or unsuccessful. Remember, it should not be possible for you to tell what the Understander thinks or feels about what the Speaker has to say.

When the Speaker and Understander have finished, lead a feedback session, contributing information about what you have observed and asking for the reactions and contributions of the Speaker and the Understander. The following questions are central.

- Did the Speaker feel well Understood? What was this feeling like?

- Did the Speaker understand his or her own ideas better after having expressed them?
- Did the Speaker's ideas develop at all as they were being expressed?
- Did the Understander succeed in helping the Speaker Focus?
- How did the Understander feel while working without revealing his or her own opinions?
- How did the Speaker feel about getting no help in the usual sense from the Understander?
- Did the Understander enjoy the discipline of working to give the Speaker space to develop and depth to explore?

If you do not work with an Observer, discuss your responses after the task, outside your Speaker/Understander roles.

✓ Task 7.2

Individual preparation. Draw four irregular shapes across a piece of paper, as in the illustration.

Think of these shapes as stepping stones in your professional life so far—four significant moments or stages at which important decisions were made or decisive events occurred on your way to where you are now. Write a note on each stepping stone to remind you of what it represents. (As you may have guessed, if you go for three stepping stones or five, that's fine too.) When you've done this, think yourself back into each situation and speculate for a while on what might have happened if you had made a different decision or if a different event had occurred.

Interaction

Speaker: Choose the two stepping stones that interest you most, and explain why they interest you to your Understander. Explain the alternative scenarios that you have thought about. Be open to the possibility of Focusing on one of them, and set yourself the task of finding something from that hypothetical past that might be useful to you now.

Understander: Attend and Reflect as carefully and empathically as you can. Look for chances to Thematize and Challenge, and try especially to help the Speaker find a Focus and explore it for a useful discovery.

✓ Task 7.3

This individual exercise is useful both for establishing a Focus for action and for establishing a focus for writing, whether you are writing for evaluation or publication. I am going to work one example through as I give the instructions. Please note that this is just a personal statement of what I thought of on this occasion, offered only to exemplify the procedure.

1. Choose a general work topic of some interest to you, an area in which you are called on to act. If inspiration fails, try one of these: *testing, choosing a coursebook, my colleagues, dealing with parents, teaching writing, plagiarism.* Write this topic down in the middle of a blank piece of paper, and draw two concentric circles around it. Here is one example:

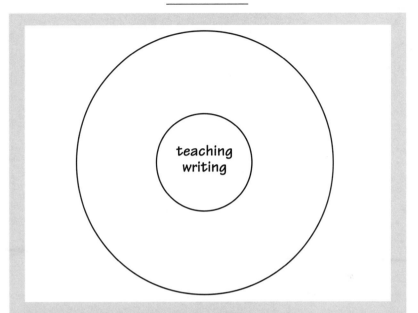

2. Break this topic down into a number of component parts, and write these parts between the circles, separating them into segments.

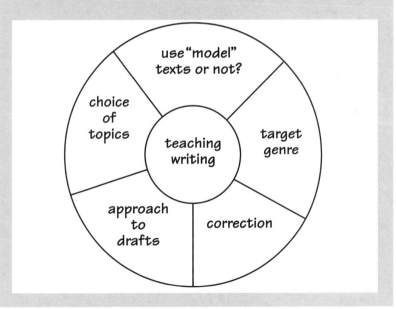

3. Choose one of these component parts, and repeat steps 1 and 2.

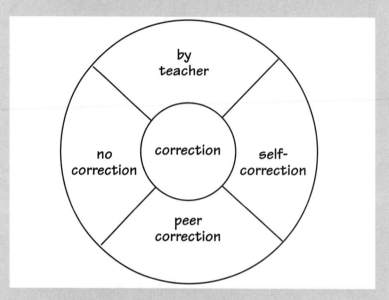

4. Repeat step 3.

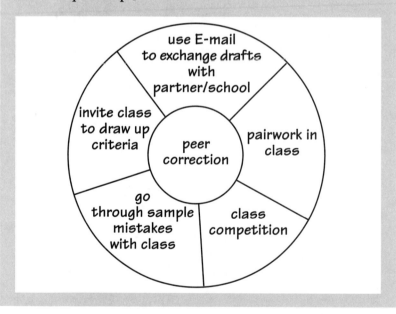

It is at this stage, or perhaps after one more circle, that I find that something very interesting happens. What had been a topic (e.g., teaching writing), something to talk about, starts to sound more like an action (e.g., making a competition out of peer correction), something that you actually do. At this point, we can say that we have focused our thinking to the point that we can act on it. We are looking for the kind of action that we perhaps have not tried before, something that we have only heard of or seen or perhaps something that we tried once and might want to try again. Anyway, it should be something that relates to our generally expressed interest and that gives us an opportunity to develop through conscious action. Once we have identified it, we can formulate a plan of action and consider how we are going to try to learn from following it through. As an extra task, if it interests you, you might try taking my ironic example from the beginning of this chapter of *teaching pronunciation* and seeing how it might break down into action research possibilities.

A further attraction common to both this approach and the next is the possibility of retracing one's steps to pick up related avenues of thought and investigation.

✓ Task 7.4

This individual task parallels the previous one. You may find one approach preferable to the other.

1. Once more, choose a general professional topic that interests you. If inspiration fails, choose one of these: *bullying, teaching grammar, groupwork, organizing programs for asylum seekers, staff meetings.* (Please note that if you don't start thinking of your own topics soon, we could be in trouble here.)
2. Draw a long line across a page, and label it with the topic of your choice. Here's my example, but once again, it's just a personal thing.

Independent learning

3. Now draw branches off this main line, and label each one.

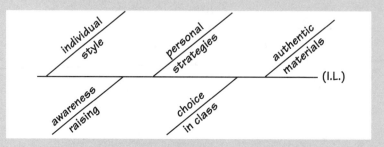

4. Draw twigs off the branches, and label them.

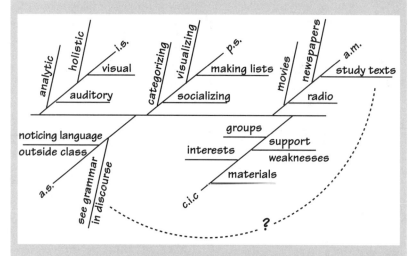

5. As in Task 7.3, what we are looking for is the point at which our topic turns into specific possibilities for action. You might find one on a single twig, or you might look across the whole set of possibilities and see an interesting connection. As I work on this one, I think I have found an interesting possibility for one EAP group in the idea of helping them see how the grammar that we learn in English classes functions in the textbooks of the subjects they specialize in. I have marked this connection with a dotted line.

Tasks 7.5–7.7

The next three tasks offer a decreasing amount of support for a Speaker/Understander session on Focusing toward direct action. You can do them all, or choose the one(s) that appeal(s) to you. Be sure that while doing Tasks 7.5, 7.6, and 7.7, you have a chance at some stage to experience the activity in more than one role—that is, as the Speaker, as the Understander, and perhaps as the Observer.

✓ Task 7.5

This is a kind of role-play for a Focusing exchange, using the individual work you have already done. It can offer good practice in Focusing for both Speaker and Understander.

Individual preparation. Choose either 7.3 or 7.4, whichever you felt more comfortable with or whichever gave you a more interesting outcome.

Interaction. Now work with an Understander. The Speaker should talk through the Focusing exercise as if he or she were doing it live. While doing this, the Speaker should keep up a running commentary on the decisions being made.

As choices are made, the Understander should reflect what the Speaker says in order to check communication. When a Focusing circle has a number of items in it or a line has a number of branches coming off it, the Understander should invite the Speaker to Focus of one or these items or branches, thus taking the Speaker into the next stage of the process.

✓ Task 7.6

Now try a real-time version of Task 7.5 with a topic of your own choice. Again, the Speaker should work through one of the Focusing tasks and talk aloud while doing so. If you would rather work without these aids, then go on to Task 7.7.

✓ Task 7.7

This time, the Speaker chooses a topic to talk about without using the circles or branches. The Understander should Attend, Reflect, Thematize, Challenge, and most of all, attempt to help the Speaker find a Focus. Remember, the purpose of Focusing is to help Speakers:

- get beyond a superficial level of talk;
- select something from what he or she has already said about which he or she wants to develop ideas in more detail;
- deal with specifics as part of a move toward action.

Chapter 8 Into Action

We have concentrated so far on the Speaker's development via the exploration of ideas, emotions, and experience. The Speaker sets out, we might say, with a secular act of faith: explore and you will discover. It doesn't always work out in big terms; it can't be Columbus and the New World every time.

On the other hand, there would not have been any point in checking with Columbus on what he had found when he was two weeks out of harbor. What is more, the Speaker is unlikely to be able to specify what it is that will be discovered—the Columbus parallel again. And from the Understander's perspective, it is also worth keeping in mind that anyone with a better knowledge of routes to India than anything that was available to Columbus could have pointed out pretty early on that he was setting off in quite the wrong direction. In the absence of that knowledge, what Europeans saw as a New World was discovered, and that discovery was not less transformational for them because what they saw as new was everyday commonplace for the people already living there. (I think I have pushed this analogy as far as it will go and I don't want to step into its shadow.)

So Speakers articulate their ideas, experiences, and feelings about their work in order to move toward a way of being a teacher that is authentic for each individual. Understanders work to foster this expression, signaling nonjudgmental acceptance and using Reflection, Thematizing, Challenging, and Focusing as they seem appropriate.

Goal Setting

It is now time to return to the point that we made when talking about Focusing: that the kind of growth that we seek through cooperative development comes through action as well as talk. Focusing, through its increase in specificity, not only facilitates depth of reflection and exploration, thus making discovery more likely; it also makes action possible. For educators, this action will involve some kind of behavior related to those for whose learning we have responsibility (and let us pause just briefly to note that this includes ourselves—if we don't remember that, we are letting down the whole educational endeavor).

The spur for this particular action will probably come out of one of three types of realization. Speakers will realize:

- that they are dissatisfied with what is happening in some area;
- that some particular success deserves wider application;
- that one area of professional activity is so interesting as to demand further investigation.

Whatever the motivation, the time for expression of ideas and values now has to be used in the formulation of a goal that can be specified in terms of the kind of action that can be implemented and evaluated. This is the **Goal setting** that the Speaker needs to accomplish if cooperative development is to move beyond talk and into the realm of learning through conscious experience.

There is no correct goal or type of goal, except that goal that provides a next step for the Speaker in the investigation of professional activity. The tasks at the end of the chapter are intended to help you establish a variety of action-oriented perspectives on your own situation.

All the efforts of the Understander are put at the service of the Speaker in this activity of goal setting. As a particular area of concern is worked on and a Focus found, the aim of the interaction is to decide, "*So what? What is to be done?*" The overall purpose of the talk is to make sure that what is done is what the Speaker wants to do, based on a coherent foundation of the Speaker's values, knowledge, experience, and purposes.

Not every session of interaction will necessarily lead to goal setting in terms of direct action. Some sessions will lead to a Focus that the Speaker wishes to take away and read about or to a Challenge that the Speaker wishes to think more about. Indeed, both Bartrick and Barfield (in chap. 11) emphasize the usefulness of CD-related work that does not lead to specific outcomes in action. Nevertheless, the articulation of a goal expressed as professional behavior is a recurrent purpose. Furthermore, people who work together on a regular basis, in a regular teaching routine, with regular, mutual class visits, should find that Goal setting becomes an easier and more normal practice.

Cooperating in a regular teaching routine also helps to keep goals to a moderate scale: the smaller the goal, the better the chance of acting toward it and being able to evaluate its worth. Working toward such small-scale goals and getting early feedback are themselves motivating; they help to keep cooperative development on the move.

So let me say this once more. A statement such as

I want to improve my students' reading abilities

expresses a large-scale aim, but it is not in itself the basis for action. A statement such as

I'll find out what the students think about having the reading passage read aloud to them

is a small-scale goal, and that is its strength. This is a goal that the teacher can aim for in the very next reading class. So, while Goal setting may begin with a broadly conceived purpose and while that purpose gives coherence to what follows, it must then be narrowed down to something that the Speaker can actually undertake as a specific piece of action.

As we have already noted, as well as being grounded in an overall purpose, a goal might be motivated by a sense of dissatisfaction with some area of one's professional life. In the following exchange (Extract 8.1), the Speaker introduces the topic with an open declaration of negative emotion. Both teachers work in a private English-language school in Europe that pupils attend after their regular school day. I include a longer extract from this inter-action and then comment on it afterwards.

Extract 8.1

01	SPEAKER	Okay, talking about feeling annoyed and frustrated, I
02		face a problem lately with giving instructions in
03		class. For some reason, the children just don't seem
04		to take any notice. I try to carry out the lesson in
05		English as much as possible, and then when it comes
06		to the, let's say, homework, comes to the point of
07		telling them what to do for homework …
08	UNDERSTANDER	Just to get this straight, you mean the junior classes?
09	SPEAKER	Yes, the problem is worse with A preliminary and B
10		preliminary, the first classes.
11	UNDERSTANDER	The first classes, yes, and you've got a problem
12		because they don't get the instructions …
13	SPEAKER	Yes, it seems that they don't understand what is said,
14		or they don't listen to what is said—I can't decide
15		what is what.
16	UNDERSTANDER	And you say that you speak English to them?
17	SPEAKER	Ah, yes, I try, as much as possible, I could say, to
18		speak in English, though lately, to save time, I
19		suppose, I explain their homework in [the pupils'
20		L1]. But even in [L1], if I say, "Chapter 35," as soon as
21		I say that, someone says, "Chapter 34?" Or, "I didn't
22		hear that, say again!"
23	UNDERSTANDER	You mean there is a problem here with the class …
24	SPEAKER	Yes, they just don't … however clearly I say it.
25	UNDERSTANDER	You mean in [L1]? Even in [L1]?
26	SPEAKER	Yes, even in [L1] they don't, they don't follow.
27		There's something I'm not doing right here, I think. I
28		find this such a waste of time and I end up shouting,
29		"Can't you understand? Listen!"
30	UNDERSTANDER	So, you think it is you who is to blame?
31	SPEAKER	Well, funnily enough, we have another teacher and I
32		wanted to watch, to observe her, and at the end of
33		the lesson she explained in [L1] very clearly what
34		the homework was, and from my position at the
35		back of the class I saw the same thing. Immediately
36		she said it, the children said, "What have we got?"
37	UNDERSTANDER	Did this give you any thoughts? I mean, did it make
38		you think of any other ways to do that?

39	SPEAKER	Mmm, maybe it's a question of classroom
40		management really, that we need to establish some
41		rules, perhaps.
42		"Right! Now we're going to give the homework
43		instructions. Everybody must pay attention!"
44		Mmm, or perhaps if I could write it on the board
45		and say, "This is what you have to do."
46		And then, they could, they could follow, they could
47		write it down, they could copy it down, yes, maybe
48		that's a good idea, to stop the confusion caused by
49		the oral explanation of the instructions.
50	UNDERSTANDER	So, you think the confusion is caused by the oral
51		explanation of the instructions?
52	SPEAKER	Eh, it certainly is a part, a major part, yeah, I think it
53		is. I think that's right. I need to try it. I do write on
54		the board sometimes, but I'm not consistent. Mmm.
55		Maybe that's the problem, then, I am not consistent
56		about it and they don't know what to expect. Mmm,
57		that could be a discovery there! (laughs)
58	UNDERSTANDER	Good! (laughs)
59	SPEAKER	Yes, children of that age especially need
60		consistency . . .
61	UNDERSTANDER	You mean, every time, the same thing . . .
62	SPEAKER	Yes. Okay. So, five minutes before the end of each
63		lesson, they know,
64		"Now the teacher is going to tell us the homework
65		so I must pay careful attention."
66		Maybe that's the way they see it. And maybe I could
67		ask how they do it at their regular school, the
68		[national] school, and see if there's anything I could
69		learn from that situation.

First of all, we might notice, as a very rough positive indicator, that the Understander has only thirteen of the fifty-eight lines transcribed. Second, check for yourself the way in which what the Understander says is almost always a Reflection of something found in what the Speaker has said. The only exceptions, I suggest, are in line 58, where the Understander is joining in the Speaker's enjoyment of a discovery, and in lines 37–38, to which we shall return shortly.

In what follows, I am blending together my own commentary with the commentary of the Speaker and Understander, who talked about the exchange later.

During the Speaker's opening statement, the Understander interrupts (08), Reflecting "children" with "junior classes" in order to make sure that she is building up an accurate picture of the situation that the Speaker wants to deal with. The Speaker realizes that he is communicating a lot of information at once and is pleased to confirm a focus on the younger learners, where the problem is most acute (09-10). The Understander then puts the Speaker back on the track of what he has defined as his problem, Reflecting "giving instructions" (02) with "don't get the instructions" (12). The Speaker said afterward that he runs into something of a dead end here (14-15) and that the Understander keeps the momentum going by Reflecting another strand of the information she has received (16). The Speaker goes on to insist that his choice of language is not the issue (17-22). At this point (23), the Understander checks the implication she is picking up that there is something wrong with the class, with the way the children are behaving, and asks the Speaker to confirm this. The Speaker does so (24) but then goes on to say (27) that he is doing something wrong. He also feels comfortable enough with his Understander to confess a lack of control in his professional behavior (27-29). He commented later that it was because he could make this admission that he was also able to make progress with the issue.

The Understander, in a move paralleling that in line 23, now (30) asks if the implication is that the Speaker himself is at fault. The Speaker responds by telling the story of a class that he observed where the teacher had the same problem (31-36), implying once again that the problem lies somehow with the learners. The Speaker later commented that he saw with hindsight that it was exactly this swinging backward and forward, looking for where to lay the blame, that had been getting in the way of his addressing the problem. We can also see, perhaps, that this was the block that he had run into in lines 14-15.

At this point (37-38), however, the Understander helps the Speaker move on from this obstacle by facilitating a shift of attention toward Goal setting. This is a firm move by the Understander, which the Speaker might have wished to reject in order to continue speaking about the topic. The Understander's sense of timing is, however, impeccable. The Speaker, now faced with questions of action, makes the fundamental, developmental step of taking responsibility for improving the quality of what is happening in class. Initially, he talks through alternative possibilities and compares them with what happens at the moment (39-49). The Understander Reflects the comment on confusion (50-51), which leads the Speaker, in the space of a few lines, both to the establishment of a workable new procedure to try out and to a breakthrough in underlying awareness that he immediately recognizes as important to him (52-57). This, in turn, leads him to refine his intended classroom procedure (62-65) and to formulate another possible plan of action (66-69).

In the next extract from the same session, Extract 8.2, the depth of exploration that the Speaker has attained, facilitated by the Understander, leads to a continuing interplay between ideas and intentions; procedures and awareness; exploration, discovery, and action.

Extract 8.2

01	UNDERSTANDER	So, you think you'll do, what?
02	SPEAKER	I think I will, er, let me see. Five minutes before the
03		end of the lesson, I'll explain to them, "Now, I'm
04		going to write on the board the instructions for the
05		homework." Of course, they are very young, but I'll,
06		I'll have to write in English. My written [L1] isn't
07		good enough to cope with these things.
08	UNDERSTANDER	So, you'll write it in English on the board, you mean.
09	SPEAKER	Mmm, yes, I'll write the page and I suppose I'll show
10		them in the book. I'll show them the book but,
11		again, this creates further confusion . . . Perhaps it's
12		part of a bigger problem, somehow, because they put
13		their books in their bags, and in and out, and
14		sometimes I feel I'm not quite in control of what's
15		going on there.
16	UNDERSTANDER	How many children are in the class?

17	SPEAKER	Eleven, twelve. There are some different ages there.
18		That may play a role because there are some who
19		are third class elementary school and some who are
20		fifth.
21	UNDERSTANDER	And you think this has to do with the confusion?
22	SPEAKER	Maybe. Or maybe I judge . . . How can I say this? If I
23		look at one of the children, if I look at Margarita,
24		who's in fifth class, and I think she knows what
25		she's doing, she's written down the homework . . .
26		Mmm . . .
27	UNDERSTANDER	You think that—if I've got it right—if Margarita
28		understands it, everybody has.
29	SPEAKER	Mmm. Yes.
30	UNDERSTANDER	You've got this impression.
31	SPEAKER	That's not good, perhaps, because maybe she's the
32		maturest in class.
33	UNDERSTANDER	So you imply that age difference makes a difference.
34	SPEAKER	Yes, that's right. I can see now that maybe I'm
35		pitching my, er, instructions at a level that's the
36		highest maturity level, and I should maybe be doing
37		it at the lowest, or at least in the middle. Right, I see.
38		So perhaps I should be—it's a more general thing.
39	UNDERSTANDER	So, you've got a problem, the class has a problem
40		because—different ages in the class. Oral
41		instructions—if I've got it right—don't work, and if
42		you write it on the board, you think they get
43		confused . . .
44	SPEAKER	So . . .
45	UNDERSTANDER	. . . but not for all the students you said, the
46		confusion is only for some of the students.
47	SPEAKER	. . . if I make sure that the least mature members of
48		the class have understood, that will make my
49		problem less. Yes. I think I need to try that now.
50		Okay.

Looking first at the Understander, we can see how she moves to pin the Speaker down to some specific action (01) and from then on Reflects back to the Speaker what she hears him saying, always using points that he has already made, expressed either in the same words or in appropriate paraphrases. The only exception to this occurs when the Speaker refers to confusion (11), which prompts the Understander, who wants to establish a clear picture for herself, to ask how many students there are in class (16).

Commenting afterward on this section of the session, the Speaker said that he felt himself obliged to clarify precisely what he intended to do in terms of giving instructions, and this led him to try to describe exactly what happens in class. Various classroom scenes came back to him (09-15), bringing out different aspects of the overall area of difficulty (17-20). He then started to hear inconsistencies in his position (22-26, 31-32), but at the same time he felt himself moving toward a kind of illumination, which came to him (34-38) as he began to see the class not as an undifferentiated mass but as a group of individuals of varying ages and stages of maturity (47-49).

He said:

Again, the prompting of the Understander helped me to Focus, not only by narrowing my scope, but by helping me to see more clearly, to see "in focus." Instead of a vague haze of frustration I had previously summarized as, "They don't listen to instructions," I could see the problem broken down into manageable parts:

> 1. *I do not use one consistent method of giving instructions for homework exercises and the class may be troubled by not knowing what to expect.*
> 2. *The class is of different ages and maturity and may therefore respond to different types of instruction.*

The negativity of emotions such as, "It's my fault" or "They are to blame" has been replaced by an analytical approach to seeing what lies behind the problem. I now wanted to investigate real classroom events to see if these findings could be substantiated.

The Speaker's move toward an action research style of classroom investigation (49-50) is not one that we can follow in detail here, but it is worth noting that as a result of this investigation, the Speaker made useful discoveries about the legibility of his writing on the board and about how much of what he said at any time was understood in detail. (In fact, we can see the beginnings of this realization in the Speaker's comment, "it's a more general thing," (38). He also came to see his students' previously annoying habit of questioning his instructions as a consequence of poor presentation, and, crucial to the practical issue of giving homework, he established with the students a way of referring to the different types of homework exercises that they did understand.

The Speaker's final comment on the above session articulates entirely the cooperative development ethos:

> *I have been given the room and the confidence to explore my own ideas and my own practice. This gives me the encouragement to try and fulfill my potential as a teaching professional. The ideas I have expressed and the practice I have described are by no means ideal, but I am sure that the voice that is heard is mine as I feel, and not mine as I would like to feel. From this point, personal and professional development really are possible.*

As we have already seen, Speakers and Understanders can usefully pursue their work beyond Goal setting into the detail of classroom procedure. At its most explicit, this can entail the Speaker working out a step-by-step blueprint for the next class or series of classes. The idea is to give the Speaker a chance to talk through what will be necessary before actually having to do it. In CD terms, we call this **Trialing.**

Trialing

In this spoken rehearsal, the Speaker gets a chance to make sure that the steps toward the set goal have been thought through and that they are coherent. The Understander follows the Speaker's description and brings up any points of detail that the Speaker might overlook. These might include, for example, clarification of exact procedure, linking of procedure to purpose, or listing of necessary aids. Thus, both minds combine to diminish the risk of the Speaker's being faced with an unexpected eventuality in class.

At this point, it is important to stress the relationship between careful planning and flexibility. The purpose of the Trialing is certainly not to produce a plan that must be followed at all costs. The point here is that the Speaker's course of action toward a goal should be organized and meaningful in its own right. At the same time, let us agree immediately that classrooms are always full of unexpected eventualities and that no amount of preparation can change this. However, when the unexpected happens, it is exactly when one has a systematic plan based on lucid ideas that one is in a strong position to be flexible, to improvise, and to react confidently to the new situation. (That, at least, is my position on this issue, but the issue itself becomes a topic that a Speaker works on in chap. 9.)

There is another point to make about the unexpected things that happen in class: they can be very useful learning experiences. So if I am not able to carry out my plan in one particular class, I do not want to spend my time and energy getting too frustrated about it. I want to learn from the unexpected occurrence that got in my way. In my next session as Speaker, I may want to take it as my Focus.

Trialing, in any event, is meant to support the development of careful lesson preparation, which can in turn support flexibility and adaptability in a sensitive teacher who is working toward a clear goal.

In the area of Trialing, it can be particularly difficult for the Speaker not to ask for advice or opinions. Again, the fundamentals of this style of cooperation are at issue. As Speaker, I am looking to develop myself to be the best teacher I can be. What sounds like a mistake to someone else might not be a mistake for me. If I do plan something that goes wrong, I can live with that and learn from it. The lessons that I learn will also be my own.

It can also be difficult for the Understander not to get involved in making suggestions. As Understander, the underlying principles of respect, empathy, and sincerity help me to remember that the Speaker is developing as an individual. Certainly, anything that I think I recognize as something that I have already done is unlikely to turn out to be a repetition of my experience when someone else does it. The Speaker will learn from it, and so will I. In fact, those readers who have by now worked as Understanders may well be experiencing an extra dimension of growth that I have not previously mentioned: Understanders who do learn to respect and empathize with views other than their own are in a wonderful position to learn new perspectives on old certainties. As we noted in our earlier discussions of Understanding (chap. 2, p. 31), anyone who is properly open to Understanding also takes the risk of being changed by what they hear.

To return to our present focus, however, the Understander has to work hard to insist on clarity and detail. During this Trialing process, one point about cooperative development as a whole should become very clear, if it is not already. The relationship between Speaker and Understander is not one of wishy-washy warmth and positivity about anything and everything. The Understander wants to accept exactly what the Speaker wants to do, but there is a discipline and a rigor involved in making sure that the Speaker is clear about what that is. The cut-off point is when the Speaker says, *"That's enough. That's how I want to leave it."* We saw a version of this in Extract 8.2 (49–50).

Extract 8.3 provides another example of two people engaged in the Trialing phase of a CD exchange. The Speaker had begun the session with a very general topic to discuss: writing. Almost immediately, however, she reported that she came to the surprising realization that she really enjoyed her teaching of writing only with her advanced classes. As the Understander Reflected back to her the picture that unfolded, the Speaker Focused on what it was that she enjoyed about her advanced classes, coming to see the key factor as the high level of student motivation, which interacted with her enjoyment at trying out different methods with them. The goal she then set herself was to use more varied procedures with her lower-level class, where writing had been mostly restricted to the use of picture-story prompts. She further refined this goal in terms of using a technique in which a piece of writing is planned out in terms of paragraphs with functional headings. As we join them in Extract 8.3, the Understander leads her into Trialing (01).

Extract 8.3

01	UNDERSTANDER	Okay, so how will you set about doing it in the
02		classroom?
03	SPEAKER	Well, I can write all these, I mean, the title, on the
04		board, and give the numbering of the paragraphs. In
05		every paragraph I could write what each should
06		contain. I can have them write one together in class
07		the first time, just to see (Understander: Yes). Then
08		they'll have a different focus at home, but they'll
09		have something concrete in their hands. They'll
10		know what to write in every paragraph, but it will
11		be more specific to them.
12	UNDERSTANDER	Yes, I see, students respond a lot if they feel security,
13		don't they?
14	SPEAKER	Yes, and they will have confidence as well, because
15		sometimes they don't know what to include in their
16		compositions. And I think I will give them a specific
17		number of words, as well (Understander: All right).
18		About 100 to 120 words. Not too many in the
19		beginning. If I give them about 120 words, it will be
20		easy for them to do (Understander: Mmm). Up to
21		120, no more, so they will start counting the words,
22		something they haven't done up till now.
23	UNDERSTANDER	Okay, so you are going to try in the classroom first,
24		to see . . .
25	SPEAKER	Yes, I think I can have them work as a group, mmm,
26		not individually, but if I assign three or four together,
27		two desks in one corner, four boys, two desks for the
28		other students, and they can work as a group first, so
29		they would have each other in doing that.
30	UNDERSTANDER	Okay, so they're going to try groupwork, then.
31	SPEAKER	Mmm, yes, I'll have them work as a group first.
32	UNDERSTANDER	How long, do you think, will the lesson probably
33		take?
34	SPEAKER	Well, we'll say about ten to fifteen minutes, I think, to
35		give them the instructions and introduce them to
36		the new method, and mmm, after that, after writing
37		everything on the board, I'll ask them for particular

38		vocabulary and I'll write that on the board. If that's
39		not sufficient, I'll give them some more words to
40		write down. Then I'll change the desks and have
41		them start writing. And I'll give them twenty to thirty
42		minutes to write their composition—to make a first
43		draft and then to copy it.
44	UNDERSTANDER	All right.
45	SPEAKER	So I think this will be inspiration and motivation, and
46		after two weeks maybe—because I can't do that
47		every week, it will be too much for them—I will
48		introduce them to a new topic of composition.
49	UNDERSTANDER	Yes, I see. How are they in groups? Do they work
50		well together?
51	SPEAKER	Eh, sometimes. When we do exercises. I haven't put
52		them in groups much because they're very noisy.

At this point in the exchange (49–52), we can note how the Understander has picked up an aspect of the proposed methodological change (groupwork) that is in fact significant. The Speaker goes on to work through how she will handle the grouping and groupwork, and then, in Extract 8.4, the session moves toward its close, with the Understander checking both how the Speaker feels about the plan overall (01–02) and specifically about the timing (08), a point of earlier concern (Extract 8.3, 34–43). The Speaker's "Okay!" (13) signals the end of the session.

Extract 8.4

01	UNDERSTANDER	Okay, so do you feel comfortable about the plan of
02		the next lesson?
03	SPEAKER	Well, I think that in the beginning it will be
04		completely different and they will like it, especially
05		the boys.
06	UNDERSTANDER	Uh-huh.
07	SPEAKER	They like new things.
08	UNDERSTANDER	Are you happy with the timing, then?
09	SPEAKER	Yes, it'll take me fifteen minutes to give the
10		instructions and write on the board, and then five
11		minutes to change the desks. I'll give them thirty
12		minutes to write the composition and edit it clearly,
13		so fifty minutes will be enough. Okay!

The only other lines that I feel I need to comment on from this session are lines 12–13 in Extract 8.3. From a fundamentalist CD perspective, this comment oversteps the line in terms of respect. That is to say, it expresses agreement with the proposition that it reflects. The Speaker reported later that she felt a strong sense of collegiality at this point, as the Understander disclosed his own affirmation of the underlying principle without in any way influencing her development of her ideas and plans. This move occurs at best on the borderline of what I understand nonjudgmental discourse to be, and while its occasional use is clearly documented as welcome, it demands a lightness of touch to make sure that it does not tip over into overt agreement with the Speaker, because of all the changes that such agreement would necessarily bring to the relationship and its discourse.

In this chapter, I have tried to explain and to exemplify how cooperative development, in the hands of empathic Understanders and committed Speakers, can move from the realm of ideas into action, in terms both of Goal setting and Trialing actual procedures.

It is tempting to me to follow up these plans with reports on and evaluation of the actions themselves. But that would be to extend the coverage of what I am trying to communicate, and in writing, as in cooperative development, you need a clear focus if you are to act effectively. If you do want to read more about the cycles of action research or about reflective teaching, then please check out the references that I give in chapter 12.

This chapter ends, once again, with a series of tasks. By the time you have completed them, I hope you will feel that you have a grasp of the style of work that I call cooperative development. There will be no more tasks, except the ones that you set for yourself.

Tasks

Feedback

In the following tasks, it would be useful, but is not essential, to work with an Observer. If you do, then the Observer should pay particular attention to the Understander, noting any nonlinguistic communication. Also pay special attention to the Understander's attempts to reflect, thematize, challenge, and assist focusing, goal setting, and trialing, noting anything that seems particularly successful or unsuccessful. Remember, it should not be possible for you to tell what the Understander thinks or feels about what the Speaker has to say.

When the Speaker and Understander have finished, lead a feedback session, contributing information about what you have observed and asking for the reactions and contributions of the Speaker and the Understander. The following questions are central.

- Did the Speaker feel well Understood? What was this feeling like?
- Did the Speaker understand his or her own ideas better after having articulated them?
- Did the Speaker's ideas develop at all as they were being articulated?
- Did the Speaker find the Goal setting and Trialing useful and successful?
- How did the Understander feel while trying to aid Goal setting and Trialing without making his or her own suggestions (i.e., while working with respect and empathy)?
- How did the Speaker feel about getting no help in the usual sense from the Understander?
- Did the Understander enjoy the discipline of working to give the Speaker space to develop and depth to explore?

If you do not work with an Observer, discuss your responses after the task, outside your Speaker/Understander roles.

✓ Task 8.1

Individual preparation. Complete the following sentences for yourself. Then see if you can add a similar sentence or two of your own. Later on, you'll be asked to choose one or two of these sentences to talk about.

- As a teacher, the type of activity I most enjoy is . . .
- As a teacher, the type of activity I least enjoy is . . .
- One type of activity I think students learn a lot from is . . .
- The kind of change I would like to make in my teaching is . . .
- One aspect of my teaching that I'm really pleased about is . . .
- One thing I would like to do more of in my teaching is . . .
- One thing I don't like about my teaching is . . .
- One technique I would like to try out in class is . . .
- The kind of student I'm best with is . . .
- The sort of student I can't stand is . . .

Interaction

Speaker: Choose one or more of these sentences to talk about. Your aim is to set yourself a goal for a future class. You may start off quite generally, but your purpose is to specify a particular piece of teaching action that you will carry out. If you find it helpful, use one of the focusing techniques from chapter 7. Start by asking yourself, *"What is so interesting about this for me?"* and move on to ask, *"What exactly am I going to do about it?"*

Understander: Attend carefully. Make the Speaker feel well listened to. Use all previously practiced skills where appropriate. Listen particularly for any potential Focus and for the chance to help the Speaker move toward action. The aim is to help the Speaker specify a small-scale goal for classroom action. In Goal setting, it is particularly important that the goal:

- is practical in terms of actual implementation;
- is coherent with the Speaker's values and purposes.

✓ Task 8.2

Individual preparation. When we move to put our thoughts and values into action, we can do so in a wide number of ways. Read this list of possibilities, and see if one area motivates you more than another. The focus of your action may be:

- *means-oriented*—e.g., We know that we are trying to teach people to speak English in this course. How can we improve the ways in which we do so?
- *ends-oriented*—e.g., We know that these students want to become librarians. How sure are we about the relative importance of teaching them to *speak* English?
- *theory-oriented*—e.g., As we investigate our teaching of spoken English, how can we articulate our increased understanding of what is happening here so that we build up our local theory? How can we link this up with what others have discovered?
- *institution-oriented*—e.g., To what extent is my spoken-English course, through its goals, its topics, and my practice, contributing to an integrated educational program through which the institution mediates between its students and its social context?
- *society-oriented*—e.g., To what extent is my spoken-English course, through its goals, its topics, and my practice, promoting values that I believe in (e.g., contributing to a healthy dialogic relationship among students, teachers, the institution, and society at large)?
- *teacher-oriented*—e.g., Where is my own personal and professional development in this? What is the contribution to collegiality and thereby to the kind of society I want to live in?

Interaction

Speaker: Choose the two areas that interest you most, and explain why to your Understander. Be open to the possibility of Focusing on one of them, setting yourself a goal and working on how to reach that goal.

Understander: Attend and Reflect as carefully and empathically as you can. Look for chances to Thematize and Challenge, and try especially to help the Speaker find a Focus and move toward action, Goal setting and Trialing some ideas where possible.

✓ Task 8.3

Individual preparation. Let's get rid of some aggression and negativity here! Think of all the things (and people!) that get in your way in terms of your doing your job well and enjoying it. Try for at least ten items and write them down as continuations of this sentence:

One problem is that ...

For example:

One problem is that the students for my Monday afternoon class always come late.

When you have done this, see how many of these sentences you can now rewrite as continuations of:

One problem is that I ...

For example:

One problem is that I haven't got a strategy for dealing with students who regularly come late.

In other words, see if you can reformulate your problems in ways that make you responsible for doing something.

Interaction

Speaker: Choose your most interesting examples, and explain them to your Understander. Be open to the possibility of Focusing on one of them, setting yourself a goal and working on how to reach that goal.

Understander: Attend and Reflect as carefully and empathically as you can. Look for chances to Thematize and Challenge, and try especially to help the Speaker find a Focus and move toward action, Goal setting and Trialing some ideas where possible.

✓ Task 8.4

Individual preparation. Read the descriptions of four styles of decision making. Can you think of examples of when you use each style in any aspect of your professional (or private) life? Do you favor any particular one?

1. *autocratic*	You make the decision and then inform others of what is expected of them.
2. *persuasive*	You make the decision and then do your best to explain it and make it acceptable to others.
3. *consultative*	You check other people's opinions before you make the decision.
4. *codeterminate*	You explain the issues and then go along with the majority or consensus.

Interaction

Speaker: Explain your ideas on decision making to your Understander. Be open to the possibility of Focusing on

the development of your decision making abilities, setting yourself a goal and working on how to reach that
goal.

Understander: Attend and Reflect as carefully and empathically as you can. Look for chances to Thematize
and Challenge, and try especially to help the Speaker
find a Focus and move toward action, Goal setting and
Trialing some ideas where possible.

✓ Task 8.5

Individual preparation. When you are setting yourself a
goal in terms of action, there are five useful criteria, listed
here, that you can use to help check on its suitability. Take a
possible goal of your own, and check it against these questions. We are looking for a "yes" answer in each case.

- *Scale:* Have I identified a course of action small
  enough for me to deal with in a reasonable time scale?
- *Control:* Have I made sure that I am not dependent on
  the permission or help of other people, and have I also
  allowed for collaboration where possible?
- *Relevance:* Is the action I am planning tied in to work
  that I have to do anyway as part of my job?
- *Usefulness:* Will the investigation itself be a useful experience for my students and others involved?
- *Motivation:* Is this issue intrinsically interesting
  enough to keep me motivated?

Interaction

Speaker: Justify your goal to your Understander in terms
of the above criteria. Be open to the possibility of Focusing where appropriate on one or more of these criteria in order to be sure that your plan of action sounds
feasible.

Understander: Use all the Understanding skills at your disposal to help the Speaker define a clear goal and possibly Trial some intended courses of action.

✓ Task 8.6

Individual preparation. Can you specify what sort of outcomes you are hoping for from the course of action you are planning? Can you describe what would count for you as success? How will you be able to tell whether you have been successful? Will you be able to find out how other people involved feel?

Interaction

Speaker: Explain to your Understander what thoughts you have in response to these questions. Be open to the possibility of Focusing where appropriate on one or more of them in order to help you be prepared to evaluate your plan of action.

Understander: Use all the Understanding skills at your disposal to help the Speaker think ahead about evaluating his or her intended course of action.

Part 3
Further Developments in Action

Parts 1 and 2 of this book have introduced cooperative development as an essentially one-to-one framework for channeling the power of nonevaluative discourse toward an individual's goals for personal and professional growth. My aims were introductory, explanatory, and pedagogic. Although I drew examples from around the world, the setting was essentially neutral.

Part 3 is different. It invites you to observe the basic principles that underlie CD as they function in related but distinct ways and in specific contexts. Once again, there is a mixture of discussion and exemplificatory data drawn from actual experience. However, although part 3 certainly also sets out to deepen understanding and facilitate action, there are no tasks set here. Instead of trying to help you structure experience of your own, I want to offer you reports of other colleagues' contextualized action so that you can decide for yourself its significance to your own situation. You might even want to make this issue of significance the topic of a CD session with your Understander.

Chapter 9 tracks the evolution of a scheme of group development, chapter 10 introduces the development forum for visiting speakers, and chapter 11 invites some guest writers into the book to report on related developments in different parts of the world.

Chapter 9   Group Development

A Significant Moment

It is around 3 P.M. on February 3, 1998. We are in the Language Studies Unit of Aston University. With five colleagues acting as Understanders, I am the Speaker. We are approximately twenty minutes into the session.

Extract 9.1

01	UNDERSTANDER	You used the word "renewal," a lot there . . .
02	JULIAN	Yeah.
03	UNDERSTANDER	. . . "CD renewal" . . .
04	JULIAN	Yeah.
05	UNDERSTANDER	. . . but I didn't actually get a picture anywhere of
06		just what that renewal meant. You talked about how
07		you might take CD into different areas?
08	JULIAN	Yeah.
09	UNDERSTANDER	I wondered if you'd actually thought about what that
10		means for you, the idea of "renewing CD," you know,
11		in what sense?

The request for clarification contained in these nine lines of dialogue marks a particularly important turning point in my own professional development. Let me first of all interpret the moment in its context and then go on to explain more about the scheme that we were operating here.

The starting point for my work as Speaker that day was the news that my book, *Cooperative Development,* had been deleted from its publisher's list for the following year. I had what I take to be the usual writer's emotions about this fact, but they were magnified on this occasion by the feeling that I was about to lose my main line of communication in terms of the project that continued to motivate me most. I had been running courses and workshops in cooperative development since 1988. The significance of the book was that before, after, or even instead of face-to-face contact with colleagues, I was in a position to communicate my ideas in written form. But as of 1999, I was to be more or less back where I had started. That was how it felt. And I did not know what to do.

At the beginning of that school year (in October 1997), my immediate colleagues at work had paid me the enormous compliment of asking me to arrange some kind of regular professional development opportunity for ourselves as a group. We had been through a series of familiarization sessions in the use of nonevaluative discourse, based on tasks similar to those provided in the first part of this book, and the session from which I take Extract 9.1 was our first full-scale attempt at what we came to call group development (GD).

In lines 01 and 03, the Understander checks that he has correctly identified an expression that the Speaker has used. He then asks for clarification of this expression. In retrospect, I see that the power of this particular move arises from the fact that it functions in at least three ways:

- it requests clarification of a repeated idea that is clearly important to the Speaker—"renewing CD";
- it invites the Speaker to consider the possibility of choosing to focus on this point;
- it shifts the Speaker's orientation from talk to action, in the sense that this idea of renewal can only be clarified in terms of proposing to do something.

Again in retrospect, I see that the Understander chose just that item from my discourse that allowed me to shift my energy away from the disappointment and frustration that had been occupying me and toward the consideration of what my next steps actually were to be. Until this point, "renewal" had been an empty con-

tainer signaling an emotional reaction. I was now called on to fill
it with the detail of a response.

As ever, I am not saying that something mechanistic or necessarily causative happened here, but something facilitative certainly
did. In that moment, I felt a flash of panic along with a sense of the
absolute legitimacy of the Understander's request. From that moment, a hugely empowering and satisfying second wave of cooperative development work has flowed, involving more than I can
take space to report on in this book and including the book itself.

The Scheme

As a group of colleagues who already shared a positive working
relationship, we agreed to explore the potential of a nonjudgmental approach to individual self-development in a group context. There were eight of us at the initial meeting where the idea
was discussed, this being the teaching team for the MSc. in TESOL
program that we shared. Six colleagues (four men and two
women) wanted to be involved, and two did not, so the six of us
proceeded. In our context, no difficulties arose from this division,
either interpersonally or in terms of program coordination: some
people were involved in this collaborative research and development program, and others were involved in other things.

Another point worth picking up here is that I am sometimes
asked how to arrange this work if people do not want to do it or
in situations where working relations are bad in the first place.
The short answer to this question is that one cannot arrange this
work under such circumstances. There is no suggestion here that
group development, or any form of cooperative development, can
be used to *make* people develop professionally or to establish
harmony in place of strife. What I am reporting on is work that we
did in the situation in which we found ourselves. In other situations, I would still look for ways to introduce the principles that
motivate me, but I am not so presumptuous or naïve as to suggest
that we have some kind of a cure-all here. One last comment,
however: I would go so far as to say that in a situation in which

people are prepared to offer a certain (if only limited) amount of trust to each other, then working with nonevaluative discourse can certainly help them deepen and extend that trust.

All group members committed themselves to attending meetings regularly and to taking turns being the Speaker at some point. We tried to meet for one hour a week during the semester, going ahead so long as four members could make the session. (I do not want to gloss over the issues of time and effort. No one *has* the time. You have to decide whether you want to *take* the time to *make* the effort. I get upset when people imply that those people who *make* the effort must, somehow, *have* more time. That's a weakness of mine. I return to this subject—in a less abrasive mode—later in this chapter in the section titled "A New Collegiality.")

One colleague chaired the meeting in terms of suggesting when it was appropriate to move to the next stage of the procedure, but all colleagues were of equal status insofar as their roles as autonomously developing professionals were concerned. The fact that one member was director of the unit was not salient in these meetings.

We had two kinds of meetings: core meetings and feedback meetings. Our core meetings were organized in three parts:

1. The Speaker identified a topic of interest on which he or she wanted to work and then presented his or her thoughts while colleagues worked as Understanders.
2. After about 30 to 40 minutes, at what seemed an appropriate point, we changed the flow of discourse so that the colleagues who had been Understanding up to that point had the chance to Speak if they so wished. They did not comment on the thoughts or intentions of the Speaker, either explicitly or by implication. Their statements had to be self-referential. Those colleagues who wished to Speak made statements along the lines of:

   > *In my terms/my world/my field, this makes me think of the following situation/issue/experience ...*

   We came to call these statements **Resonances.** The intention was to allow colleagues to explore angles relevant to themselves and to give the Speaker a chance to hear different perspectives that were neither intended, nor to be interpreted, as suggestions, evaluations, or advice. The Speaker or other colleagues could Reflect or ask questions to clarify the resonances expressed.

Intercollegial exchanges were not to be pursued at this point, though matters of interest could be noted for later discussion or possibly as subsequent topics for exploration.

3. The focus shifted back to the Speaker, who might respond to some of the Resonances while reviewing or updating his or her position, making statements such as:

> *What I'm thinking/feeling now is ...*
> *What I have learned is ...*
> *This helped me ...*
> *This got in my way ...*
> *My next move is ...*

The Speaker or chairperson then closed the meeting.

Afterward, of course, colleagues sometimes wished to pursue points arising from the GD meeting. We agreed, however, that our usual, socially sanctioned patterns of discussing, agreeing, disagreeing, advising, etc., should not be taken up immediately, particularly not with regard to the Speaker's expressed opinions or intentions, in order to give the dynamic of self-development a little more space in which to work.

These core meetings were taped, and a part of my work as development coordinator was to go through the tapes and extract what I took to be significant incidents. We would then discuss these extracts at feedback meetings interspersed among the core meetings. For the most part, especially in the early stages, these discussions turned around issues of the legitimacy of Understander contributions in terms of the model we had agreed to work with.

Whenever, for example, a colleague said, *"Ah, I'm not sure if I'm supposed to say this here, but I think it might be useful if I...,"* this was a pretty clear signal that the Understander role was about to be abandoned. But there were more subtle diversions to discuss, and a great deal of learning took place for us all—about ourselves, about each other, and about the processes we were involved in. In time, we moved ever closer to implementing the idea that the Understanders' interventions are intended to serve the self-development of the Speaker.

We had wondered about how Understanders would manage turn-taking among themselves and decided to let matters follow their own course. This did not turn out to be a problem as such, but it remained the case throughout that some Understanders intervened more than others. This was due to some extent to familiarity with the style of discourse, to some extent to the amount of affinity individuals developed with the role, and to some extent to more general issues of personal style and preference. We certainly never felt that it would be useful to formalize taking turns. In retrospect, however, I would add one further comment. We discovered that, as with one-to-one CD, it is very useful to get a Reflection in early. It settles the Speaker, pulls the group together, and reaffirms the style of the discourse. I now feel that the role of providing this early reflection is one that we might have shared out on a turn-taking basis. But that is an idea for the next time, and I am getting ahead of myself.

What I want to do is introduce what happened through the data of the sessions themselves, along with some parallel comments elicited by an E-mail questionnaire. There is an important point to bring out here about what I am trying to communicate. This work means a lot to me, and I would be very happy to know that other people want to get involved in it or in something like it. But I have by now covered enough waterfronts not to want to suggest to people in circumstances other than my own what they should or should not be doing. So it has to happen like this: I'll tell you about the work we did and why I value it. You decide to what extent and in what ways you see anything useful to you.

It is a coincidence of my involvement in this work over time and with different colleagues that the one-to-one CD featured in part 2 of this book relates almost entirely to topics directly concerned with classroom teaching, while the topics here do not. I know of no reason why GD should not be carried out among full-time class-room teachers of ESL, but that has not been my experience of it. I have chosen to keep the data authentic and allow my readers to make their own decisions about the usefulness for themselves of the work on which I am reporting. That seems to me to be in line with the principles of respect, empathy, and sincerity that under-pin all these efforts. As I said in the opening lines of chapter 1, the issue is not whether we are teaching preschool or supervising doc-toral students but how we can develop as professionals.

We are going to look next at three GD sessions in some detail in an attempt to track significant moments in episodes of individ-ual development. After that, we will look at the work again from the viewpoint of an enhanced collegiality. The names used in the extracts are pseudonyms. Everyone concerned has read this chap-ter and had any input that they wish. So right now, let us return to Room 742. It's sunnier now. We're in June 1998, and Bill is Speaker.

Bill as Speaker

Particularly on Bill's mind is the need to give a talk at an upcom-ing conference, but the issue he is working on is one that is com-mon to other situations in a teacher or teacher-educator's profes-sional life. Here is how the Focus comes to be articulated (01–08) and Reflected (09–17). Notice how the Reflection leads to a fur-ther articulation of the Focus (18–22), making explicit Bill's feel-ing of failed communication when he gives a planned talk.

Extract 9.2

01	BILL	For whatever reason, I've got a strong sense that I'm
02		much better at improvising and off-the-cuff talking
03		than I am at planning. As soon as I enter into a
04		planning world in terms of talking, it seems to put
05		on some kind of stress, which I feel imposing on me,
06		and this imposition, this structure that I've
07		preplanned, is, is a saddle, a chain, something that
08		inhibits me.

09	JOE	So, if I can just check that with you, this area of
10		focus that you want to work on is a preference for
11		off-the-cuff talk, as opposed to planned talk (Bill:
12		Mmm). You feel that when you plan something, that
13		when you start to talk, you feel that plan as an
14		imposition on you and it constrains you and ties you
15		down, and you feel that you're not being as
16		productive as you could be in your talk (Bill: Yes). Is
17		that right?
18	BILL	That's right. It has a . . . in the experiences of public
19		talk that I've had, where I've planned to a higher
20		degree, I've had a very strong feeling that I haven't
21		ended up communicating very much at all, because
22		of that structure.

At this point (in Extract 9.3), Harry asks for further clarification of the stress/pressure/inhibition that Bill has Spoken of (01–06). While GD does not usually favor the use of either/or questions (and Harry tries to back away from making such a move (05–06)), one can appreciate here the sensitivity of Harry's question, which Reflects quite explicitly the two aspects of difficulty that Bill has indeed expressed, but not articulated separately. As he is asked to dig deeper into this area, Bill makes a de facto Focusing choice (07–08) and also develops further the communication element of what he has said (08–27), drawing on his earlier background in acting (10–15, 18–19) and also making an analogy with music (15–18). The length and enthusiasm of this turn indicates how helpful Harry's previous move has been, and its closing lines (24–27) suggest that there is a long-standing personal preference here that Bill is bringing to bear on professional duties, which have perhaps sometimes been more shaped by his ideas of what a person is *supposed* to do. Sara's Reflection (28–32, 35) picks up the audience/communication Focus that is clearly important to Bill, and Lucy's simple but powerful metaphorical Reflection (40–42) allows him to express the depth of the constraints that he feels (43).

Extract 9.3

01	HARRY	Can you just clarify something for me about this
02		pressure? When you say it's like an imposition, is that
03		an imposition in the sense that consciousness of the
04		plan places a psychological pressure on you, or is it
05		that having the plan constrains what you can say? Or
06		is it both?
07	BILL	I think it's both, and the interesting thing about the
08		second one, the constraint element, is that a lot of
09		the thoughts, or this vague thought that I've got,
10		relates to drama, where you have a choice between
11		scripted performance and improvisation. Back in
12		the eighties, I was part of a theater group, Improv, it
13		was called, where you had very loose structures,
14		and you'd walk onto stage as a group, and you
15		improvise . . . I suppose this is very much like jazz,
16		where you play together and the more you get to
17		know each other, the more you know what you
18		might do . . . But the actual line that you're going to
19		take is often supplied by the audience. And I think
20		there's a parallel there with the kind of public
21		talking that we do, where the more constrained you
22		are, the more planned it is, the less able you are to
23		respond to your audience, the people you are trying
24		to communicate with. And I think for a long time
25		I've believed that really I would be better having a
26		very loose structure and walking in to do whatever I
27		do, a lecture, a presentation, a talk . . .
28	SARA	Just picking up on what you said about the
29		audience, do you feel that you've had experiences
30		where you've received some kind of signal from the
31		audience and you've been unable to change in
32		response to it?
33	BILL	I think it's partly that and partly the fact that I don't
34		feel open to any signals.
35	SARA	So, you don't feel that you see them?
36	BILL	I see the two things, you know, in opposition: this
37		driving force to get through the plan does mean that
38		I don't even see the signals, let alone invite them or
39		deal with them.
40	LUCY	As though you're looking back into your head all the
41		time, rather than looking out to your audience and
42		communicating with them?
43	BILL	Yes!!

Later in the session (Extract 9.4), Paul takes Bill back to his drama analogy, reflecting his Understanding of what is involved (01-03) and checking how this transfers to Bill's present situation (05-09). Again, this elicits quite a lengthy response (10-26), one that turns out to be significant to the session as a whole in that it foregrounds a distinction between preparation (11-14) and having an explicit, planned structure (18-26).

Extract 9.4

01	PAUL	You mentioned audience involvement, audience
02		participation, or the audience actually changing the
03		story line . . . Have I got that right?
04	BILL	Yeah, yeah.
05	PAUL	Is that right? How important is that element in this?
06		In other words, I can understand that you don't
07		know where to go . . . *Is* it the case that you don't
08		know where to go until somebody has made a
09		contribution?
10	BILL	I think there are plenty of places I *could* go with a
11		talk opportunity. I'm not talking about knowing
12		nothing about the area you've allotted to talk about.
13		I'm not talking about no *preparation,* no *reading,*
14		no *thinking* around the area, but the more
15		experience I have of this kind of teacher education,
16		the more comfortable I am with the idea of taking
17		my thoughts and my current understanding in,
18		without a clear structure (Joe: Mmm). And at the
19		same time, I know that audiences sometimes like to
20		see a clear structure, because they take that as the
21		sign of a good, of a professional, somebody who has
22		planned, and I think there will always be those who,
23		if you don't say, "Look, there are five stages to the
24		presentation today and I'm going to cover this, that
25		and the other," then they will assume that you
26		haven't *prepared,* even.

Joe then (Extract 9.5) offers the two terms *planning* and *preparation* that Bill has used in Thematizing a possible contrast (01-08). Bill is enthusiastic about this (09), and the insight he achieves through reseeing preparation in this light is articulated via another analogy, this time having to do with sports (09-15).

Extract 9.5

01	JOE	Mmm. And that's the big distinction I hear now in
02		what you're saying: between being prepared to enter
03		the arena, and to deal with the topic in the context
04		of the people, on the one hand, which is what you
05		do want to do. And the idea of having a plan (Bill:
06		Mmm), which you think will ride roughshod over
07		the discourse possibilities that could have occurred
08		in that arena.
09	BILL	Yes, yes! And another thought hits me from that,
10		from this preparation/planning distinction, is that an
11		athlete doesn't necessarily prepare for a hundred
12		meters by doing a hundred meters. They prepare in
13		lots of different ways. That to *plan* for a speech
14		event, if you take the metaphor to its conclusion, is
15		not a good way to *prepare* for a speech event.

Bill talks more about audience and student expectations of plans and also about a distinction that is important to him—between a debilitating *tenseness* that he sometimes feels and a creative *tension* that is necessary to high-quality performance. He then (Extract 9.6) returns to the warming-up metaphor (01), and we see—marked by pauses as well as explicitly signaled (04-05) and expressed (05-07)—how Bill's developmental goal is taking shape for him. Joe's Thematizing (08-10), which is over-explicit in purist CD terms, again draws an enthusiastic response (11), and Bill's Goal setting is now articulated in terms of possible action strategies (16-20).

Extract 9.6

01	BILL	That's where the warming-up comes in, the
02		preparation, you need to reach that pitch where
03		you're excited enough to talk and I think that, what,
04		one realization that is becoming even clearer to me

05		now is that I need, I need to *try* to not wrap myself
06		up with a highly planned product, and to take a few
07		risks with a couple of presentations.
08	JOE	Because the highly planned product brings you
09		tenseness, whereas a well-prepared improvisation
10		gives you tension?
11	BILL	Yes! Yes, I've got to, I started to say this earlier and I
12		somehow got sidetracked, but, in terms of
13		preparation, I have never been able to say, "Right, this
14		presentation is an hour, I'm going to rehearse this.
15		I'm going to put a clock down and give this
16		presentation to nobody." I just can't do that. And
17		there are, there are other things: I can do snippets, I
18		can read, I can voice things. There are other forms of
19		warming-up that I think, that I feel more comfortable
20		with.

It seems fair to describe what happened in this session in the following terms. Bill articulated important personal preferences in terms of his own style of communicative action and also identified other people's expectations—and his need to live up to them—as getting in his way. He discovered a way of expressing this contrast that allowed him to evaluate his preferred style highly enough to validate goals and actions based on it. In these necessarily brief extracts, I have tried to present the essential data of this process.

As well as the developmental progress achieved here by the Speaker, there were other outcomes. The planning/preparation distinction, capturing as it does two important dimensions of how we work, has become a part of our everyday discourse in the Language Studies Unit. Lucy commented, *"This has definitely sharpened my thinking about preparing talks, and has had a real developmental effect for me."*

For me, this session also provided an example of how Understanders must be willing to be changed if they are to be open enough to Understand. I state my general position on planning and flexibility in chapter 8 (p. 117). Faced with the prospect of giving a talk at a conference, my preferred strategy involves producing a full written text of an appropriate length, which I then read onto a tape. I listen to the tape a couple of times and make headline notes from it. On the way to the conference, I listen to the tape while reading my text. Before my talk, I listen to the tape while looking at my notes. When I get up to speak, I am not only prepared—I am *planned!* I do not find this constraining. I find the procedure lengthy and arduous but eventually liberating. I find that *my* best chance of communication lies in the clarity that I believe I produce with this kind of planning. This is how I am best prepared.

But there are occasions when I cannot achieve this kind of planned preparation, and I have found that reflection on the distinction between planning and preparation, which had not been explicitly available to me before this session, has proved enormously helpful to me in avoiding the kind of tenseness that can interfere with anyone's performance. I see more clearly now that a planned message without personal preparation may not communicate well at all, whereas if I am prepared in myself to communicate, then I am likely to have things to say that will be meaningful to my audience. To give a specific instance, I recently ran a weekend workshop for participants in our distance-learning MSc. in TESOL program. In the time available to me, I reduced the period I might have spent planning content and prepared myself by rereading the participants' background files. The workshop went well.

We have looked at the way in which Bill used his personal experience and analogical thinking to bring individual preferences to bear on professional difficulties and goals. In the next session, we deal directly with contending personal and professional demands, although that's not where we begin.

Sara as Speaker

During 1998, our MSc. in TESOL teaching team organized a series of mutually supported periods of study leave. In May 1998, Sara was coming toward the end of her ten-week sabbatical period, in which she had been working on her Ph.D. She was concerned about what was going to happen when she returned to full-time work. This concern is what she chose to Speak about.

Extract 9.7

01	SARA	. . . and that led me to think that perhaps a
02		reasonably fruitful topic of discussion for today
03		would be if I, we, tried to talk about how I'm going
04		to carry on with it once I've finished this wonderful
05		experience of a sabbatical.
06	JOE	Okay, so you, you're staying with the topic that
07		you've headlined for us before, "working (Sara: Yes)
08		on the Ph.D."—not in the sense of there being any
09		specific problem you want to work on, but with a
10		focus on how you're going to handle that when
11		you're back at work.
12	SARA	Yeah, I think so, yeah.
13	HARRY	Can I also clarify something, that that comment at
14		the end, this "wonderful" period of a sabbatical, was
15		that significant (Sara: Oh, yes!) in the sense that, that
16		you have, you know, you have doubts about what's
17		coming up . . .
18	SARA	Oh, yes! (laughs)
19	HARRY	Yeah, right, Okay, thank you.
20	SARA	Yes, definitely. The reason is, I mean, it's obvious, but
21		the sabbatical has made a tremendous difference
22		because, from an academic point of view, the Ph.D. is
23		all I've been concentrating on. When I return to
24		work in just two and a half weeks' time, that won't
25		be the case anymore, and especially now that I'm
26		nearing the end of the project, and therefore have to
27		hold it all in my mind, whatever bit I'm working on
28		(Harry: Yeah). The idea of doing that when also doing
29		all the other things I'm supposed to be doing is very,
30		well, it's worrying in two senses: in one sense it's
31		worrying because, erm, I think it will be much
32		harder to do the Ph.D. that way, and it's also
33		worrying because I think that in my attempts to do
34		that I risk, not doing other things quite so well as I
35		might, so it worries me two ways.
36	JOE	So, you're concerned that going back to work is

37		going to "get in the way" of continuing with the
38		Ph.D. . . .
39	SARA	Yes! (laughs)
40	JOE	. . . and balancing that is this concern that your
41		determination to get the Ph.D. done and finished
42		now it's entering its final stages might get in the way
43		of your doing the job as well as you want to—(Sara:
44		Yes)—both those.

By the end of these introductory exchanges, Sara's topic has been clearly stated. After her opening (01-05), Reflections by Joe (06-11) and Harry (13-17) have helped her deepen her original formulation by bringing out the importance of the timing of her return to full-time work in terms of her completing her doctorate (20-30) and have separated out the two-way difficulty she feels she will have when trying to make a good job of doctorate and teaching (30-35).

Shortly afterward, however, as we see in Extract 9.8, the picture changes significantly.

Extract 9.8

01	PAUL	We work here flexi-days rather than flexi-hours (Sara:
02		Yeah). What kind of a time scale do you think in—in
03		terms of weeks, or days, or hours, when you see
04		these conflicting interests?
05	SARA	Days, days.
06	PAUL	And you don't think that you have in fact got control
07		over your days, after coming off sabbatical?
08	SARA	Well, I think I have very limited control over them. I
09		mean, that this is in my, this is further compli-, since
10		I've had Adam, this is an extra factor that complicates
11		things for me (Paul: Ah), erm, inasmuch as I, that you
12		know, I've got days that are days that I spend with
13		him and that I wouldn't want to break into.
		[Sara talks here about earlier periods before Adam
		was born of working on her research for long,
		uninterrupted stretches.]
14	SARA	It's as if, because, because, Okay, you know, a person
15		has their home life, their social life, but among
16		adults, you know, say in marriage, there's always

17		possibility for negotiation (Bill: Mmm) but I don't
18		think, you know, when toddlers are involved it's not
19		like that. Erm, I wouldn't want ...
20	LUCY	Especially if you're around in the house and they
21		know you are.
22	SARA	Yeah, er, I wouldn't want to anyway. I don't think it's
23		fair on, on Adam, so. So, it's as if if, it's as if balancing a
24		job and a Ph.D. might have been a bit difficult but it
25		was perfectly possible; managing a job, Ph.D. and a
26		toddler (Joe: Mmm) really seems to me like the limits
27		(Lucy: Mmm) of what is humanly possible.

I should perhaps explain Paul's use of the expression "flexi-days" (01) here. As most of our teaching is through a distance-learning program, it is possible for us to move our work around, to chunk it in different ways, to work from home and go into the university more in order to meet with people than to teach. In this later extract from the session, Paul asks his question about time scale in order—as he commented later—to help him get a better view of how Sara saw the demands on her time. In explaining her perspective further, however, Sara introduces into the equation the presence of her young son and of her determination to safeguard extensive periods of time with him (09–13). At this point, therefore, the two conflicting pulls on her time that she originally identified as the nub of her problem have become three (25–27).

Another point to note here is Lucy's intervention (20–21), which is not really legitimate in terms of our rules of procedure. What Lucy is doing here is introducing an element of her own experience and attitudes, based on an evaluation of the practicality of getting work done when a toddler is in the house. The sympathy expressed is undeniable, but as an attempt to express empathy it fails (22) because it is not in fact based on an Understanding of what Sara is saying; Sara does not *want* to act in this way.

Sometime later, Sara is again exploring her attitudes toward various aspects of her work and has just talked about a feeling of having lost touch with course participants as individuals during her time away. She continues:

Extract 9.9

01	SARA	I suspect that another reason is because, as I say,
02		with Ph.D., job and toddler, you know, things are just
03		getting so squeezed and that worries me because I'd
04		rather, erm, be able to, you know, have a level of
05		emotional investment with the participants I'm
06		working with that I'm comfortable about. So again,
07		it's that, I'm sort of feeling gosh I must I really must
08		make space again for those people. I mustn't see
09		them as getting . . . you know . . .
10	HARRY	Getting in the way, yeah?
11	SARA	When I receive a query from a participant I must
12		not see this as getting in the way of my Ph.D.!
13		(Harry: [laughs] Yeah) I mean, you know, I just (Bill:
14		Mmm), it's supposed to be job first and people first
15		(Harry: Yeah) (Lucy: Mmm).
16	HARRY	So what you're saying, if I understand you correctly
17		is there's a big psychological weight, as well as the
18		purely practical weight of having to complete the
19		Ph.D.
20	SARA	I suppose there is, yeah.
21	HARRY	And that's, that's . . .
22	SARA	I suppose there is, yeah.

What Harry picks up in his Reflection (16–18) is that Sara is struggling with more than a question of how to schedule a certain number of tasks into a given amount of time—that she also has a set of expectations regarding emotional investment and her own attitudes with which she needs to find a sense of comfort or well-being. The moment of insight that Sara achieves here is caught in her thoughtful, repeated acknowledgment (20, 22) that something important is happening here and in the fact that Harry, recognizing this, does not go on (21) to spell out the importance that he sees in this.

When we moved into the Resonances phase of the session, Paul set out to say that for him it had been interesting to hear an apparently familiar situation described from a perspective so different from his own.

Extract 9.10

01	PAUL	The point being that your situation is not for me, it's
02		for my daughter and my daughter-in-law. They're
03		both in identical situations, one has got an MBA to
04		finish and one has got a PGCE [teaching
05		qualification] to finish and they've got kids, little
06		ones. And they are both in exactly this kind of bind,
07		but without a sabbatical. And, er, we have a solution,
08		and that is that my wife goes and takes over, to let
09		those pieces of work continue and, er, be finished.
10		And I was just dwelling on the enormous impact of
11		that, it simply makes possible what would otherwise
12		be impossible (Sara: Mmm). But it's not so much the
13		circum-, my private circumstances, but the fact that
14		I'm in a different context (Harry: Yeah) (Sara: Yes). So
15		I hear it with different ears (Joe: Mmm).
16	SARA	Yes, but what you say still gives me an angle on the
17		nature of the thing, inasmuch as, I think if I wanted
18		to, well, I think unquestion-, unquestionably, if I
19		wanted to get more help with childcare I could. But
20		I don't (Paul: Mmm). I don't want to.
21	PAUL	Oh, er, a grandmother looking after the child is not
22		the same as . . .
23	SARA	No, but I mean I have that . . .
24	PAUL	. . . "childcare."
25	SARA	It is to me! I mean, my mum looks after Adam
26		sometimes when I'm at work and, and I'm very
27		happy with the arrangement, but I wouldn't want to
28		extend it any, I mean, there's a certain amount of
29		time when I want to be the one who is looking after
30		Adam, and it doesn't matter if it's Ted, if my mum, it's
31		me, I want it to be me.
32	PAUL	It's a totally different ball game.
33	SARA	Yes (laughs) (Paul laughs). It's, but what you said is
34		helpful to me, because it helps me to, it concretizes
35		for me that in that sense my problem is not a
36		practical one.

While Paul is thinking about the experience (and the difficulty) of
what he calls, "hearing with different ears"—a very Understander-
related experience (01–15)—Sara chooses to relate his situation

more directly to hers and to evaluate Paul's family's response in terms of her own preferences (16-20). We are on the borderline of our procedural agreements here, but I believe that we stay inside them in terms of Paul's Resonance being neither intended nor received as a suggestion as such. Where we almost short circuit is with Sara's use of the expression "childcare" (19) and Paul's feeling that he, in turn, has not been well Understood (21-22, 24). Sara's definition of this concept for herself (25-31) seems to mark out another highly significant incident in this session, in that it becomes very clear to Sara that her problem is "not a practical one" (33-36).

At the opening of the GD session, Sara identified her topic as a pragmatic problem of how to fit in her teaching and her doctoral study. By the end, she sees it rather differently, as a complex situation involving her family relationships, her levels of emotional investment with course participants, and the psychological weight that her definitions and expectations create for her.

This is how the session closed:

Extract 9.11

01	JOE	Is there anything you want to say to round up?
02		About how the topic, or responses to it—anything
03		you want to say?
04	SARA	Mmm. Just that the way I've experienced the session
05		has been looking in much more detail and from
06		many more angles about the, at the, situation, or
07		problem, or situation that has been problematized
08		for the purposes of this session (Joe laughs) and that
09		has been interesting and I think I have a fuller sense
10		of it than I did when I walked in. I think I probably
11		have more of a sense of why it was getting to me,
12		actually, inasmuch as it's in a sense been shown as
13		more of a problem than I would have said it was!
14		But that's good, because otherwise you're aware on a
15		subconscious level that it's a problem. If you haven't
16		made it conscious it can bother you more actually
17		(Lucy: Mmm), you know, it can get to you more. Erm,
18		I don't feel particularly at the moment moved
19		forward in terms of possible solutions, but I
20		wouldn't expect to and . . . I'm quite happy to just

21	now go to sleep on the train on the way home and
22	just see what happens (Harry: Yeah). Yeah. And that's,
23	that's all I have to say.

In the earlier chapter on Reflecting (chap. 5, p. 68), I use a quotation about how the Understander can sometimes be frustrated by the feeling of not having helped enough. I suggest then that this is one of the hard parts of learning to be an Understander—that making suggestions is a lot easier than creating an opportunity for self-development. The quote that I use came, in fact, from feedback on this session. I introduce it again here, now in its proper context.

Lucy:

My feeling was one of frustration as Understander—I understood her problems so well I didn't need or want to simply reflect (having been through similar conflicts myself). I interpreted her speaking on this as a cri de coeur and desperately wanted to take an active role as sympathizer and a suggester of solutions. We did discuss these things in a separate chat later on, but somehow it was not the same. Maybe, having acted as Speaker, she had got it off her chest publicly and was slowly coming to her own solutions. Hope so—though I can't be sure.

Sara:

That session really did help me to clear my thinking on the point I discussed and it has helped me shape my priorities and feel less conflict afterwards. This I find interesting because I don't think it was a session where "outcomes" were particularly salient at the time.

Sara completed her doctorate on schedule, now has a second child, and has changed her employment pattern for the medium term by entering a job-share arrangement with another colleague on a fifty-fifty basis. None of us would claim that all this flowed from our one-hour GD session! But neither would we dismiss the significance of such sessions to the facilitation of an individual's developmental decision making and the building of a collegiality in which such development can flourish.

Bill as Speaker (Again)

Why Bill again? Why not Paul, Harry, Joe, or Lucy this time? Might it be that Bill is a person who gets more out of this sort of work than the others? Well yes, it might. That is how things work out; nothing is equally good for everyone. On the other hand, feedback from the group suggests that all members have benefited significantly from their work as Speaker and Understander, as well as from the new collegiality that I discuss further below. Harry is on record as saying that one of his sessions as Speaker *"ultimately changed my way of working."* Paul's session on the coordination of our research efforts not only enabled him to discover strengths in his work that he had not been aware of (see Data 9.19) but also took us all very meaningfully into areas of common ground and differences between and among us, as the Resonances show.

So why Bill again? Because I need to select data that seems to me most coherently extractable in terms of communicating with my readers. The issue is not whether development took place but whether it can be shown to be taking place in the explicit record of a few snippets of data. Here again, in February 1999, I think that this is quite demonstrably the case.

When I took on the role in the unit of special responsibility for our professional development, Bill took on a similar responsibility for what we refer to as the pastoral care of our course participants. Generally speaking, this refers to the ways in which an institution looks after its students outside the purely academic demands of its courses. As our MSc. in TESOL is a distance-learning program taken by mature people (usually in the 25–45 age range) living in countries all around the world, the issues to be dealt with that fall outside purely academic ones constituted little less than life itself. What can pastoral care mean under these circumstances, either as a concept or in terms of our actions? This was what Bill wanted to work on.

In his opening statement, of which only the last, summarizing sentence is given here (Extract 9.12), Bill emphasizes the issue of interaction. Let me highlight again the early Reflection. In this instance, we might suggest that Bill's explicit summarizing of his goals (01–03) can be seen as a signal to the Understander that this would be an appropriate time to come in, that this is the end of his opening statement and that it should be checked. Notice how Joe's Reflection (04–07) presents pastoral care and interaction as two topics to bring together. Hearing the image in the Reflection ("when you say that") allows Bill to recognize and move on from this separation (08–11):

Extract 9.12

01	BILL	So, they're my goals, I suppose, to try to get this, to
02		develop this sense of where we're going with
03		pastoral care, but also tie in this idea of interaction.
04	JOE	So, pastoral care, but specifically interaction (Bill:
05		Hmm) is the, is the, that's what you want to bring
06		together: pastoral care and how we interact with our
07		participants, that's what you want to explore.
08	BILL	Yeah, and when you say that, I wonder if there is
09		actually anything else? Is there anything else in the
10		field of pastoral care that isn't interaction in some
11		way?

Bill then Speaks about the various forms of interaction that take place between our participants and ourselves. As he does so, he warms to his insight regarding the inseparability of pastoral care and interaction (Extract 9.13, 01–03). Joe attempts a Challenge in terms of Bill's earlier statement (04–05), but Bill's exploration has brought him to a discovery ("I've realized") that is important to him, as is clearly signaled (13–14) by the comment, "I've never understood as clearly as I do today."

Extract 9.13

01	BILL	Yes, interaction in all those senses because I think
02		that that is what pastoral care is, it's almost
03		synonymous with the idea of interaction.
04	JOE	So it's not . . . is that a change? Have you just
05		changed what you mean by interaction?
06	BILL	No, I think what I've done is I've realized that when
07		I talk about pastoral care, I've thought about pastoral

08	care—it's one of those words which, which I've
09	been living with for a long time . . .
	[Here Bill gives some autobiographical details.]
10	. . . and I think I've always thought of it as a system,
11	and now I'm thinking of it more as interaction, and I
12	think it's a difference in emphasis. And maybe the
13	two things . . . I've never understood as clearly as I
14	do today that really there is nothing else except
15	interaction, as long as you include any printed
16	matter that we might send, or any future websites
17	that we might put together.

Bill continues to explore the possibilities of what interaction-as-pastoral-care might mean, and one of the group Reflects back a problem-solving scenario as an example to check whether or not he has Understood. In Extract 9.14, Bill confirms the accuracy of the Reflection (01) and also uses it ("hearing you talk about that has made it clearer") as the basis for a new discovery (02–07). Paul Challenges Bill with regard to his current and previous definitions of *interactive* (08–10), and Bill, after a significant pause to think (11), uses this Challenge to clarify the relationship that he sees between the two definitions (11–15). When Paul Reflects this relationship (16–17), Bill takes a further step to establish a three-part characterization of pastoral care in terms of interaction (18–20). He refers to this as a genuine discovery in GD terms ("a real sense of outcome"). The unusually long pauses here also mark significant moments when Bill is doing a Speaker's work in Understander-supported silence (11, 18).

Extract 9.14

01	BILL	Yeah, I think so. I also think, and hearing you talk
02		about that has made it clearer, that one of our duties
03		is not just to respond to problems, as a pastoral role,
04		our duty, or part of that role, is to anticipate what
05		these problems are going to be and be well ahead of
06		them, and that might mean looking at trends and
07		trying to see what's going to happen.

08	PAUL	Have you moved over the last half an hour, a little
09		bit, from the purely interactive to the more
10		proactive?
11	BILL	(five-second pause) Yes, I think so. I think that's true.
12		That interaction feeds from that sense of being
13		proactive and trying to anticipate what the problems
14		are and then we think, well, how can we best, how
15		can we best work with this possible problem?
16	PAUL	Does that mean a dual relationship between pro- and
17		inter-?
18	BILL	(three-second pause) Yes. Yeah, I like that distinction,
19		and then we have, we have, *reactive, pro*active and
20		*inter*active
21	PAUL	Reactive being the "fire fighting"?
22	BILL	Yeah.
23	LUCY	So, our first telephone call would be proactive ...
24	BILL	I think you might have given me a nice title there,
25		Paul! I like it! Yeah, I think that's a really good
26		distinction for me. That maybe we've been living in
27		reactive worlds with our pastoral care. I think that's
28		a real sense of outcome for me, that distinction.
29		Thanks.

Bill's use of "given" (24) and "Thanks" (29) draws a response from Paul at the Resonances stage of the session. Paul expresses his Resonance in terms of the process we are involved in (Extract 9.15, 01–11), which draws in Bill, Joe, and Lucy in a celebration of what has happened.

Extract 9.15

01	PAUL	This is a part of the joint discovery that we've
02		commented on before (Joe: Mmm). Yes, exactly. And
03		this is looking at the process, and Bill imagining that
04		I had actually given him something! Which I didn't!
05		That's an entirely wrong way of looking at it,
06		because I wasn't aware, yeah? I didn't have anything
07		up my sleeve at all. They were just little pieces that
08		came together in the way that you were Speaking
09		and it seemed to me, you know, in what you were

10		saying, those pieces were there rather than I was
11		telling you anything.
12	BILL	I think so.
13	PAUL	They just came out.
14	LUCY	Mmm.
15	BILL	Definitely, that was my sense. But I think there's a
16		sense of "being given" something by the very clever
17		pulling out of two things.
18	JOE	Again, it's the power of Reflection, isn't it?
19	BILL	Yeah, I think that's a really good example. Because I
20		said both those things, proactive and interactive . . .
21	LUCY	. . . and reactive . . .
22	BILL	. . . but I wouldn't have seen that relationship if you
23		hadn't reflected that back.

Finally, when the Speaker role returns to Bill (Extract 9.16), he confirms his sense of a discovery that can form the basis of professional action. Where he had previously been concerned that his vagueness was at fault, he now feels that there is real complexity to deal with, and he has the confidence to employ the framework that he has worked out in order to move forward with his special responsibility for pastoral care.

Extract 9.16

01	BILL	I've probably had the same feeling that most of you
02		have that really quite a lot of issues were raised
03		today and I think that I'd started off with a feeling
04		that if I'd been more organized about this, there'd
05		have been a clearer sense, but the more we talk
06		about it, the more this pastoral sense of it gluing
07		together all the things that we do, and all these
08		different interactions, there are so many things
09		involved in pastoral care, that talking them through
10		today and hearing some of your Reflections and
11		Resonances, has kind of given me the confidence that
12		those things are multifarious (Joe: Mmm) and that if I
13		start with that perception, then I can work with this
14		model thing, I can start to look for these interactions
15		and present choices to you, and we can decide what
16		we as a group, collectively, think is best.

Once again, it is tempting to detail the work that has arisen from the discoveries and goals signaled here, but that is not my specific focus, and space is limited. It will have to suffice to say that we feel that we now have proactive, interactive, and reactive systems for taking care of our course participants with which we and they are well satisfied, even if there is always room for improvement.

I have repeatedly stated the importance to us of the reflexive relationship between individual and group development. Having concentrated so far on individuals, let us now turn to a group perspective.

A New Collegiality

In this section, I draw on responses to a brief questionnaire that I e-mailed to GD colleagues. The questionnaire itself is reproduced at the end of the chapter. As I have already emphasized, we began our group development work in a positive, collegial atmosphere. This was already the kind of place where, if you needed a helping hand, you would not often have to ask two people. So that is where I was starting from. Another important way of describing our situation would be to acknowledge explicitly again the level of commitment that leads a group of professionals to take the time out of their busy schedules in order to meet for an hour most weeks and work together in this way. We tried a few scheduling tricks (none of them successful) in order to enable ourselves to clear a few minutes' space before our meetings, but in the end we had to admit that life was too hectic. As one colleague put it:

> *Though I do know it would be more productive and re-warding not to go into a GD session feeling, "Oh ****! I still haven't . . . ," it always happens. If only I were better orga-nized, I'd do 5 mins Tai Chi before each session!*

Once we were in a GD meeting, it also took some time for us to come together in terms of what we were trying to do, rather than just going through the motions. It took a while for the out-side world to slip away or for us to slip away from it.

The first five minutes are always spent feeling pressures fall off. The immediate question is always, "Can I afford the time?" when the real question is, "Can we afford not to?"

We took that time on the initial premise that we would be using it in specific ways in order to further individual professional development. One of our earliest formulations of this was made in comparison to the time that we spend in our regular unit meetings, at which we exchange opinions, argue, make suggestions, and behave in all those socially sanctioned ways that one expects to behave at meetings. In the unit meetings, we said, the individual works for the good of the group. In the GD meetings, we wanted to create a situation in which the group worked for the good of its individuals. In the ways that I have sketched above, I believe that we have had some success in this. The following piece of feedback came in response to the first question on the E-mail questionnaire, in which colleagues were asked to recall one particular moment from the sessions so far:

The thing that comes back to me most vividly is the memory of telling everyone in the resonances phase of Sara's last session that I rarely say, "I know just how you feel . . ." but that I thought I could make an exception in this case, only to hear her say in her response that my description bore no relation to the way she felt. Two things learned:

- *In future, NEVER think I know how someone feels.*
- *Being an Understander in the way we're trying to be Understanders at least minimizes the chance of coming away with self-satisfied illusions about the extent to which we've really understood: the aim of these sessions is to help the Speaker, not to come away impressed with our own powers of insight.*

However, it is precisely in this new style of focusing on the individual that what I am calling our new collegiality is based. Sustenance of the individual is a social phenomenon; we did not work to promote the individual as separate from the group, but as a member of it. In an important sense, this type of individual is impossible without the group; such an individual is in the group, of the group, and for the group:

> *For me, whatever else this may be, it's a weekly demonstration that as colleagues we really do have time for one another and respect for one another. To know that at some point my colleagues are going to give five hours a week of their combined time to something I think is important enough to tell them about fills me with a sense of wonder, surprise, gratitude, and, most of all, faith in what we can do together. It's a weekly affirmation of our sense of shared responsibility and commitment.*

So our focus on individual development has led toward a growth of collegiality that had not been foreseen, even if it should not have been surprising. In other words, we knew that the original form of CD pairwork has clear outcomes for Speaker and Understander, not only in terms of specific goals achieved and in terms of more general communicative attitudes and abilities but also in terms of relationship. Similarly, our group development work added a layer of outcome in terms of enhanced collegiality that we all felt and commented on.

I'm not going to try to weigh that and count it out for you. I don't know what the units would be. Instead, I'm going to look at some of the ideas that arose in our feedback sessions and, as we go along, try to tie them into this concept of collegiality.

The Whole Person and Multiple Identities

A great deal of work that has been done in TESOL over the last twenty-five years has turned around the idea of language learning being a whole-person process, as distinct from simply an intellectual one. All the materials and techniques, now commonplace, that invite students to invest their opinions, emotions, and experiences in their language learning are based on this fundamental principle. At the same time, a great deal of postmodern writing in different fields has emphasized the idea of each one of us having different identities at different times. Sometimes I speak as a motorist, sometimes as a cyclist; sometimes I argue against censorship of any kind, and sometimes I argue as the father of a teenage daughter. As we have already seen in this chapter, a person might sit down with a self-image of two competing identities, that of teacher and that of student, and discover that it is a third identity, that of mother, which is at least as important.

As the Reflecting, Thematizing, and Challenging moves interwove over the months, we also talked about how these two views—of wholeness and multiplicity—are two ways of looking at the same phenomenon, of the whole person not as an undifferentiated whole but as the meeting place of different roles and identities. What we all seek is awareness and coherence. As each one of us in the group came to insights that helped us think about our own individual coherence, we came as a group to have a much clearer picture of how we fitted together and to have more acceptance of those aspects of others that might perhaps have otherwise been unappreciated or even found annoying. We saw how one person might find linear thought liberating and another might be constrained by it, how one person might use hyperbole without intending to express anything more extreme than what another would express through understatement, how one person might move their ideas forward via constantly shifting analogies while another might find this process disorienting. These propositions are perhaps commonplace as abstractions, but it is a rich and binding experience to have them unfold in personal terms within a group of colleagues.

Being involved in the GD interaction helped us all work on ourselves as colleagues, as well as working on ourselves as individuals. To clarify this, here are two more items of feedback from the questionnaire that well represent, I think, the depth of commitment that was made. Once more, in response to the first question:

Q1: Does any one moment from the GD sessions come back to you particularly?

I recall not one moment, but one kind of moment. A combination of:

> *(a) an awareness that the persona into which I had developed, for reasons I consider natural, meant that much of my past understanding had been in terms of situations and problems, rather than people, and the expectation, what was really wanted, was that I would* deliver, *rather than Understand in the GD sense. Which called for a more sensitive output monitor than I had so far developed.*

and

> *(b) an awareness of the nonhomogeneity of the group with regard to that generosity of spirit, or the experience which breeds it, to Understand sympathetically, rather than silently bridle.*

This kind of moment was occasionally uncomfortable.

And then, after colleagues had been asked to respond to a number of lexical prompts that I had chosen:

Q7: Is there a different key word or phrase that you would have put in that list?

Personality. An odd one, but it keeps cropping up in my thinking. Do I need to become in some sense a different person in order to be an Understander? I'd like to think not, but I have a growing feeling that in some respects I do. It's easy for me to be nonjudgmental because that's the way I've always been, more or less, but I can't easily hold back on the philosophical, and I wonder whether sometimes I manage to convince myself utterly that what I'm doing really is no more than Reflecting, when in fact . . . The same applies to other colleagues in different ways, I think. Perhaps the biggest challenge is to remain yourself and be a genuine Understander.

Differentiated Understanding

We have already talked (chap. 5, p. 65) about the inevitability of some element of difference between what the Speaker says and what the Understander re-cognizes and then re-articulates as a Reflection. This slippage between the two is the dialogic strength of the Speaker/Understander engagement—it is what makes the difference between the Understander and a tape recorder or a diary. When we have more than one Understander involved, however, this dialogic strength risks becoming a problem.

When Understanders who know relatively less ask for clarification, this should present no difficulty, as both the Speaker and a better-informed Understander can use this as an opportunity to check common ground and enhance empathy. But when an Understander who shares with the Speaker a higher level of knowledge about a given topic asks for clarification of a point, this may appear to be a mystification to the other Understanders. It may appear that this Understander is looking to contribute to a discussion or to lead the Speaker. In Extract 9.17, the Speaker is working on her ideas regarding the identification of lexical chunks and their use as teaching material.

Extract 9.17

01	LUCY	In other words, a chunk might have slots in the
02		middle, or they might come at the end, that can be
03		changed, but the basic frame of the chunk itself is
04		static.
05	PAUL	Are you referring to changes of tense, or the use of
06		pronouns, that might change, but it's still the same
07		chunk?
08	LUCY	Yes, very often they're grammatical choices.
09	PAUL	It's "tweakable." Grammatically tweakable.
10	LUCY	Yes, er, sometimes they're grammatically tweakable,
11		sometimes they're not. Sometimes they have a kind
12		of . . .
13	PAUL	Does that correspond . . .
14	LUCY	. . . an environment that's favored, like "set eyes on,"
15		which is almost always present perfect and almost

16		always on "her" or "him." So there are favored
17		grammatical environments.
18	PAUL	You mentioned DeCarrico [Nattinger and
19		DeCarrico], does this correspond with their
20		canonical and noncanonical contrast?
21	LUCY	Yeah, roughly . . . er, no, sorry it doesn't. Because
22		they . . .

In lines 01–12, the Understander is checking that his Understanding is true to the idea that the Speaker wants to develop. From line 13, however, the Understander wants to introduce the Nattinger & DeCarrico comparison. Between himself and the Speaker, based on their shared specialist knowledge, this seems to be a legitimate move; indeed, it does help the Speaker to clarify her position further. For the perspective of the other Understanders present, however, the significance of this comparison was only partially accessible.

It is from this kind of experience that we formulated the term *differentiated Understanding*. It is a feature of GD, but it need not necessarily be seen as a problem. To the extent that it proves to be one, I know of no straightforward solution, other than what we might call ongoing sincerity checks by the specialist Understander as to the nature of the interventions. In the above extract, for example, the issue for Paul at line 13, and more particularly at line 18, is to be very sure that he needs to introduce this distinction in order to Understand what the Speaker is saying. If so, he should. Any other motivation would be dubious. What quality of attention was available to the Speaker during lines 14–17? You cannot read this from the data, but this is what counts.

Nonspecialist Understanders must assume sincerity and can choose to ask for further clarification if they wish. Occasional retrospective discussions of these interventions on the basis of taped extracts proved extremely helpful to us. In retrospect, moreover, we also see that it is in identifying and negotiating a response to this phenomenon that our collegiality has been further enhanced.

Choice of Topic and Focus

There is another strand of our weave to pull in here. Apart from differences of content, are there fundamental differences of kind between the topic brought to the group by Sara (Extracts 9.7–9.11) and this last one, brought by Lucy (Extract 9.17)? Between what we might call the personal and the academic sides of the professional? For me, there is no easy answer, but it was the concept of differentiated Understanding that helped us clarify the issue somewhat.

In one way, it seems clear that the pedagogic use of lexical chunks is a topic about which one can claim to have, or not to have, specialist knowledge (of concepts, of terminology, of the literature) and experience (via corpus linguistics, materials writing, classroom teaching). Balancing the demands of one's personal and professional lives, on the other hand, is a challenge that we all face on a regular basis. It is essential to remember, however, that we are not talking about a discussion here.

In the terms of group development, it is in both cases the Speaker who is the knower, and it is from this knowledge base that we want to proceed. Although it is the academic/professional topic that throws differentiation into greater relief, Understanding is always differentiated, and it is always up to each Understander to negotiate an Understanding that is useful to the Speaker without disassociating the Speaker from the other Understanders present. While we all have experience of balancing personal and professional demands, none of us has inside knowledge of Sara's experience of those demands, and it is to achieve empathy with her experience that we all have to work. Through the Resonance provided by Paul, we get an insight into the differentiation that he has been working to escape in his Understanding. Furthermore, it is in the differing definitions of childcare, as a technical term, that some part of the differentiated Understandings is made clear and through which the Speaker moves toward her own discoveries.

Another important lesson that we learned through the personal/academic contrast relates to the way in which the Speaker initially presents his or her topic. With a more academically oriented topic, there is a temptation for the Speaker to slip into the more familiar seminar-presentation mode of talking, in which the Speaker sets the scene, explains the background and history of the topic, and carefully moves toward the issue of concern. If the Speaker takes up this stance, the Understanders risk being reduced to the role of listeners. The Speaker needs to work as soon as possible at the cutting, or crumbling, edge of their thinking; this is where Understanders can be of most help, and if they need background, they will ask for it.

This whole issue of topic and focus is not simple, nor am I trying to present it as such. It may be that a Speaker wants to approach a session with only a hazy idea of a topic area to explore (see Bill's pastoral care session, Extracts 9.12–9.16), in order to see what discoveries might arise. It may be the Speaker's purpose to explore the history of a project, perhaps in the search for alternative avenues that might have been taken or in order to identify mistakes that were made, in which case it is this history that is the focus of the initial exploration. What the Speaker needs to avoid, however, is the type of scene-setting introduction so necessary— or at least usual—in other kinds of discourse that one associates with serious professional, academic, or research-oriented topics. If the Speaker does have an academic issue to deal with, then, as Lucy put it, the Speaker must look for a way of:

> *starting slap in the middle, and then unfolding outwards, petal by petal, rather than building up to it chronologically.*

To sum up then, we found different dynamics and different learning opportunities associated with different choices of topic and with different Speaker stances in relation to their topics. Fundamentally, however, I find that any topic chosen by a Speaker has more in common with other Speaker topics than it has differences from them. Furthermore, it is from the common respect for all Speaker choices that another element of our enriched collegiality is woven.

Individually Owned Coconstructions

While it is the Speaker's responsibility to bring a topic on which to work, we have seen that a specific Focus may arise unexpectedly in the interaction between Speaker and Understanders. And if the Speaker's exploration leads to an overt discovery, whose is it, this concept, this plan, this analysis, this technique?

If what we are saying about the value of re-cognizing—and the value of this approach as a whole—is true, then what we have is a coconstruction in which a group of people has been involved. We have seen a striking example of this in Paul's Reflection to Bill during the pastoral care session (Extracts 9.14, 9.15). We have a more borderline case when Paul himself is Speaker (Extract 9.18).

Paul has special responsibility in the unit for coordinating our individual research efforts into what might pass for a coherent profile. He has been Speaking about his plans to do this, outlining a framework constructed by sets of rules organized hierarchically. As the Speaker makes the rules and their relationships clear, Harry Reflects this in a way that Paul accepts. After a few further comments from Paul, Harry says:

Extract 9.18

01	HARRY	So it's also a heuristic among ourselves for clarifying
02		decisions about our research?
03	PAUL	(laughs) I hope you're clarifying my thoughts,
04		because I didn't know I'd had that one!
05		(general laughter)

This was a discovery, and a very useful one, but whose? The Understander had no doubt that he was Reflecting what he Understood the Speaker to have told him and that this was the best way of checking that Understanding. The Speaker recognized the discovery as arising from his work, although the term *heuristic* was not one that he had used, any more than he had intended to develop the idea of a heuristic at this time.

In the sense that the discovery was even more than usual one that arose unbidden from the discourse and that it was made possible only by our interaction as colleagues, it seemed to develop our collegiality further. It also made us think more deeply about the matter of ownership of the ideas produced in our GD sessions.

Such a discovery may lead to other things. There may be financial implications arising from a talk, an article, even a book. Our suggestion is that the ethics of the approach lead to a distinction between involvement in construction and ownership. When the people of the neighborhood come together to help me put the roof on my new barn, we have built two things: a barn and a community. The barn alone is mine. The community and the building of both barn and community belong to all of us. Similarly, the Speaker's discovery, coconstructed with the help of Understanders, belongs indisputability to the Speaker. One might expect due acknowledgment to be made of the others' involvement if this intellectual property were invested further. The collegiality and the process of discovery belong to us all.

A different situation arises if an Understander has taken an idea from a session and then done his or her own work with that idea. There must come a point at which the former Understander earns the right to claim the idea that he or she has in the meantime developed. The ethics of this situation suggest to us that it is the Understander's responsibility to keep the Speaker closely in touch with such developments and the Speaker's responsibility to be prepared to acknowledge a point at which an idea has left his or her domain of development and is flourishing elsewhere. At best, this might lead to a more orthodox form of collaboration between the two or more people concerned, outside the Speaker/ Understander relationship.

Resonances

When I first suggested this stage of the GD procedure, I was mostly motivated by the prediction that maintaining a Speaker/ Understanders relationship over a whole hour would not be optimally profitable, especially when the majority of the group had no experience of it. I wanted to make sure that everyone in the group had the chance to express something for and of themselves in each session without compromising the discipline of the discourse.

However, things turned out better than we had the right to expect, and the Resonance stage of the sessions turned out to have its own dynamic and its own interest. During one of our feedback sessions, we came to distinguish differently weighted types of Resonance, including personal, professional, and procedural elements. We have already seen how an essentially personal resonance of Paul's helped Sara clarify aspects of her dilemma (Extract 9.10) and how his essentially procedural Resonance helped our thinking on the issue of ownership (Extract 9.15).

On occasion, the Resonance phase exceeded itself, in the sense that one or more of the group took extended turns in terms of the development of their own thinking. It was also the case that we sometimes slipped into what I would have to call a listening-discussion mode, when the intensity of the Understanding and the desire to develop carried over into what looked like, but did not feel like more usual turns in a discussion. The following extract (Extract 9.19) begins with Harry's (essentially professional) resonance following Bill's Speaking in what we came to refer to as the preparation/planning session (Extracts 9.2-9.6). Harry's Resonance has less to do with preparation or planning itself and more to do with how and when he feels that he achieves his best communication (01-07): when "something goes wrong."

Joe's Reflection (08) leads Harry to articulate his idea further (09-12), but he is explicitly dissatisfied with what he has said (12-13). Joe, however, has shifted enthusiastically into Resonance, rather than Understander, mode and wants to articulate his own, very different, view of when he himself is at his communicative best as public speaker (14-18).

In a way that will continue for much of the exchange, Harry insists that their two views are compatible (19-22). While Lucy's Reflection (23-24) helps Harry articulate his position further (25-34), this only serves to reconfirm Joe in his sense of difference (35-36). Surprised, in fact somewhat taken aback, Harry invites Joe to explain (37).

Extract 9.19

01	HARRY	What excites me is that I am never completely sure,
02		when I stand up and I start talking, whether people
03		are listening to me or the message, and whether
04		we're really connecting. And when something goes
05		wrong, all of a sudden I get that feeling that there's
06		me and the people out there, and there isn't, there
07		isn't anything . . .
08	JOE	There's no message getting in the way?
09	HARRY	Yeah . . . There's no *preconceived* message getting in
10		the way, there's no what-they-expect-to-get, or what-I
11		expected getting in the way of my direct contact
12		and my direct delivery of this message now. It's very
13		difficult to put this . . . Okay. Let me start again . . .
14	JOE	No, no, that's tremendous for me! That's now made
15		me think . . . oh . . . when I engage, there is really
16		only the message (Lucy: Mmm) (Harry: Yeah) It's not
17		really them and me at all . . . it's being involved in the
18		message . . .
19	HARRY	That's it! That's what I mean. I put it the other way
20		round. It's not me and my preconceptions or them
21		and their preconceptions, it's just the two of us and
22		therefore the message.
23	LUCY	But the message is like it is because of them, and
24		how they react to you.
25	HARRY	Yeah, mmm, well, I guess I'm trying to do it here!
26		The image I have is of something between me and
27		my audience, and when something goes wrong, it
28		shatters that, and there's just me and them, and we
29		can wing it together from then on and I feel really
30		close and the messages that come out then seem to
31		me to be genuine, and it's not connected with the
32		title of the talk, or the theme of the seminar—it's
33		just what I'm putting across right now in this
34		moment.
35	JOE	Yeah, I think we are talking about very different
36		things.
37	HARRY	Yeah? Well that's what I'd like to know.

In Extract 9.20, we see Joe take up the invitation. He begins with
a careful Reflection (01–06) of Harry's position that Harry con-

firms as correct. Harry's further elaboration (07-08), however, leads Joe once again to differentiate between their two statements (09-10). At the same time, Joe realizes that he is acting outside the agreed GD framework and tries to withdraw (10). Harry encourages him to go on (11) and the two go once again through an exchange of Reflection and confirmation (11-15).

We then see Joe struggling to articulate a position that is clearly new to him and one with which he seems uncomfortable, a position that has "very little to do with people" (16-24). When Harry once more insists that their two statements are alternative expressions of the same position (25-30), Joe finally distinguishes the two in terms of the way he feels about what he is saying (31). At this point, and once again genuinely surprised, Harry concedes the difference and the tension is released in laughter (32).

Joe is left quite alienated from the image of his current position that he has come to create, but this represents a potential growth point for his own future Speaking. After a long pause (32) that acknowledges the difficulty that Joe is in, Harry affirms the different mode that the discourse has moved into and asks to maintain it (33-34) while he expands on a type of communicative experience that gives him a particular kind of satisfaction (35-47). In effect, this functions as a more orthodox statement of a Resonance, and soon afterwards the group returns to Bill for his rounding-up statement.

Extract 9.20

01	JOE	For me, what I heard you (Harry) saying was talking
02		about those moments when some unforeseen event
03		(Harry: Mmm) takes away the expectations, the
04		planning, the preparation, the everything else, and
05		allows you to get into real, immediate, here-and-now
06		contact (Harry: Yes) with those people.
07	HARRY	That's what I meant . . . . (Joe: Yes) . . . and getting the
08		message across like that.
09	JOE	Ah, well, it's that last bit that you said there that for
10		me is the distinction . . . Oh, I'm sorry . . .
11	HARRY	No, get it! Really!
12	JOE	Well, because of that interconnectivity, you feel you

13		can communicate the things you want to
14		communicate.
15	HARRY	Exactly!
16	JOE	Yes, and somehow I was feeling, and I'll just have to
17		think a lot more about this because I've never
18		thought it before, but I was feeling that, when I'm at
19		my best (four seconds pause), I don't think there's
20		very much of me, or them, it's ... it's the message.
21		It's those meanings out there in the world, and it has
22		very little to do with people ... (general laughter) ...
23		I'm afraid ... it's nothing to do with getting close to
24		people, it's ... phew! Woah! It's *this!*
25	HARRY	Yes, but the point is that when you get that close,
26		the *this* is all there is. You're not conscious of this
27		being me and that being them, you're just conscious
28		of a connection. You're talking about a message,
29		we're talking about a connection, but the thing is the
30		same, it's ...
31	JOE	Yeah, but I *hate* what I'm saying!
32	HARRY	Oh, really?! (general laughter) Oh, I love it! (four
33		seconds pause) I'll tell you what, while we're
34		opening up like this, can we carry on in this mode?
35		(General: Yeah, Mmm) Because we were talking
36		about planning and messages, and I know that for
37		me what's best is when I've got a really simple
38		message and I actually could say it in one sentence,
39		but I'm going to take an hour, and at some point that
40		message is coming across in just the right way and
41		what the hour is about is finding the right moment
42		that gives me the opportunity, do you see what I
43		mean? And when that goes across, you know it, and
44		it only comes through that point of human contact,
45		and you can feel it, it's visceral. And sometimes you
46		walk away and you haven't felt it, and they've been
47		listening to me talk about something, and that's all.

I am motivated to comment further on what Harry can have meant by the expression "in this mode" (34). There is an amount of linguistic investigation to be done before anything could be said with any level of certainty, but I believe that what is happening here is a halfway house between conversation and what we had actually aimed to do in the Resonance part of the session.

At one level of analysis, Extracts 9.19 and 9.20 together comprise Harry's Resonance and, inside it, Lucy and Joe work to Understand him. Running parallel with this Understanding, however, Joe is articulating his own Resonance from what Harry has said. Joe's Resonance is both intellectually and emotionally dissonant with Harry's and, while Harry initially takes it to be in tune with his own, it is Joe's affective evaluation (31), rather than an intellectual clarification that makes Harry realize that it is not.

What remains consistent throughout these extracts, and what I believe Harry is referring to when he talks about carrying on "in this mode" is the quality of the attention which is given to each person as they speak. People *are* trying to articulate different ideas, but there is a group commitment properly to Understand all of them. While the Speaker/Understander role is not clearly maintained, the ability to offer cooperative understanding is massively present. This is something that we have added, as a group, to our communicative repertoire, and which has, in turn, enhanced our collegiality. I believe that I am reporting here on processes and experiences similar to those that Anne McCabe writes about in chapter 11.

The feedback discussion on this session made a specific point of the need truly to live with the frequently asserted observation that different people work at their best in very different ways.

A Kind of Conclusion

The phase of work I have described in this chapter came to an end in the summer of 2000. One member of the group reached retirement age, and two decided for different reasons to shift to job-sharing arrangements, thus bringing in two new team members. Also, the work that we had been doing and the obvious satisfaction that we were getting from it had attracted the attention of other colleagues in other sections and departments of our school.

The work now faces new challenges. Can the group renew itself? Can it grow bigger? How many members would be too many? How much explicit training should new members have before they try the whole format in real developmental terms?

Would it be better to start new groups with only new members so that they can negotiate the finer details of their own interactions, as we did ours? To what extent is it even true that we renewed CD in a group format, following guidelines that I suggested? This was not Paul's perspective.

> *I do not see things so much in terms of Speaker and Understander. More a group consciousness. The development has been social. I could not go to another arbitrary group and (alone, ipsissimus) Speak or Understand. I could only become more aware of the degree to which different rules operated.*

Responses to these questions take me beyond the scale of this book. I haven't gotten there yet. There is one issue that Paul raises, however, that has received some kind of a response. The experience of our group development sessions was so positive that we began to wonder if it might be possible to offer it to others, who might indeed be able to come along and Speak and be Understood. We turn to a brief account of this experience in the next chapter.

To close this chapter, let me make one final and explicitly evaluative comment in the general area of working for a living. This period of time, this work, with these people: as far as I know, this is as good as it gets.

The E-Mail Questionnaire

Hi,

This is the promised (threatened) request for feedback on our group development work so far. As you can perhaps guess, I am stuck between asking lots of specific questions and none at all. I have come around to what follows.

Hey, don't do this now if you're feeling frazzled. Excuse my temerity, but make an appointment with yourself for when you can meet with yourself for a while and do it then.

When you find you want to take the time, please type your responses into this message and send the whole thing back to me. I look forward very much to hearing from you. I'll then get back to you with a summary-cum-response of my own.

REFLECTIONS ON LANGUAGE STUDIES UNIT GROUP
DEVELOPMENT 1998

1. Does any one moment from the GD sessions come back to you particularly? Any idea why?

2. Does our GD work remind you of anything else? Any idea why?

3. What is the general emotional response you have right now as your mind turns back to the GD sessions?

4. Are there any comments you'd like to make about your experience as Speaker, either during your session as Speaker or when reflecting on it?

5. Are there any comments you'd like to make about your experience as Understander?

6. Do any of these words facilitate any response from you?

   skills, concerns, values, changes, doubts, wishes, language, pressures, reservations, recommendations, requests

7. Is there a different key word or phrase that you would have put in that list?

8. If I wasn't getting in your way like this, what would YOU like to say?

Thanks,
Julian

Chapter 10 Visiting Speakers

Extending Invitations

The work I report on in this chapter arose directly from the perceived successes of our group development work. We asked ourselves to what extent it would be feasible to place the Understanding potential of our group at the service of our wider peer group of teacher-researchers. Whether they saw this work in developmental terms or, more pragmatically, as a way of moving some ideas forward, we hoped that the possibilities might be attractive to them.

Once again, let me make this point about the story I am telling. On one level, this is a narrative tied into a certain time and place, involving actual people with their real concerns and aspirations. On this level, I hope that it is interesting. On another level, for some readers, I hope that the story might also be significant. It will be significant if it helps these readers see possibilities for themselves in their own times and places. At this level, the story is not about which Speakers addressed which topics, and what they explored, discovered, or planned. The examples might be of a professor of linguistics Speaking about lexical cohesion, or of a teacher educator Speaking about materials for the teaching of reading, or of a ESOL teacher Speaking about motivation problems with children who have to attend extra language classes at the end of a full school day. The function of these Speakers and their topics in this sense is to exemplify the potential of the process and the power of the discourse. Each reader will have to decide for her- or himself the extent to which the examples achieve this kind of significance.

We expected three major (and, of course, overlapping) problems:

- *Intellectual:* Without a lengthy introduction, it was unlikely that a visiting Speaker could create enough common ground to enable us to Understand the critical point on which he or she wanted to work.
- *Emotional:* Without the close affective bonds of mutual trust that we had developed, visiting Speakers might not be able to open up sufficiently to work in public on their own professional development, not even on the academic/professional side of the coin.
- *Procedural:* With no experience of the kind of discourse we had developed, Speakers might not even be able to proceed.

We addressed the first problem by inviting visitors to attend two sessions. In the first, they gave the usual type of talk about their work that visiting speakers give. This was an open session for anyone among students or staff who wished to attend. We asked visitors to choose the topic of their talk, however, with the specific criterion in mind that it should also brief Understanders for the restricted-access, developmental session that would follow. In this second session, the visitor would Speak about some aspect of the talk that he or she wanted to focus on in an attempt to take his or her thinking further. On one occasion, the visiting Speaker did not give such a talk, but sent us a paper she had written as background to her session as Speaker.

As for the emotional and procedural hurdles indicated above, these were the very issues that we wanted to explore, and we saw no equally explicit way of addressing them in advance of the sessions themselves.

I contacted potential visitors first by E-mail and then by phone, when I talked them though our idea for an invitation. Afterward, I followed up with a letter which is reproduced at the end of this chapter. Three proposed visits fell through for various reasons, but we still had seven visitors, four men and three women. I knew two of them personally quite well, two of them slightly, and three not at all. We taped the sessions, and I extracted data that seemed particularly interesting. I then set tapes of the whole sessions and of the extracts to the Speakers and fixed dates to get together with them to discuss their reactions. Finally, I reported back to our group, and we discussed the sessions further. Everyone concerned has read this chapter and provided any input to it that they wished.

Unanimously, the visiting Speakers reported positively on the experience, at least to the extent that they found it "interesting"! The two difficulties most commented on were the lack of normal, evaluative feedback from listeners and the awkwardness of going beyond what one felt sure about being justified in saying. In other words, the pressures that characterize CD discourse from the Speaker's point of view were immediately apparent to them. Nevertheless, in four of the seven cases, there were explicit discoveries, clearly identifiable in the data and afterward corroborated by the Speaker. We, in our turn, learned more about Understanding and gained new perspectives on our own work in GD.

From this point, I have organized the rest of this chapter in the following way. Initially, I set out to build a composite view of the visiting Speaker sessions, drawing on data from all of them and from the follow-up interviews. Here, I use a range of extracts from different sessions in order to demonstrate this outgrowth of the cooperative development scheme in its various aspects. I then look at three longer data sets in order to give a sense of individual events in their own right. As we go along, I draw out what we as a group learned from the visiting Speakers, and I close the chapter with a personal meditation of my own.

The names of the visiting Speakers are included in chapter 12. In my discussion of their work, I use pseudonyms and either *he* or *she* to refer to each visiting Speaker. In order to provide a greater element of anonymity, I do not guarantee that either the name or the gender of the pronoun chosen reflects the sex of the person referred to. In this chapter, I do not usually identify individual group members as Understanders, because I want to foreground the relationship between the Speaker and the Understanding group. I discuss the background to these decisions further in chapter 12.

A Composite Image

Visiting Speakers would be unusual people indeed if they had not felt a little apprehensive about what they were letting themselves in for. This feeling was expressed explicitly by our first visitor before the session began:

> *I am, to be honest, I think quite naturally, worried that if I tell you what I don't understand, then you'll think less of me.*

The Speaker also chose to address this emotion in his opening to the session (01-15).

Extract 10.1

01	SPEAKER	I was expressing my nervousness beforehand and I
02		think it might be useful to start from that
03		nervousness (Understander: Mmm). I'm nervous
04		because this is the first time you've done this with
05		an outsider, and also because, like everyone, I'm
06		insecure, really (laughs). The places where you are
07		doing your creative thinking are also the places
08		where you are easily most vulnerable (Understander:
09		Mmm). So, I feel I'm exposing myself to you, and
10		what I'm going to expose is areas where I think I
11		might be muddled (that's why I'm nervous and
12		embarrassed in a way), but also by exposing the
13		muddle, I thought, these are the areas that I am also
14		most interested in, and most anxious, in a way, to
15		work through.
16	UNDERSTANDER	So, as a basic attitudinal set, then, you are saying that
17		you do feel nervous about engaging in this (Speaker:
18		Mmm) exchange, because it's a new one and we …
19	SPEAKER	Yeah, I suppose what I'm saying is that I've always
20		done my thinking privately and then exposed it
21		when I thought it was safe (Understander: Mmm)
22		and you're inviting me to expose my thinking before
23		I was ready to expose it (Understander: Right). I
24		don't mind doing that—well I do mind doing it in a
25		way! (general laughter)—but I am quite happy to do
26		it because it seems to be a sensible position to put
27		oneself in.

The Reflection here (16–18) is the kind of thing that we would think of as quite normal by now: an early move to settle the Speaker and cue the style of discourse that the Speaker should expect. The Understander Reflects the emotion not only because this is frequently a useful move to make but also because on this occasion the Speaker himself has highlighted it.

In a later interview, the Speaker commented on this opening exchange:

> *Having had some experience of counseling, I recognized this kind of response and it felt rather mechanical. The interesting thing then, though, was that it did give me the chance to say an important part of what I wanted to say— about exposing private thoughts—and when I heard myself say that it made me realize that it's also true generally that I am essentially a private thinker—I don't usually work my ideas out with someone else, I tend to keep my thoughts to myself until I'm ready to go public with them.*

So, what was initially perceived as a mechanical procedure nevertheless facilitated improved communication and a more relaxed atmosphere for that communication (19–27). Furthermore, in a way that could not be obvious to us at the time, it enabled the articulation/creation of a meaningful personal insight for the Speaker (19–21). Notice, in the commentary, the key statement, *"when I heard myself say that it made me realize."* The interactional space that the Understander has made available allows the Speaker this unusual opportunity to hear himself and to realize the significance of what he has said.

As a group, we found in this commentary a confirmation of the power of Reflection in terms of keeping the Speaker's ideas available for the Speaker to work on. It also lent support to the idea of getting on board with an early Reflection so as to help the Speaker experience and identify the style of the interaction. The Speaker also affirmed that it was the assumption of a supportive attitude and his predisposition to trust us that allowed him to take these first steps on what he called *"a journey into the unknown."*

The Speaker's further comments reveal how in tune he was with the style of work, recognizing intuitively through this experience the purpose of our undertaking as a whole:

> *The nervousness faded after about five minutes. Perhaps addressing it directly helped to deal with it. Looking back on the session, it was a useful—in a sense liberating—experience. The ideas that you normally present in a talk have stopped being your thinking because you tell people what you know that you know. In this environment, you have a chance to do what you can't normally do, to follow routes that aren't yet ready, but seem like they may be important.*

Visiting Speakers generally commented positively on the early Reflection, with one saying that it had helped her *"find my start,"* adding that having the emotional side (being worried) of her experience Reflected helped her *"put that aside and focus on the topic."*

In an initial Reflection from a later session (Extract 10.2), the Understander works to capture the not quite explicit attitude behind the Speaker's opening and comes up with the expression, "worth it" (12). The Speaker, who is developing an approach to teacher education, partly accepts this Reflection but is also motivated by it to articulate further the criterion that, in his terms, would make the effort worth it (14–18).

Extract 10.2

01	UNDERSTANDER	Just before you go on, can we just clarify that base
02		position? (Speaker: Yes) You've said that there is this
03		question of an "enhancement paradigm," and what
04		does that mean? And you want to work on that, not
05		just as a concept, but the detail of how that would
06		be implemented (Speaker: Mmm). And you said
07		earlier that you feel a particular—I'm not sure that
08		"pressure" is the right word—but there's a life-cycle
09		element to this as well (Speaker: Mmm), and you're
10		looking to evaluate what it is that you're getting into
11		here, because you want to commit to something that

12		(Speaker: Mmm) you feel is *worth* it, almost
13		(Speaker: Mmm), is that right?
14	SPEAKER	Yes, that's right. I mean, I'm not . . . it could be, it
15		might turn out to be just a waste of time, in the
16		sense that it's a blind alley. Right? It might be
17		something that sounds very good, but then when
18		you get down to it, is actually not very *useful.*

He later commented:

> *This was a very productive way to begin. In the articulation of my thinking, the concept of* usefulness *became highlighted, and I think this is in fact the touchstone of my whole approach to professional development.*

The issue of people speaking from different roles or identities also surfaced again in these sessions. One Speaker was both a practicing therapist and the director of a university-based counseling service. The two roles did not always easily coexist, and this Speaker (who was, of course, a sophisticated user of a related style of discourse) used the group to try out various ideas and consider what was reflected back to him. Prior to Extract 10.3, he had Spoken about short-term and long-term educational goals and had distinguished between helping people to deal with an event that is troubling them and helping people in a more general, holistic sense. Understanders combine to Reflect (01–12) and Thematize (14–18).

Extract 10.3

01	UNDERSTANDER	Do I get the sense here that, going back to the
02		beginning again, when you talked about the
03		university and the essential journey toward the
04		degree which you want to help students to make
05		(Speaker: Mmm), and taking this event/person
06		distinction, that at one time perhaps the focus was
07		on a particular event that might get in the way of
08		that, but now you're dealing with the person who

09		actually sets out on the journey (Speaker: Yes),
10		having brought with them all sorts of problems
11		(Speaker: Exactly). And that's a big change in terms
12		of orientation.
13	SPEAKER	I think it is, yeah, yeah.
14	UNDERSTANDER	And is that, what Harry just said there, is that
15		connected to the earlier distinction you made
16		between education in the narrow sense of a course,
17		and education of a person in the longer
18		life-sense?
19	SPEAKER	I think it is. I think it is. Yeah, yeah. It is. I suppose
20		I'm also, while we're on that, I have to ask myself, I
21		guess, if a student comes in their first year, with
22		quite severe difficulties, what can we offer them?
23		Can we offer them help for the next three years?
24		(Understanders: Mmm, Yeah) Or can we say, "Well,
25		within the university, what we can help you do is, a
26		short piece of counseling work that might help you
27		to cope with this year (half-laughs) (Understander:
28		Mmm). And when you might be welcome to come
29		back in, say, your final year, if you want a bit more
30		help, to see you in your final year."

The Speaker said later:

> *I was trying an idea out here, and I don't like it at all. Our work should be to make ourselves redundant in the life of our clients, not just to do some patching up till the next time.*

In another section (Data 10.4), the same Speaker takes the Understander's Thematizing (01–11) as an opportunity to explore beyond the connection made (12–29) in a way that provoked the following comment later:

> *This really was a chance to explore by thinking aloud—not exactly free-association, but I felt I had the space to look around without having to construct an argument or come up with a definite answer to anything.*

Extract 10.4

01	UNDERSTANDER	Is there also a connection between—sorry, I'll have
02		to work at this (laughs). When you made the contrast
03		between someone in private practice and your
04		institutional position (Speaker: Mmm), is there a
05		suggestion then that the institutional role of
06		counseling has been traditionally seen much more as
07		helping someone deal with events, and that this
08		change of purpose [toward dealing with the person]
09		is one of the issues that's (Speaker: Yes, yes, I think
10		so) that's right there in the broad theme that you're
11		dealing with?
12	SPEAKER	Yes. Yes (three-second pause). And again, that's
13		sparked off another thought, in that I would be
14		tempted to say that the traditional view of the
15		counseling service in a university has actually not
16		been how to help an individual deal with events, but
17		to help the rest of the university feel that there's a
18		place where students can deal with distress
19		(Understander: Right, yes, yes). So the university
20		(Understander: Mmm), in its psyche, says to itself,
21		"Well, this isn't our problem, there's a counseling
22		service that deals with that" (Understander: Mmm).
23		And I think that's quite dangerous (Understander:
24		Mmm), because I don't think it's just the counseling
25		service's responsibility to deal with distressed
26		students. Okay, I think we have a lot to offer! But it's
27		a university concern. What does the university do
28		with the increasing number of students who have
29		severe mental health difficulties?

The three-second pause and the introductory comment that follows it (12–13) are significant here. The former indicates where the Speaker's preparatory work is being done, and the latter signals the onset of the exploration that follows. Discussion of this extract of data also helped us as a group to understand the whole idea of exploration better: sometimes it means setting off into new territory and sometimes it means getting to know better areas with which you are already familiar.

On other occasions, of course, combinations of new faces, unfamiliar discourse, and differing personal styles meant that we did not move along in quite such harmony. One visiting Speaker session began:

Extract 10.5

01	SPEAKER	Okay, I'm just starting down a few sort of areas that I
02		think about, and ah, I'll just mention one of them. Ah,
03		can I take two or three different things, yeah?
04	UNDERSTANDER	Sure.
05	SPEAKER	In case I don't want to stick to one thing, yeah?
06	UNDERSTANDER	Yeah. As I say, then, our effort will probably be also
07		to try to help you decide where you want to Focus,
08		so you can push something further.
09	SPEAKER	Yeah, Okay.

With hindsight, it is fair to say that the Understander's probably over-explicit insistence on a Speaker/Understander relationship along linear tracks (06–08) and the Speaker's rather dubious response to this prospect (09) signaled a standoff that was never properly resolved, although a lot of interesting things were said.

In the following extract from the same session (Extract 10.6), the Understander is attempting to Thematize from what the Speaker has said in hopes of offering a Focus for further Speaker exploration (01–06). The Speaker recognizes where the Understander is headed and goes there immediately (07), but the Understander soldiers on to establish the connection more formally in his own terms (12–15). Once he has done so, however, the Speaker barely stays to acknowledge the link that he confirms he has just made (16–20) before going on in the next utterance to a different issue (20–22).

Extract 10.6

01	UNDERSTANDER	So, if I can just check with you there (Speaker:
02		Mmm), the point for a potential Focus is that you
03		start from the Prabhu distinction between the
04		teaching "event" as something you call technical: a

05		syllabus event, a piece of classroom methodology;
06		but another way of looking at it is . . .
07	SPEAKER	Yeah, it's a step to the traditional debate.
08	UNDERSTANDER	. . . as a sociological . . .
09	SPEAKER	Oh sorry, yeah.
10	UNDERSTANDER	Sorry, that's the other perspective, yeah?
11	SPEAKER	Right.
12	UNDERSTANDER	And now you're saying perhaps this relates to the
13		old debate about teaching as part art and part
14		science, and you're wondering if these two
15		perspectives can match up with that?
16	SPEAKER	Yeah, yeah. I've actually thought about it. It's two
17		different things I've thought about recently. I've had
18		conversations where both have come up. But just a
19		few moments ago I was thinking how they parallel
20		each other. Now, related to that is working in
21		language education, or working on an aid
22		programme . . .

Some time later in the same session, the Speaker has been describing a television program he has seen about a language teacher who uses unorthodox methods apparently to great effect. In Extract 10.7, we see how the Understander tries once again to establish thematic links across the Speaker's discourse (04). Once again, the Speaker sees it coming (05), and once again the Understander doggedly perseveres (06). This time, however, the Speaker confronts the mismatch of styles explicitly and then jokingly acknowledges a personal preference for nonlinear thinking and talking (07–10).

Extract 10.7

01	SPEAKER	He was dealing with these sixteen-year-old kids at
02		school in Islington. So he, you know, cannot, be as an
03		individual, replicated, you know?
04	UNDERSTANDER	Mmm, so, this is another input into . . .
05	SPEAKER	Yeah, it could be.
06	UNDERSTANDER	. . . your terms of art and science?
07	SPEAKER	It could be! It could be! You see, you're going to
08		discover my dark side! Which is that I sort of talk

09	around in circles for a long time! But that's Okay, I
10	think. You keep trying to bring me back on! (general
11	laughter)

Once it had been brought out, this issue of individual style resurfaced periodically throughout the session, perhaps becoming the unspoken (and certainly not Focused!) topic of the session as a whole. The Speaker referred to *"my tendency to drift"*; the issue of *"Where do I stand?"* is common to three of the topic areas he addressed; and he reported a criticism of his writing as being good on summary and analysis but lacking in conventional argument. At one point (Extract 10.8), he explores briefly the idea that there is perhaps a distinct type of contribution to be made by a discourse style outside the normal rhetorical expectations of the modern academy but concludes that there is little possibility of having such a piece published.

Extract 10.8

01	SPEAKER	What if, you know, what if that's just a different way?
02		I mean, that could have a function as well, just sort
03		of talking around ideas (Understander Mmm). And so
04		then, going back to what I was saying before about
05		reading authors from previous decades, who actually
06		got away with that sort of thing—maybe because
07		there was no one else around who could organize
08		their writing any better (smiles)—so, I mean, I don't
09		want to get into saying that I could be Max Weber
10		(general laughter), but the thing is, there's just no
11		niche for that.

This was not a session, then, that followed clear-cut lines or that led to Speaker discoveries identifiable in the discourse. For me, however, this was a session that stood out in terms of Understander learning—my learning. It was a powerful reminder to me that although language itself has some necessarily linear features and rational thought (as understood in contemporary Western culture) also has some necessarily linear features, neither personal nor professional development is linear. Anyone looking for the footprints of development in the data of discourse does well to remember this fundamental mismatch. In other words, the tracks of what cooperative development looks to facilitate through language will not always be demonstrably there in the record of the language used, even if the development is taking place.

But if I am to communicate more to you than assertions of value, it is in the language data that I have to search for evidence. I believe it is fair to say that all the visiting Speakers felt that they had spent their time usefully and that the comment reported in Extract 10.9 is typical of one kind of outcome, even where no explicit discovery could be documented.

Extract 10.9

01	SPEAKER	I am just kind of struck by (seven-second pause), I've
02		just been reminded, perhaps, of what it is like to be
03		listened to. Because, obviously, while I was just kind
04		of sharing these thoughts, just that sense that you
05		were kind of listening, felt very supportive . . . It was
06		the process, the feeling that you were being (two-
07		second pause) attentive, kind of there, in there with
08		it. Sometimes, someone would say something and I
09		thought, "Oh," and I'd have another thought and that
10		would spark off another. So, on that level, that was
11		kind of (two-second pause) creative, for me.

Having given this composite image of visiting Speaker sessions and provided some examples of how Speakers interacted with our Understanding procedures in general terms, I now want to look at connected extracts from three individual sessions in order to investigate how the Speakers concerned moved toward their own outcomes. It is not an easy ride through these rich and complex exchanges, but as you have come this far with me, I hope you will buckle up for the extra mile.

To give one advance organizer, in the terms of how thought

and action interact that I use in Task 8.2, I would say that Rebecca brought along a means-oriented problem, which she explored to pragmatically useful discoveries at the theoretical level. David explored details of linguistic theory and discovered links toward coherence in his own personal and professional development. Liz's focus was means- and ends-oriented, and her explorations opened up personal, professional, and institutional dimensions of discovery regarding her research goals.

Rebecca as Visiting Speaker

Interviewed a couple of weeks after the session, Rebecca commented on the distinctive nature of the experience in terms of its being *"neither explaining to students nor discussing with colleagues."* She said that we had not given her any new ideas but that we had provided her with a framework. Illuminatingly for us, she referred to this framework as being *"like Vygotsky in reverse."* In Vygotsky's theorization of child development, the child can be helped beyond its current level of ability by working with an adult, with someone who knows how to function at a developmental level just beyond where the child is at any given time. This is what Vygotsky calls the zone of proximal development. Rebecca suggested that our group inverted this relationship, providing the possibility for the person who knows to *"see at a greater level of delicacy"* and thereby *"to learn more about what they already perceived."*

When listening to the tape of her sessions, she noticed the silences before she spoke in a way that she had not been aware of at the time, indicating, she thought, the mental work that she was doing. She enjoyed the Resonances section, saying that it was intellectually stimulating and useful to hear them and that it was also rewarding in an affective sense to see that one had touched people in individually meaningful and necessarily unpredictable ways.

Rebecca had brought along a specific problem. She was devising a research project concerning the use of reading texts in

TESOL classes, with specific reference to gender issues. She knew that something was not quite right about the project design, but she wasn't sure what the problem was. She later singled out three specific outcomes from the session, and I shall try to capture these as discoveries in the data of the interaction.

Initially, Rebecca told us about how data had been collected in different countries and then (Extract 10.10) she introduces the need for a model of analysis, one which would enable the researchers to identify different types of text and different ways of using texts.

Extract 10.10

01	SPEAKER	So, we had three sets of data there and it became
02		fairly obvious that what was lacking in this was a
03		way of analyzing it . . . What we were actually trying
04		to do was somehow relate the teacher treatment to
05		the text, right? So you need a model in which you
06		can analyze teacher treatment in relation to a text.
07		So, you might have, you might want to categorize the
08		texts into types, right? (Understander: Mmm) And
09		also categorize the treatments into types, right?
10		(Understander: Mmm) So you've got at least a
11		double-layered model.

The analytical framework that Rebecca had developed (in a simplified version sufficient for our purposes here) comprised three lines of questioning:

1. Does the text concern people? If so,
2. Does the text represent people in traditional roles or nontraditional roles?
3. Does the teacher (a) ignore the social significance of this representation, (b) endorse it, or (c) subvert it?

A key moment comes (Extract 10.11) when Rebecca is asked for clarification of the importance of teacher intention in the third line of the model (01).

Extract 10.11

01	UNDERSTANDER	Are the teachers' intentions involved here?
02	SPEAKER	This third line does not allow for teacher intention
03		at all.
04	UNDERSTANDER	Ah. Okay, good. That clarifies it to me. Because this is
05		an *observational* model (Speaker: Yes) of a certain
06		paradigm of social science (Speaker: Yes). It isn't in
07		any sense a participatory, "Let's try to understand
08		what people think they're doing" (Speaker: No) type
09		of research. It's, "This is what happened (Speaker:
10		Yes). I identified this behavior in this sense"
11		(Speaker: Yes). It's that tradition of observational
12		research.
13	SPEAKER	Yes, yes. It's not ethnographic (Understander: Yes,
14		right). If it were, then I suppose you could replace
15		that third line completely, and then you'd need a
16		separate model rather than an additional line.

The clarification effected by the Reflection (04–12) was crucial to the Understanding that the group could offer. In terms of communication between Rebecca and the group, it was important that the matter be spelled out so explicitly because the Understanders were more used to working in a research tradition that inquires into the meanings that people attribute to their actions, hence the initial question in this extract. The significance of this spelling out, however, proved also to be of great value to Rebecca, who was, as is evidenced by her six *Yes*'s (04–12) and explicit distancing statement (13), firmly committed to working in a tradition based on an external observer of objective behaviors. Her comment on "a separate model" (16) will prove significant later.

After she had talked for some time longer about problems associated with the different levels, or lines, in the analytical model, she is invited to Focus (Extract 10.12, 01–04). This Focusing and a Thematization (21–33) lead to what Rebecca later described as an important outcome for herself, the identification of the "double-layered problem" in the second line of the model (34–35).

Extract 10.12

01	UNDERSTANDER	Can we invite you, then, out of these areas you've
02		touched on, to decide which area you want to Focus
03		in on right now? Is that second line the area you
04		want to focus on?
05	SPEAKER	The second line, I mean, I would love to focus on it. I
06		can't see . . . what can I say . . . I mean, I'm open
07		really to the idea that a text, I mean, in some ways I
08		can see that a text has got limited meanings, it hasn't
09		got infinite meanings, but I like the idea that a given
10		text, anything can mean anything, you know, because
11		I think that anyone who uses language in all sorts of
12		ways is aware that things can mean huge amounts
13		(Understander: Mmm) depending on all sorts of
14		codes and what people mean by them. So to me, in a
15		sense, that second line is sort of unresolvable in
16		some ways and it is hard, I mean, especially if you
17		take, say, [a certain text], how do you solve it, you
18		know? How do you decide which role it is? Even if
19		you decide that it has got one meaning? Or maybe
20		two boxes are not sufficient for that . . .
21	UNDERSTANDER	So, is the difficulty there: you've got the issue of, to
22		what extent do we want to limit the potential
23		meanings of the text?—that's an issue in itself?
24	SPEAKER	Yes, yes.
25	UNDERSTANDER	And did you just say that another problem is that
26		even if we can come to a working agreement on that
27		and say there is a relatively delineated meaning for a
28		text, we would still, when making this choice, have
29		the problem of, conceptually, will this person decide
30		that that is a traditional role (Speaker: Yes) whereas
31		another person will decide, "No, that's not a
32		traditional role," even though they both agree what
33		the text says?
34	SPEAKER	That's an additional problem, yes! So, it's a double
35		layered problem, yes. Yes, yes.

The Understander carefully restates to Rebecca the points that she has made in order to check for connections, and Rebecca makes the discovery (34–35) that she later described to me as *"more important than you realized!"*

Shortly afterward (Extract 10.13), in what is almost an aside but clearly related to the above, Rebecca comments:

Extract 10.13		
01	SPEAKER	Whether it's just playing with words or not, I don't
02		know, but somehow these two labels
03		[traditional/nontraditional] in the second line
04		seemed a little bit more neutral. Or maybe that's an
05		illusion. I'm not sure. But, you know, you've made me
06		realize, it's interesting, the second line is sort of a
07		philosophical problem (Understander: Mmm), and
08		the third line, maybe it's a data problem
09		(Understander: Yes). So it's different levels, it's maybe
10		different issues for each line (Understander: Mmm).

As the Speaker also discovered, the unspoken interplay between observer categories and participant categories was causing problems at the level of research paradigm. We can follow the route to this discovery via a string of exchanges (Extracts 10.14–10.17) that, in real time, ran parallel to the above extracts.

At an early point in describing her model of analysis, Rebecca explains:

Extract 10.14		
01	SPEAKER	You need a lot of data to do this, on the grounds, I
02		guess, on the grounds that you start with what
03		you've got: "What does the teacher do?" Because
04		"What does the teacher do?" can be incorporated
05		into a model. And you might add into the model,
06		"What could the teacher logically do?" Right? And
07		you'd want the model to cope with both situations.

Later, when invited to Focus (Extract 10.15, 01–03), she comments on her model further (04–14).

Extract 10.15

01	UNDERSTANDER	Where's your thinking going at the moment? Do you
02		want to push any further in the directions that
03		you're currently working on?
04	SPEAKER	Well, I shuffle backwards and forwards between
05		being puzzled about the second line and being
06		puzzled about the third line (Understander: Mmm), I
07		think. I must admit, I would like more data. I mean,
08		for one thing, this "subversion" box—I haven't got
09		any, you know! I mean, it's there because it's logical,
10		you know (Understander: Oh yeah!), somebody
11		*could* do it. And because it could be done, even
12		though it hasn't been done, it should be in the
13		model. So, I would see this model as being both data
14		generated and logical, or visionary, or whatever.

In another part of the session (Extract 10.16), Rebecca introduces her preferred metaphor for discussing research questions in general (01–09). She applies this to her current project and, in so doing, draws back in the issue of teacher intentions (07–09), although her use of "somehow" suggests how troublesome this concept remains. Rebecca then accepts the Reflected Understanding (10–17) with enthusiasm (16–18).

Extract 10.16

01	SPEAKER	My personal vision is that it [a research project] is
02		like a carousel. It's all going round and the research
03		question is actually the pole in the middle, and
04		everything else, your data collection, your analysis,
05		somehow has to relate, somehow, right from the
06		horses on the outside to the pole in the middle
07		(Understander: Mmm). It's almost as if it all goes
08		round and somehow you pick up teacher intention
09		on the way, you know?
		[This line of thought is set aside for a few moments as Rebecca Speaks about the importance of student-generated data, too.]
10	UNDERSTANDER	So what you're saying is, if I've understood you
11		correctly, if you watch, if we can carry on with this

12		metaphor, if you watch the horses these horses
13		moving up and down, if you watch a sufficient
14		number of horses and sufficient amounts of
15		movement, you'll understand more about the
16		mechanism that's actually (Speaker: Driving it)
17		driving it, yeah.
18	SPEAKER	Yes. Mmm. Yes!

Shortly thereafter (Extract 10.17), an Understander attempts to pull together some of the points that Rebecca has made (01-17). Unlike the Thematization illustrated in Extract 10.12, this constitutes a Challenge, and the Understander is particularly careful to check each point with the Speaker. Rebecca's initial response resists the Challenge and includes a highly creative extension of the original metaphor (18-20). At this point (21), the Understander almost steps out of the Understanding role and into a discussion. He recovers after a pause but then fails to deliver a reasonable Reflection of what the Speaker did say, ending with an apology (21-23). Rebecca, however, acknowledges the difficulty here and works on it (24-36). The long pauses here are indicative of the exploration going on behind the words, and Rebecca later confirmed the articulation of "mixing your research paradigms" (36) as a discovery in CD terms. The Understander then affirms that it was this "mixing" that he was feeling as "tension between the two" (38-39), which in turn leads Rebecca to a good humored acceptance of the need to work more on this paradox (40-44).

Extract 10.17

01	UNDERSTANDER	Can I check a couple of points together that I can't
02		fit together at the moment? It goes back to this
03		metaphor of the carousel (Speaker: Yes). We've got
04		this action going on at the periphery (Speaker: Yes),
05		and we said that that could be seen as the data being
06		collected (Speaker: Yes) and we said that if we get
07		enough of that (Speaker: Yes), if we get a sense of
08		the patterns (Speaker: Yes), that could help us
09		understand the mechanisms (Speaker: Yes) that are
10		more central to the whole issue of gendered texts

11		(Speaker: Yes, yes). That's one point. Does that fit in
12		with the, with the idea of building the model partly,
13		but only partly, through the collection of data—and
14		partly as a set of logical constructs? You know, we
15		have this space here [for teacher subversion], even
16		though it might not happen? Are those two ways of
17		model building, sort of, compatible?
18	SPEAKER	I do not like to lose the idea of something that could
19		happen, you know? I mean, you can have a sort of
20		ghost horse (laughs). Yeah?
21	UNDERSTANDER	Yeah, I see the (two-second pause). Yes. Yes. You say,
22		yes they are compatible. Well, no, you didn't say that.
23		You said you like it. Sorry.
24	SPEAKER	I would like them to be compatible (Understander
25		laughs) (Speaker laughs). I mean, it would be very
26		sad to me if your model was only built up of data
27		generated categories. I think it would be a loss (six-
28		second pause). I mean, if you were being completely
29		positivist about it, that's precisely what you would
30		do, right? But I think if you're allowing for the
31		possibility of subversion, then you need to have a
32		ghost horse in there somewhere (Understander:
33		Mmm). Or one trotting around the outside waiting to
34		jump on, if you like (five-second-pause). How
35		compatible they are, I don't know. I mean, you are
36		sort of mixing your research paradigms
37		(Understander: Mmm).
38	UNDERSTANDER	Mmm, maybe that's what I was feeling—some kind
39		of tension between the two.
40	SPEAKER	Because you're being sort of intuitive (Understander:
41		Mmm), and positivist at the same time, which don't
42		really go together—(Understander: Mmm) (two-
43		second pause). Usually! (laughs, general laughter)
44		Maybe they could here! I don't know.

Rebecca later described the opportunity to unpick the nexus of difficulties around paradigm conflicts, data, philosophy, ethnography, and observation as not at all confrontational but very challenging. There had been some discomfort, she said, but the fact that she had been able to do the work was a confirmation of the positive attitudinal space that we had created together. It is also, of course, a confirmation of the open, positive, and collegial attitude that Rebecca brought with her to what we might want to start calling our development forum.

David as Visiting Speaker

This session reported here contains more technical terminology than any of the others. I include it in part for that reason. Professional development must mean different things for different professionals. One meaning it must have for colleagues in higher education, a part of whose responsibility it is to contribute to the intellectual growth of their discipline, is conceptual development in terms of the issues with which they deal. There is no doubt that this visiting Speaker was operating at a level of expertise in advance of that of his Understanders. And still, I want to claim, we can demonstrate that the framework that Rebecca described as *"like Vygotsky in reverse"* was helpful to David in taking these ideas further. I ask you here not to worry about unfamiliar linguistic terminology but to read for the developmental points that are germane to our topic. (In other words, perhaps, to do the kind of thing that we regularly ask language learners to do when they read texts that contain words they don't know!)

As we join the session, David has already distinguished between information that is *explicit* in a text and information that is *evoked* in a reader by a text. He has also used the term *transformation,* which he marks as difficult because of its history in linguistic theory. At the opening of Extract 10.18, an Understander tentatively Reflects (01–10) what he understands the term *transformation* to mean in terms of these two types of information:

Extract 10.18

01	UNDERSTANDER	Can I pick that one up? Because you've mentioned
02		that, and it's very powerful, and you moved back
03		from it—"transformation"—and I understand, I
04		think, why you moved back from it but it was, as you
05		were talking earlier on it came back into my mind,

06		when you talked about this relationship between
07		what is there, what is explicit, and what is evoked.
08	SPEAKER	Mmm. Yeah.
09	UNDERSTANDER	Is that where that transformation, is that what it's
10		trying to bridge? Or have I misunderstood that?
11	SPEAKER	Erm, I think in a way you've misunderstood it.
12	UNDERSTANDER	Right. Okay, yeah.
13	SPEAKER	But I'd like to take that opportunity . . .
14	UNDERSTANDER	Yeah.
15	SPEAKER	. . . to explore it a little more.

David's rejection of the Reflection (11) is hedged, of course, and triply so, by "Erm," by "I think" and by "in a way," but the assertion "you've misunderstood it" remains an unusual one that might be found abrasive in regular discussions. An interesting insight here arose from David's later comment:

> *I felt very comfortable with the Understander's Reflection and the chance to clarify for him and for myself what I was saying here. Under these circumstances, I didn't feel a need to worry about the Understander's "face," and I didn't think that he did, either.*

The Understander confirmed that this feeling was indeed shared. In other words, it seems fair to claim that the trust and respect being extended in this style of discourse, the sensation of being on the same team in terms of the search for new meaning, can also simplify communication with regard to at least some of the need to hedge for politeness. Rather than have an adverse effect on collegiality, this straightforwardness can serve to affirm the affective and intellectual bond between Speaker and Understander.

We have seen how David explicitly marks the failed Reflection as an "opportunity" (13), and it is one that he seizes enthusiastically and at length. In this regard, he commented later, *"Mistaken Reflections are inherently self-justifying, which is not to say that others don't have their own value"* (see, for example, Extracts 10.21 and 10.22).

Moving on, David retrospectively characterized what followed as *"working out more fully some thoughts that I had had."* In CD terms, we would call this exploration, which is also what David calls it (Extract 10.18, 15). In order to explain his use of *transformation,* David began by making some background comments on genre studies and semantic patterning in text. Extract 10.19 picks up his exploration at the end of this introductory phase (01–07). David points out explicitly (02–03) that he is working with ideas that he is not sure about, and he then continues with a flow of creative discourse that takes him "out to the very fringes" (14–16) of his thinking.

Extract 10.19

01	SPEAKER	. . . So I think the genre thing needs mapping in
02		some way onto my categories and I don't know how
03		to do that. That's another of my insecurities there.
04		But the transformation idea comes from this. I want
05		to set up two kinds of transformation, and I mean it,
06		in a sense the two terms, I'm almost using
07		"transformation" polysem—polysemously.
08		Erm, at the first level, I want to say the archetypal
09		structure is Situation, Problem, Response, Evaluation
10		and so forth, and I'd want to say that there are
11		transformations of sequences of this, so that you can
12		have the Response first and then the Problem, or the
13		Response and Evaluation and then the Problem, and
14		I'd want to be able to say in principle (and this is
15		right at the very fringes of what I've explored, and
16		I'm not sure whether I'm right in saying it anyway)
17		that there are also certain sequences that
18		transformationally wouldn't occur. So you wouldn't
19		get, erm, Response and a Situation together and then
20		a Problem and then the Evaluation. I think you
21		always, if you did combine them, you'd have
22		Response, erm, Problem, or you'd have Response and
23		Result, but I don't think there's a reason, er, in a
24		Situation before a Problem arose I don't think would
25		be necessarily encoded. So I'd want to say that
26		certain kinds of sequence are in fact variants within
27		the use of the code. That's one sense.
28	UNDERSTANDER	Mhmm.

David then moved on (in Extract 10.20) to deal with the second of the two senses in which he wanted to use the term *transformation,* a sense which he said he found more interesting. Leaving aside, to the extent that one can, the detail of the linguistics, we have further clear indications here of the exploratory nature of the work that David is doing in real time. We find explicit reference to the newness of the work (01-02, 45-47), significant pauses and asides as he thinks of and comments on examples (05, 22, 27-28), and particular care over the use of emerging technical terms (35-38). Moreover, there are distinct changes in delivery from the speed and relative lightness of Extract 10.19 and 10.20 up to the strongly emphasized "So" (07) which marks the importance of what follows, into the preparatory period of 08-24, and then on to the much slower and increasingly thoughtful work of 26-48.

David's retrospective comment on this stage of the session was: *"The link with Offers and Requests was new. I was making this up as I went along."* It seems fair to claim, then, that Extract 10.20 provides us with an example of exploration pushing on into discovery.

Extract 10.20

01	SPEAKER	One of the things that I've tried to explore, and I'm
02		not yet very far down the road with it, is that each of
03		the patterns that I've talked about actually has a
04		correlation with a quite specific set of syntactic
05		statements—in an archetypal form (two-second
06		pause).
07		*So,* for example,
08		[an aside here about not having some data with him]
09		Problem is, using Halliday's categories, is
10		characteristically represented in terms of a relational
11		process with a carrier and attribute: "Something is
12		bad." That's the archetypal structure. And is followed
13		by a statement of a material process, not necessarily
14		directly, but shortly afterwards, with an actor and
15		material process: "Someone is doing something," and
16		there's a causal connection between the two. So,
17		erm, "The weather was bad, so I put my umbrella
18		up." Archetypal structure. The Desire/Arousal pattern

19		takes a positive evaluation: carrier/attribute,
20		relational process, carrier/attribute, but the attribute
21		is positive. Er, "The video was exceptionally cheap, so
22		I bought it." The, erm, (four-second pause) but you
23		can see immediately that that could also be
24		categorized as an Opportunity/Taking pattern
25	UNDERSTANDER	Mmm. Aha.
26	SPEAKER	It's cheapness, whether it arouses a desire, or it's an
27		opportunity you take, that's a third thing, about the
28		blurring of categories. On the other hand, the
29		Goal/Achievement pattern, the Goal will be
30		formulated with with a Purpose clause, syntactically,
31		Goal is marked out by a Purpose clause. Erm, a Gap
32		in Knowledge, on the other hand, er, is formulated,
33		can be formulated, in ah, simply as a question. Erm,
34		and there you go into Opportunity again when an
35		Opportunity can be formulated as an Offer. And so
36		you can start categorizing the different kinds of
37		trigger, no, I don't mean trigger there, the different
38		kinds of starting point in terms of: are they
39		statements, offers, requests or, or questions. Now,
40		there's a statement kind, that would be Problem, that
41		would be Desire/Arousal. And there's an offer kind,
42		that would be a certain subset of the Opportunities.
43		There's a question, that would be the
44		Question/Answer pattern, and to some extent the
45		Gap in Knowledge pattern. There ought to be a
46		Request pattern, but I'm not sure what it is, if it
47		exists. But syntactically, the four basic categories
48		seem to map.

In contrast, and without wanting to underestimate the usefulness of articulating a review in its own right, David said of what followed later:

> *The last part was making public something I had already worked out. I found it difficult to concentrate when listening to the last part again, but even now I find listening to the other parts interesting—I want to hear what I say! You can tell how new most of this is by the fact that so little of it exists in written form.*

Perhaps picking up subconscious signals that the Speaker is losing enthusiasm, and certainly under pressure to keep up with what is being said, an Understander Reflects his own partial Understanding of where the Speaker has reached (Extract 10.21, 01-12). The Speaker responds to this by confirming the Reflection (13) and then going on to amplify the claim (13-20). We have here one of the values of an accurate Reflection—the Speaker is motivated to take the point further and to articulate a far-reaching goal of the work he is engaged in.

Extract 10.21

01	UNDERSTANDER	So, can I check this with you? If we take the, the
02		dynamic between Situation 1 and Situation 2 and we
03		say that Problem/Solution is one possible dynamic,
04		Question/Answer is another possible dynamic and,
05		erm, Goal/Means of Achievement is another possible
06		dynamic, what you are positing at the moment is the
07		idea of certain syntactic realisations of those
08		dynamics, where the—you can map a certain sort of
09		syntactic choice onto the kind of, let me use
10		"Problems," the instigating item of the pattern that
11		links up with the choice in the "Response," whatever
12		we decide to call it . . .
13	SPEAKER	Yes, that's right, that's right. Yeah. So, what you'd have
14		is, if you like, the El Dorado of being able to kind of
15		link the syntax in with the text structure in such a
16		way that you'd have a relationship that was, that was
17		clear. Erm, if that could be shown to be true on a
18		general level, it would mean that you would have, for
19		the first time, text-structural descriptions that link
20		directly into syntactic choices.

Next, as David pauses in his expansion of the claim (Extract 10.22, 09), an Understander picks up his return to *transformations,* (01-02) in order to check a slight shift that has taken place, namely that the Speaker has now outlined a greater challenge that goes beyond his earlier use of the term (10-20). David enthusiastically confirms this interpretation (13, 16-17, 19) and expands on it (21-27).

Extract 10.22

01	SPEAKER	If it's going to work at all, though, it's got to work
02		through transformations. Because you, it's self
03		evidently true that quite a lot of patterns don't have,
04		don't have those things. So you've got to have a way
05		of getting to . . . the other possible structures. You
06		know, if it's just simply true that a lot of the time . . .
07		it's interesting. But if one could show that the other
08		versions are, in some sense, genuinely new versions
09		of the original structures, then, mmm . . .
10	UNDERSTANDER	So, if I've understood you then, and again, perhaps
11		I've misunderstood, the challenge lies in actually
12		finding those transformations.
13	SPEAKER	Yes, it's
14	UNDERSTANDER	It's not virtually the things you've talked about—
15		that's where the, the real . . .
16	SPEAKER	Yes, the challenge, you're absolutely right, the
17		challenge lies in finding
18	UNDERSTANDER	those steps
19	SPEAKER	those steps, those further steps.
20	UNDERSTANDER	Yeah
21	SPEAKER	And if I could do that, that would be very exciting.
22		And it might link in with the work, the other work,
23		the "other me" which I have talked about which is
24		the collocation/colligation me, because it may be
25		that what I am about to want to say is that there are,
26		that these syntactic patterns are ultimately the result
27		of the conflations of various colligations, and it
28		would be nice to think that . . .
29	ALL	(gasps and laughter)
30	SPEAKER	(with humor, in acknowledgement of the size of
31		the claim) . . . that one could make that connection.

Now, leaving aside again the nature of the linguistics involved here as a topic, notice how, as a result of a further amplification based on an accurate Reflection, David reaches out intellectually to formulate, in this social situation, a vision so tentative (and so powerful) that he prefaces it with, "it may be that what I am about to want to say is that . . . " (24-25).

And this is not the only outcome. David's extension of his

intellectual conceptualization enables him to establish a highly resonant connection between two periods of work in his academic career (22–24, 27–28, 31). David later said of this:

> *I realised at this point that I have lost touch with a part of my work that was, and still is, very important to me. I don't see how this connection can be fitted into the book I've almost completed, but I do see the need to make this connection and I think I can see in the future where to start.*

It seems fair to claim here that the discourse is functioning not only to serve issues of exploration and discovery in terms of David's specific disciplinary focus but is also facilitating the kind of discovery that might be important in terms of a larger-scale sense of coherence in a person's working life. For some people, at least, at some stages of their professional life cycle, such a realization can be importantly affirming, as David found it here.

Liz as Visiting Speaker

Our work with Liz started off with a fundamental misunderstanding of her topic. We had understood that she intended to work on the issue of how she was going to take her research forward. After she had sketched three possibilities in an opening statement, therefore, our early Reflection and invitation to Focus were not out of the ordinary.

Extract 10.23

01	UNDERSTANDER	So, there are three possibilities (Speaker: Yes): there's
02		"a new direction," "text and patterning" and "local
03		grammar" (Speaker: Mmm). Are those the things you
04		want to talk about this afternoon? Or one of those,
05		or was there . . . ?
06	SPEAKER	Er (three-second pause). Yes, I suppose it is. I mean,
07		it's the choice (Understander: Mmm), it's knowing
08		how to choose between them.

09	UNDERSTANDER	(ten-second pause). Do you want to start with one of
10		them ...
11	SPEAKER	It might be an idea! (laughs)
12	UNDERSTANDER	... and talk it through? Or ... do you want to do it
13		comparatively, or ...
14	SPEAKER	(seven-second pause) Yes, the "local grammar" ...

Liz explained later that it had not been her intention to go through her research possibilities and make a concrete decision in terms of content or method. She was feeling *"down in the valley,"* as she put it, and wanted to address the more abstract issue of how one went about making such decisions. The pauses in Extract 10.23 (6, 9, 14) mark her mental reorientation to the approach that we were (all unawares) offering her.

As we Understood Liz through her different research possibilities, we Reflected at one point a sense of different levels of excitement. Later (Extract 10.24, 01–07) we would take up another aspect of affective undertones. At this point, Liz's exploration of the areas she had initially laid out lead her to one kind of breakthrough. In the time indicated by the long pauses (08), she retakes control of the agenda, deepens her focus in the area of text and patterning, and starts to talk about "another issue": an automatic pattern recognizer (11–13).

Extract 10.24

01	UNDERSTANDER	Can I just pick up something that Joe said? When he
02		talked about "a scale of excitement," I sensed, I may
03		be wrong, but I sensed in your reply, there was
04		something more like a "scale of concern" that it
05		might not be doable, or there might not be anything
06		there (Speaker: Yes). Is that right? (Speaker: Yes) Do
07		you want to explore that a little bit more?
08	SPEAKER	Erm (ten-second pause), I think (three-second
09		pause), I think there's another issue, actually, which
10		is that what I'd *really* like to do at this stage, as far as
11		patterning is concerned, is to get an automatic
12		pattern recognizer—this hypothetical program that
13		someone is going to write for me.

As she explores this theme (Extract 10.25), it becomes increasingly apparent to Liz (as she later confirmed) that the research she wanted to carry out was consistently "tacked on" to something else (01-04), that her enthusiasm was consequently diluted (05-08), and that she was involved in a series of "pretences" (09-12) involving some putative "application" in order to proceed (13-15).

Extract 10.25

01	SPEAKER	. . . so, one of the problems is that in order to get
02		what I want, which is this program, I'm always
03		having to tack it on to something else that I'm less
04		certain of.
05		. . . so, you know, you get tied into this, this *project,*
06		half of which you're very, very enthusiastic about,
07		and the other half of which you're very much more
08		tentative about.
09		. . . so it's as though you've got to pretend that your
10		main research aim is to discover life on Mars, and
11		then you say, oh and by the way, we'll have to build
12		this telescope.
13		I don't think I'm really implying any applications at
14		all, other than the application of knowing what
15		language is like and how it works.

In some ways, it is here that Liz succeeds in reestablishing her agenda for herself. A clarification process is engaged. It is here for the first time that she comes to the realization-cum-decision that she would not pursue any more research grants that involved her in projects to which she did not feel fully committed. This is articulated (Extract 10.26, 08-17) when an Understander picks up on her enthusiasm and Reflects what he heard as a potential focus additional to the ones she had initially stated (01-07).

Extract 10.26

01	UNDERSTANDER	Unless I'm mistaken, you seem to be saying that
02		there are in fact four ways you could go, rather than
03		three: one, the unknown; one, the patterns; one, the
04		local grammars; and one, this analytical computer
05		track (Speaker: Erm . . .). Or would you say that that
06		is not one? You have spoken of that with more
07		enthusiasm, I thought.
08	SPEAKER	Yes, well, that is the one I'm enthusiastic about! But
09		it seems, the advice I've had, is that it's not possible
10		to get that done by itself, because it needs to be paid
11		for, and people won't pay for it because they don't
12		see the outcome of it. I mean, I think, actually, I've
13		got several sort of research proposals going in to
14		various bodies, and I think that if they all fail, I shall
15		forget the advice and (laughs) do what I want to do
16		and try to get money for that, and if that fails as well,
17		then I'll think about that!

From this point on, and despite our occasional misfires in Understanding as we invited her to pursue matters of research content, Liz worked increasingly on the original question that she had brought to the development forum: how does one go about making the choices that one has to make in a situation where one's research enthusiasms are not likely to be funded and the research projects that may have funding available are relatively uninspiring?

In Extract 10.27, she initially indicates that there are issues beyond the software program that she wants as an end in itself (01-07). After a detour into patterning, an Understander reaches back to recall enough of the expression "the question of what I personally do" to Reflect it back to the Speaker and ask if this question is one that she wants to pursue (08-13). There is another long pause (14) in which Liz demonstrates her willingness to do Speaker work. She then takes us through an extended example of what she might achieve in terms of local grammar (14-17) before reaching into a deeper level of attitude and affect, from which she addresses the dilemma that concerns her beyond the specifics of research content (18-31).

At this point, Liz has brought herself face-to-face with at least a significant element of the issue that she had initially brought to the development forum. Underlying (and some would say undermining) all decisions on research direction is the knowledge that a commitment to any research effort will be judged not only in terms of its theoretical interest or practical significance but also in terms of whether it will be seen by panels of evaluators (in whom the academic community has little faith) and by one's employers as useful in the sense of earning high marks and thereby bringing in government funding. When an Understander draws out and Reflects the key emotive terms that Liz has used (32–35), her laughter is of surprised recognition, and she suggests an implication (36–38) that the Understander denies (39).

Extract 10.27

01	SPEAKER	There's also a question that, if I were to get what I
02		wanted, and got money for somebody to write this
03		thing (Understander: Mmm), there's also the
04		question of, erm, there's still the question of what I
05		personally do. In a sense (Understander: Mmm). If I
06		have a research day—when I am so lucky as to have
07		such a thing!—what do I sit and do with it?
		[The talk moves to the need for more research on patterning.]
08	UNDERSTANDER	Is there any way we can pursue that line that you
09		said a moment ago of, "What is it that I actually *do?*"
10		In a different way than we have so far? There was
11		something about the way that you said it: "There's
12		still the question of what I actually *do*" (Speaker
13		laughs). Is there any more to say about that?
14	SPEAKER	Erm (eight-second pause). The things that I've talked
15		about, like the local grammar, one of the things I
16		could do is write a local grammar, and one of the
17		things I'm particularly interested in is attribution.
		[The Speaker says more about this grammar of attribution.]
18		And I suppose I have a fear of saying, "Right, this is
19		the next thing I'm going to do. I'm going to use all
20		my research time for the next three months, six

21		months, or whatever, and at the end of it I'm going
22		to have a local grammar of attribution." Is that
23		something I dare spend that amount of time doing?
24		Is that going to be a useful thing to have at the end
25		of six months? Is it going to be publishable?
26		(Understander: Mmm) Is it going to go into the
27		Research Assessment Exercise in some form? You
28		know, that sort of question. Is it, er, the most valuable
29		thing? Or should I, you know, is there another form
30		of sitting down and finding something out and
31		writing about it, that would be more useful?
32	UNDERSTANDER	When you use words like "dare" (Speaker laughs),
33		"fear," "useful," "RAE" (Speaker laughs) and "should," is
34		there (Understander laughs), is there, I mean
35		(Speaker laughs), anything else to talk about there?
36	SPEAKER	(Speaker laughs) Oh, you think I should be talking
37		about what I would *enjoy* spending the research
38		days working on!
39	UNDERSTANDER	Those words came out very strongly there, that's all!
40		(three-second pause)

Of Extract 10.27, Liz commented later that she had not previously realized that she spoke in such terms about her research and that it was very useful to have it Reflected back to her. In the pause that followed (40), the talk was turned back to the pattern recognizer. Then, in Extract 10.28, an Understander invites Liz back to that earlier point of silence (01–05). Liz later identified the five-second pause that follows (06) as being particularly important, because there was a set of other project possibilities about which she could have Spoken. Significant for her (and this is what is happening in the silence) was the in-the-moment realization that none of them was worth mentioning, in the sense that none of them rated highly enough to interfere with the important point of principle that she was formulating regarding how to come to a decision about what to do next. So saying "No" (06) was highly significant.

In the rest of her statement (06–22), Liz rearticulates a version of her original question in the light of the work she has done during the session. Motivation for a reorientation is assessed in comparison with the significance for her of her earlier work (06–14); the pressure of research evaluation is acknowledged and put in its place (14–17). Then, after another significant pause (18), Liz quietly acknowledges the condition of her current motivation (18–20), orients it firmly with regard to her established research (20–21), and identifies the key to her next step (21–22).

Extract 10.28

01	UNDERSTANDER	A while back, when you said, "Do you mean things
02		I'd enjoy more" (Speaker: Yes). Was there anything
03		else, at the end of that?
04	SPEAKER	Was there anything else?
05	UNDERSTANDER	Things you'd enjoy more?
06	SPEAKER	Er (five-second pause). No. I think if there was
07		something where I thought, like the first time I saw
08		corpus output, I thought, I looked at it and I
09		thought, "That is what I must do!" I mean, from my
10		own internal imperative (Understander: Right). There
11		isn't anything at the moment where I look around
12		and say, "I'd really love to do research on that! That's
13		the thing I most want to do research on." There are
14		items of interest, things it would be nice to do. I
15		mean, if I had that very strong enjoyment motive, the
16		"shoulds" and the "RAEs" and all the other modals
17		(general laughter) wouldn't matter (Understander:
18		Mmm) (four-second pause). So it's that sense of the
19		coal that was burning brightly is sort of spluttering,
20		to a certain extent. It's not that I'm not interested in
21		corpora (Understander: Mmm), but it's a question of
22		how to take it forward. What is exciting?

Or as she later expressed it, in terms that I believe almost any teacher, researcher, or committed human being would find poignant, *"When the flames aren't burning brightly, how do you tend the fire?"*

When Liz is asked to sum up (Extract 10.29, 01–05), her statement addresses first of all her original, more subtle question of how to approach the choices that one has to make (06–20). Possibly because she has done the work in this area, she is then also in a position to review her actual research choices in terms of content and direction (21–28) and demonstrates in so doing how their articulation in the session has helped her to prioritize them. Finally, (29–43) she comments on her work with the group in terms that move us all quite deeply, so that only laughter (46) provides an appropriate release.

Extract 10.29

01	UNDERSTANDER	What we do, then, is come back around to you and
02		just ask you if there are any closing reflections that
03		you've got on the ideas that you had when you came
04		about what you wanted to talk about. If you feel that
05		you have anything that's shifted—or not . . .
06	SPEAKER	Erm, I think what I've had really clarified for me is
07		the sense that (six-second pause) that you have to
08		do, in a sense, what grabs you (Understander: Mmm).
09		That I think I've been putting too much, setting too
10		much store by what would look good on the forms
11		(Understander: Mmm). What are other people going
12		to find? And that when it comes down to it, if you
13		are going to sit there in front of a blank piece of
14		paper, on your research day, you have to do what it
15		interests you to do. And sometimes, just look at that.
16		Not look a year ahead, but just look at this, and if
17		this is interesting, then do it because it is interesting.
18		Forget about where the long-term goal is for the
19		moment and just do it and see what happens when
20		you've done it.
21		Erm, I think as I've been trying to explain the
22		different possible routes, the "unknown" route is still
23		unknown, but I think that was inevitable. Of the
24		other two routes, as I've tried to explain it, I've been
25		conscious that the local grammar route I'm able to
26		explain a lot better (Understander: Mmm) and so I
27		think that, of the two, that is the route that I will
28		probably now pursue, one way or another.
29		Finally, I think that what I've got from this and from
30		you, very much, is a sense of confidence to do what

31		I think I ought to do. I think I'd got very much into
32		this "somebody from outside"—it's a bit like when
33		you start your Ph.D. or something, you want
34		somebody from outside to tell you that your
35		proposal is the right one, and I think I was sitting
36		here thinking that I need someone to tell me which
37		of these, you know, what I can do that is going to be
38		productive in the long run and, of course, nobody is
39		going to do that. But what I think I've got from you
40		is a sense of confidence that, failing anybody from
41		outside to tell me what to do, I'm going to do it
42		myself! (laughs) So, it's taken away some of that fear,
43		I think.
44	Understander	Oh, that's a tremendous thing to hear somebody say!
45	Understander	Isn't that nice!
46	Understander	That sounds wonderful! (general laughter)

Interviewed later, Liz felt that she had perhaps picked up the expression or perhaps just a mood of doing "what grabs you" (08) in the group, but not that we had tried to move her toward that as an outcome. She thought she had felt, at first, an inclination to hear suggestions where we had not intended them. It is difficult, she said *"not to resist what is actually a genuinely natural question."* The significance of "had . . . clarified" (06) was that she wanted to stress the importance of the interaction with the group, the most useful part of which had been when people helped her see what it was that she was saying.

Liz's "as I've tried to explain it, I've been conscious that" (24–25) signals the facilitative nature of the articulation process; and her saying "what I've got from this and from you" (29–30) meant, she later explained, that she wanted to refer to the process ("this") and also to emphasize the importance of the interpersonal interaction and the contribution of the people in the group ("you") but not to separate the two.

Once again, our visiting Speaker had matched us in respect and empathy and had sincerely engaged in the process of climbing the scaffolding that we worked to put in place.

A Personal Meditation

In sum, these sessions were immeasurably more rich and rewarding than I feel we had the right to expect. It was a risky proposition to begin with, and there were awkward moments as we went along, but both in terms of Speaker outcomes and group process, I don't think that success is too strong a word to use. I have tried to sketch some distinct Speaker outcomes above. Here, I want to add just two comments, one about the group and one about myself.

Having outside Speakers brought us closer as a group in the sense that we all acted as Understander and could talk as a group about that shared experience. The most profound effect of this was a deepening discussion of the interlocking concepts of respect, empathy, and sincerity; it was at this point that Paul introduced the illuminating idea of the *mutually defining set.* I shall not go over the definitions again here, because I give that my best shot in chapter 2.

Looking back across this chapter, I find that I have to return to the importance of what the Understander can learn through Understanding. There was one very specific outcome for me, for example, from Rebecca's session as Speaker—an investigative technique that I learned as an Understander and that I will, with due acknowledgment, adapt for my own use as a teacher-researcher.

And in a broader sense than that, the experience of Understanding this range of fellow professionals—who had the remarkable openness, trust, intelligence, creativity, and resilience to work with us in this way—taught me two things that I struggle here to articulate.

First, there are thoughts that I know relate to all the sessions I have described, to group development and to visiting Speakers, but that came closest to conscious formulation following the session from which I have taken Extracts 10.5–10.8, the last session of the visiting Speaker series.

The person who teaches (researches) is so much larger than the functions of teaching (research). Aspects of this largeness may inform the person's teaching (research) in various ways. Conversely, the person may gain awareness from and through teaching (research) itself, and this awareness may enhance their personal life. This does not mean that teaching (research) is necessarily sufficient to nurture personal development or that other activities in which the person finds nourishment have any necessary input to teaching (research) other than the enhancement of the person as a person-who-teaches (researches).

Is this obvious? I think it probably is, but I also think it bears saying. I am perhaps influenced in this by the mounting political pressures in my own teaching context, where the government makes increasing demands on teachers (researchers), while simultaneously wanting more and more control over what and how they should teach (research).

Second, and despite the momentary gloom of my last sentence (to say nothing of the continuing gloominess of the situation it describes), I feel so lucky to be involved in this work. I find it impossible to interact with people in this way and not believe that there are good reasons to look ahead hopefully. We can make a difference by the ways in which we behave in our own immediate contexts. It is worth it.

The Invitation

Dear _____ :

Further to our conversation, I'd like to extend our invitation to you to come to Aston as visiting Speaker. As you know, what we have in mind is rather different from invitations we have issued in the past, and I'd like to outline our thinking here.

A number of us in the Language Studies Unit meet for an hour on a weekly basis in order to work on our continuing professional development. One mode of work that we have developed involves one individual being the Speaker for the session.

The Speaker chooses the topic that he or she wants to work on. Some recent examples have been:

- improving pastoral care provision for distance-learning students;
- clarifying ideas for an upcoming conference presentation;
- balancing the demands of teaching, research, and family commitments;
- the pedagogic relevance of lexical chunks;
- coordinating individual efforts into a coherent Language Studies Unit research profile.

These examples are meant only to emphasize the breadth of topics covered, in the sense that whatever the Speaker wants to work on in terms of his or her personal/professional development is by definition appropriate.

The procedure we follow is this: the Speaker talks on the chosen topic in an attempt to further his or her thinking, to clarify ideas, see connections, identify objectives, make plans—whatever seems useful.

The rest of the group makes every effort to understand the Speaker. They do so in a nonjudgmental way, neither agreeing nor disagreeing with what is said. They will sometimes ask questions, but more often they will reflect back to the Speaker what they have understood in order to make sure that we all have the same picture.

After about 30–40 minutes of this, we change the nature of the interaction. Each of the Understanders takes the opportunity, if they wish, to make a statement of any "Resonance" they have felt in the Speaker's work with ideas or experiences of their own. The Speaker should not understand these statements as comments on what he or she has said, or as advice, because they are not meant in this way. They should be taken at face value, as Resonances honestly reported by the Understanders. These "Resonances" may also be reflected back, either by the Speaker or by other Understanders, in order to check that they have been well Understood.

Finally, we move the focus back to the Speaker, who makes a closing, round-up comment on the session, usually in terms of what he or she has discovered or felt during the hour.

As you can imagine, all this puts unusual pressures on both Speaker and Understanders, and that is what interests us. We are investigating the idea that our usual, evaluative, sometimes adversarial exchanges, fundamental as they are to the forging of new ideas, might also mean that some (aspects of some) ideas that could also be interesting never get thought through. We are very excited about this developmental forum that we are building for ourselves, and we would like to find out if it might be of use to other people.

What we would like to do is to provide a somewhat unusual collegial environment, outside your normal working context, in which you could work on an "idea-in-progress." We are inviting you to be Speaker in the group on any topic that interests you, at whatever stage of development you find it. I cannot emphasize enough that we are not asking you to bring along a presentation for this session, but rather a point of interest, an issue that concerns and motivates you, a practical problem, an unlikely aspiration, an idea for future research, perhaps something that has been in a drawer for years and you cannot take the time for in the normal run of events. The main purpose of the session is to help you develop your line of inquiry, but in more oblique ways than is the norm.

With your permission, we should like to audiotape the session, but would not play any part of it to anyone outside the group without your permission. What we would like to do is to analyze the session for incidents that seem to us to be interesting. We would then like to send you a copy of the tape with our comments and interpretations. Finally, I would like to visit you and spend an hour going through some incidents with you in order to check our perceptions with yours.

We are making a conscious effort here to establish additional possibilities in our culture of inquiry, and the discourse of that culture, and especially of this effort, interests us greatly.

One more piece to this jigsaw. As you and we don't work closely together, there is a good chance that you would need to spend a fair amount of time filling us in with background information before being able to move to a potential "growth area" of your own thinking. If you feel this is the case, we would be keen to read something you have written in the area that might fill in this background. Alternatively, or additionally, we would be very happy to invite you to give, first of all, a regular 45-minute-plus-questions talk in your area of interest, which we and probably some of our graduate students would attend in the normal fashion. This talk, which we would welcome in its own right, could then form the common ground on which you could take on the role of Speaker in the professional development session.

We would arrange the talk before lunch and the development session after lunch on a Tuesday that suits you. We would pay normal travel expenses and a small fee for each session.

I look forward to hearing from you.

Best,
Julian

Chapter 11   Kith and Kind

Some Introductions

The attractions of nonjudgmental discourse in professional self-development are, as I have said to a perhaps wearisome degree, more obvious to some people than to others.

However, we find each other.

I have invited some friends and colleagues into this chapter to give you their perspectives, tell you about their experiences, and to open up some different possibilities. As the purpose of this chapter is to make space for their voices, I do not want to fill it with mine, but I am going to allow myself a few words of introduction. I note with interest that only one of my guests is a woman, but having noted the fact, I find that nothing need be said about it.

My first guest is Steve Mann, a colleague at Aston and a founding member of the group development work that I discuss in chapter 9. Steve is writing out of that shared experience, and one thing I cherish about his contribution is that you get to hear about that experience from another person's perspective. Another is that while I have been emphasizing possibilities, he highlights difficulties. Armed with such awareness, you may find that the possibilities increase.

My second and third guests are Neil Cowie and John Bartrick. In their very different teaching contexts—Japan and Greece, respectively—Neil and John have addressed the possibilities of carrying out CD-like work at a distance. In very practical terms, how do you make this kind of developmental possibility available to yourself when there is no one in your immediate neighborhood with whom you can cooperate? The possibilities depend in part on the level of technology available. Here, Neil reports on his experience using E-mail, and John writes about exchanging cassette tapes. I hope, of course, that reports of video conferencing, computer conferencing, and dedicated chat rooms on the Web will follow, but that will happen later, and only if people who live with such technology become convinced of the usefulness of nonevaluative discourse. You can keep up with the developments that I know about at <www.les.aston.ac.uk/lsu/staff/je>.

My fourth and fifth guests also make a complementary pair, in the sense that one deals with pairwork and one with groupwork. Andy Barfield teaches at a Japanese university, and Anne McCabe teaches at a U.S. American university in Spain. Andy reports on how he and a colleague found a sense of renewal through the use of nonjudgmental discourse in mutual self-development. Anne reports on the ways in which she and her colleagues increased group cohesion through learning to listen to each other in a nonjudgmental style. Both writers point out differences between their work and the CD format that I introduce in this book. What holds us all together is a raft of shared principles regarding the importance of nonjudgmental discourse at the service of self-motivated and self-directed development.

My sixth and final guest is Bob Oprandy. Bob now teaches in California but previously spent many years at Teachers College in New York City, where he worked with the leading figures in the fields of Counseling-Learning and community language learning. In his generous and insightful way, Bob uses the data of an exchange between himself and me to provide a C-L perspective on the work I have introduced here. I find myself cringing as I see the data of my contradictions (regarding, for example, the use of either/or questions), but it is good that the record stands as it is! I return to the C-L tradition briefly in chapter 12, but for now, I shall leave you in the very capable hands of my guests.

CD: Cooperative Development or Continuing Difficulties?

Steve Mann

Setting

This piece offers a perspective on some of the discourse difficulties experienced in being an Understander during the group development sessions in the Language Studies Unit. In presenting this perspective, I rely on data extracts from both the group development meetings and the follow-up meetings described in chapter 9. I also draw on retrospective comments from interview data.

Analysis and Interpretation

Much of the difficulty of being an Understander results from the challenge inherent in changing discourse style. This cognitive effort can sometimes manifest itself in three related and overlapping types of problems:

Concentration Difficulties: You may be aware that you are not successfully concentrating and focusing—your attention is not being sustained at high enough levels to Understand properly and therefore help the Speaker.

Contribution Difficulties: You may want to contribute a legitimate Understanding move, but before making it, you have to work on getting it right. This internal processing has implications for turn-taking.

Content Difficulties: The desire to supply your own information or evaluation may get in the way of Understanding. Understanders are sometimes conscious of editing or rejecting such a move or of suppressing an urge to evaluate.

Concentration Difficulties

The first issue of concentration, in terms of settling down and tuning in, is already raised in chapter 9 (pp. 156–57). Even when this has been achieved, however, there is the further difficulty of just how much processing energy is called on in order to listen to someone else in this new and demanding way. In this extract, Sara and Lucy are discussing the difficulties of concentrating on what the Speaker is articulating.

Extract 1

01	SARA	My feeling was that I was really needing to use all
02		my concentration to follow you, but that I was
03		following you, so therefore why Reflect now, or now
04		or now?
05	LUCY	Yes . . . I hadn't—I was following so hard and I was
06		noticing your furrowed brow at one point and I
07		couldn't formulate what I wanted to say. I knew I
08		wanted to in fact ask the question that Harry finally
09		asked, but I couldn't formulate it because I was so
10		busy listening.

Sara (01–04) links the difficulty of concentrating with the difficulty of knowing at which point to offer an Understanding move. Lucy's point (05–10) is that the difficulty of "following so hard" means that it is difficult to formulate the Understander move internally. To be a good Understander you need to follow, internally construct Understander moves, and decide on the best point at which to offer them. In a later follow-up session, Lucy resolved this potential difficulty to the group's satisfaction by suggesting that in this sort of case, when you feel you need to Understand but *"can't quite work out what it is you want to say,"* then one possibility is to "just jump in and say, *'Okay, I need to Understand, can you give me a few moments to work this out?'"*

This kind of follow-up group discussion has helped us develop a shared understanding of what we are doing in the GD meetings themselves. Furthermore, this understanding feeds directly back into the internal processes of editing and decision making that must take place in real time in GD meetings. This last comment applies equally well to issues of turn-taking, which are addressed in the next section.

Contribution Difficulties

It is difficult to speak at length about internal monitoring because obviously enough, it is not demonstrable in the transcripts of meetings. In interviews, however, the issue does arise, as Sara has explained:

> *if I do want to check an Understanding, by the time I get it right the Speaker has often moved on somewhere different.*

Sara also remarked that some Speakers create more *"reflection opportunities"* or *"pause points"* than others. As a group, we developed a distinction between these *pause points* and what we call *grab points,* at which the Understander has to interrupt the Speaker in order to reflect. Harry pointed out the interestingly different orientation between grab points, when the motivation arises from the Understander's need to understand, and the pause point, when it arises from the Speaker's desire to be Understood. This distinction reinforces the perception that from the Understander's point of view, grabbing needs to be practiced, because it is more difficult than responding to the Speaker's pause.

We see here again that insight into internal processing arises from a group-critical process and that the follow-up meetings provide the criteria that we feed into the Understanding framework.

There are also, however, external pressures to consider. The greater the number of Understanders trying to check their Understandings, the greater the competition for Understander space.

There have been sequences when one Understander seems to be dominating the Understander space. This competition for the floor is less of a problem if the other Understander is clarifying issues that you want to clarify (see Lucy, Extract 1), but if one Understander is taking things in a different direction, this can cause some discomfort and leave another Understander with a dilemma. Should you interrupt and go through with your different Understanding, or should you allow the Speaker to carry on with his or her articulation?

If everyone is to have their say, the Understander space can become crowded, with more than one Understander trying to check an Understanding. This results in two problems:

1. The different Understandings can pull the Speaker and Understanders in different directions and cause problems for Focus.
2. They can cut down on the space available for the Speaker (and providing that space is our primary aim).

So what is the optimum number for GD work? For me four is probably best—three Understanders work well. Six certainly *can* work well, but there may be instances of the kinds of pressure mentioned here.

Content Difficulties

Getting used to the level of concentration required is one aspect of difficulty, and organizing one's contribution is another. In this section, however, I want to focus on a different form of difficulty, that of not being able to resist adding to the exchange a view, an experience, or an attitude of one's own.

Using Halliday's (1978) categories of field, tenor, and mode, we might say that the introduction of expert knowledge leads to a field-oriented difficulty, while a desire to contribute sympathy leads to a tenor-oriented difficulty, and these both result (and are observable) in dislocation in the mode of discourse.

Field-oriented difficulties may arise in the area that we have called **differentiated understanding** (chap. 9, pp. 161–62). It could be possible for an Understander to be genuinely trying to relate the Speaker's ideas to his or her own and in the process get in the way of the Speaker. Looking back at Extract 9.17 (pp. 161–62) and listening to the tape, there is an element of irritation in line 21 when Lucy says, "Yeah roughly." Also, there is competition for the floor from lines 05 to 22. The vast majority of Understanding moves do not look like this exchange. Certainly in lines 09 and 18 we could argue that Paul does not allow the Speaker space to develop her line of thinking. It may be that Paul's self-confessed passion for lexical studies creates an excitement that pushes him to slip into a knock-about Understanding sequence.

With regard to tenor-related difficulties, we have already seen in chapter 9 (Extract 9.8, 20–21) that a conversationally "natural" desire to demonstrate care on Lucy's part is not legitimate in the group's terms. Earlier in the same session, we see a similar difficulty.

Extract 2

01	LUCY	Something that you said earlier rang a bell with me,
02		erm, you said it's difficult . . . you've got so many
03		things in your head that are almost intangible
04		almost—and you're raring to go on . . .
05	SARA	Yes.
06	LUCY	. . . and when you've got to stop because there's
07		going to be an interruption—it's a meal time or a
08		waking-up time or something—you've got to keep
09		them . . . and that's difficult . . .
10	SARA	Yeah.
11	LUCY	Is that what you were saying?
12	SARA	That's part of it definitely, yeah.
13	LUCY	(two-second pause) And there's—I don't know
14		whether we're into the discourse of giving tips,
15		but . . .

Lucy's initial turn (01–04) is arguably marginally "on-side" at this point. Although the presequencing move, "something that you said earlier rang a bell with me," suggests this would be more appropriate at the Resonance stage of the group development meeting, there is a legitimate checking of Understanding. However, after lines 06–09, Sara needs the space to articulate why what Lucy has said is only "part of it" (12). Instead, the earlier intrinsic difficulty in "rang a bell *with me*" has set up an orientation of appeal to Lucy's own experience that leads to the urge to give "tips" (13-15). Giving advice or suggestions is explicitly not what we set out to do as a group, and the group subsequently made this view clear.

Although it is never easy to say definitively that any move is either an unwelcome addition or a genuine Understanding, we all feel that we occasionally find the temptation too much to resist. It is something that you have to work at, and the creation of the resonance stage has definitely helped. As Harry put it:

> *Yeah, it's a bit like, you know, in a conversation sometimes, that you're bursting to say something, 'cos if, you know, if you don't say it soon you'll forget it—it's gone and it was really worth saying, whereas if you know there's a slot for saying that particular thing, you can sit back. We've now got the slot—you don't have to sit there bursting, you can just give your attention to that and know that when the time comes there'll be space for it.*

When Harry says here that *"there's a slot for saying that particular thing,"* he is referring to the Resonance stage. This slot is still not a place for evaluation of the Speakers' comments nor for suggestions, but it is place for delayed download of something that you were "bursting" to contribute while you were working on the Speaker's ideas.

Outcomes

In my title, I use a question mark after the expression, "Continuing Difficulties." For the most part, I do not think that the difficulties that I have raised are ones that *do* continue in the sense of devaluing the work that this discourse makes available, and I offer this piece not to put people off the journey but rather to point out some of the difficulties along the road. What I hope the discussion has made clear is that these difficulties themselves comprise learning steps integral to the acquisition of the discourse itself. It *is* difficult to have the discipline and commitment as a group to adopt a radical form of group development discourse, but there are tangible and ongoing rewards in terms of concrete development outcomes and strengthened group solidarity and support.

The key to resolving difficulties is open and honest discussion of how group members feel at particular times, either as Understander or Speaker. Discussion of these critical incidents, both good and bad, works in complementary directions toward a shared understanding. On the one hand, there is a group process of tuning in to a shared discourse style and agreeing on what is appropriate and inappropriate in Speaker and Understander behaviors. This process is one of creating norms and synthesizing. On the other hand, the more the group works together, the more sensitive its members become to individual differences. This process is one of analyzing and accommodating. In other words, GD discourse behaviors move toward shared norms, and where individual differences remain, they are more accepted.

In the end, it is perhaps a simple choice: to live on, possibly in a professional world of half-understandings and mutual misunderstandings, or to create an opportunity to talk our way into fuller understandings of ourselves, our discourses, and our possibilities.

CD by E-Mail

Neil Cowie

Setting

Over a period of twelve weeks I wrote back and forth by E-mail to another EFL teacher, Cheiron McMahill (CM), in a Japanese university similar to but distant from my own. Using the framework of cooperative development, we wrote about a number of teacher and teaching issues that concerned us, each trying to support the other in developing further.

Procedure

The framework of CD takes time to work out and get used to in both written and spoken modes. CM and I were constantly writing to each other about how we should interact and in the end found our own way to label our discourse. We would make our intentions very explicit with a label for each turn in the conversation: Reflecting, Thematizing, Challenging, and so on. In addition, we made up other, non-CD labels such as "metacomment" or "question." Although somewhat mechanical, this had the twofold effect of making our intentions clearer and less ambiguous and of showing exactly when we were stepping outside the roles of Speaker and Understander. I wrote later when reflecting on the experience:

> *I feel that such parts of the interaction were a positive thing because they increased our knowledge of each other's situation, and increased our fund of ideas and issues, which in turn led to further inquiry.*

Here is an example of this type of discourse, taken from our exchanges. CM copies back to me a move that I had labeled as Goal setting (01–05) and responds to it as a Speaker would, by pursuing her plans further than she had previously (06–17), as is indicated by her "I guess" (06).

She then takes another section of my previous letter (18–26) and sensitively reflects back to me a concern of mine (27–28), before inviting me to explore these issues further (28–30) in my next message.

Extract 1		
01	*NC:*	GOAL SETTING: So what do you intend to do? What
02		changes are you going to make (aside from the
03		changes in video you mentioned)? How are you
04		going to increase the input? How will you decide
05		what to include? Are you going to "lecture" more?
06	*CM:*	I guess I will go with the home videos I have, and if I
07		don't get any more from other teachers abroad, I can
08		use excerpts of movies that I think are telling, and
09		also clips from late-night newsfotainment shows
10		from the U.K. and the U.S. Some of these are very
11		interesting, actually. I could bring up stuff about
12		gender roles and sexuality too in the context of
13		current events and keep things enough away from
14		my own experiences that I could feel safe. I guess
15		I'm still going to avoid lecture for any but five to ten
16		minutes at a time. I still want them to be riveted and
17		hungry rather than oversatiated.
18	*NC:*	I'm envious as I still have to do that. I find that I can
19		have a general plan of work for the term but I have
20		never mapped it all out before I start, and then it
21		always changes anyway as we go along. You
22		mentioning class packets of handouts reminds me of
23		Oregon where I had to go to the printer's to get
24		forestfuls of photocopied notes—it was big business,
25		but I always wondered where did the copyright laws
26		fit in?
27	*CM:*	REFLECTING: Are you saying you are worried about
28		still having to plan your course for this fall? Would
29		you like to tell me your particular concerns for the
30		upcoming semester and why?

We also explicitly labeled our commentaries on our exchanges and on the scheme as a whole, as this extract shows.

Extract 2

    CM: METACOMMENT: I think this is something that CD doesn't cover, but which I am interested in, which is the sociopolitical aspects/constraints on teachers. As I understand it so far, CD encourages us to look just at ourselves and our classrooms, but sometimes (every time?) there are greater external forces, such as being foreigners in Japanese universities, that cannot be solved by improving our teaching. Or perhaps we can modify CD so that it includes this big-picture awareness.

I termed the resulting collection of twenty-three letters a collaborative journal (after Brock, Yu, and Wong 1992), an analysis of which revealed that we:

- discussed and thought through various teaching ideas with direct application in the classroom;
- identified a number of issues that we went on to examine through action research; and
- were able to clarify, articulate, and justify our beliefs about teaching and learning.

CM and I found that through our dialogue we could identify, reflect on, and develop a series of themes and issues that were probably typical of many other teachers who have done CD. I would now like to go a little further and examine briefly how a written version of CD contrasts with a spoken version and whether there might be some advantages to the former.

Some Features of Written Cooperative Development

1. When we were writing, there was no immediate feedback on whether our message had been understood, and as a result we very carefully reflected on what we wrote, perhaps more carefully than might be possible in a real-time spoken interaction. After we

had finished our journal, CM wrote the following note that I think nicely illustrates the point:

I think I put a lot more time into thinking about and writing comments on E-mail than I would have done in person. I had time to pause and think, respond to only part of what you said and then come back to it again later. . . . I could also be in a relaxed and comfortable atmosphere at home and work at times when my mind was ready for it.

CM's last comment hints that one possible benefit of collaborating by E-mail is the nonthreatening nature of the discourse and the chance for "observation at a safe distance" (Brock, Yu, and Wong 1992, 300). Of course, this should also happen in face-to-face CD, but perhaps for some people writing may add an extra element of distance that makes a supportive rapport more likely. As there are none of the paralinguistic clues we use in speaking to interpret one another's utterances, writing may force us to be extra careful and clear.

2. A second distinguishing feature of using E-mail is the ability to recycle topics effortlessly into a conversation through the cut-and-paste function. Topics can easily be rewritten and hence revisited without the original message being lost or distorted, which is a very useful tool to use in order to focus more finely on issues. As CM wrote later:

in other words, the redundancy and repetition of theme seems to deepen my concentration and loosen little bits of repressed memory and awareness.

We returned again and again throughout our journaling to several themes that we may well have ignored, forgotten, or gotten tired of if we had been talking about them. The mere fact of having a written record of the dialogue was a very powerful tool for reflection.

3. After several exchanges our letters consisted of a number of parallel themes with several different topics being addressed on one

page. These topics were all at different stages of the CD cycle: some exploring, some discovery, and others heading toward action. This varied approach is probably not so possible in a spoken mode, where it is more likely that only one topic at a time will be focused on, although of course topics will change through time. The advantage of addressing a number of topics simultaneously is that the interest of participants can be maintained at different levels. If one theme seems to be going nowhere it can be dropped and another taken up; in particular, the Speaker can decide which one of several options he or she wants to follow up on, giving the Speaker considerable freedom in choosing what he or she wants to develop. It is also possible that the juxtaposition and interplay of different themes can be helpful in looking at them more creatively.

Outcomes

Having experience of CD in both written and face-to-face modes, I prefer to meet and talk to a partner since I want the immediate response and warmth that speaking can provide. However, doing CD by E-mail is a viable method of professional self-development for teachers who are in very isolated work environments and may not have opportunities to talk regularly with colleagues. In addition, E-mail may also appeal particularly to some teachers, as writing can provide safety at a distance, clarity of expression, a variety of topics, and opportunities for focused reflection that may not be so easy to achieve in the real-time world of spoken discourse.

CD by Cassette

John Bartrick

Setting

Liisa Ioannidou (LI) and I (JB), two teachers working in different parts of Greece, decided to experiment with CD techniques in order to collaborate in a situation where we could not meet face-to-face. Despite making significant departures from the original model, we sought to conform to the principles of nonevaluative discourse.

Procedure

The Speaker records his or her thoughts on the topic he or she has chosen and sends the resulting cassette to the Understander. Having received the cassette, the Understander first listens to Speaker and then sets about responding. Using the pause button and dubbing option on a double cassette player, the Understander inserts comments directly into the flow of "Speaker talk" and produces a new cassette on which both participants talk. Superficially, at least, this gives the impression of interaction. For example:

Extract 1		
01	SPEAKER	Unfortunately, I don't have any colleagues at this
02		point and I don't have a classroom. I'm only tutoring
03		with individual students, so it makes it a little bit
04		hard to carry this out. Not the ideal conditions.
05	UNDERSTANDER	I hear you say that it's, it might be hard to carry out
06		CD and you say this because you're, you're on your
07		own as it were. I wonder if we could talk a bit more
08		about that, what the complications are, why you feel
09		it would be such a problem?

Discussion

There are several issues to discuss. I begin with two related points that arise from any attempt at non–face-to-face, nonsychronous interaction: extralinguistic signaling and the feeling of being well listened to.

Extralinguistic Signaling

The absence of extralinguistic signals between Speaker and Understander is a major difference from conventional cooperative development. Signals such as eye contact, nodding the head, body posture, and back channeling are very important in giving support and encouragement to the Speaker. They also allow the Understander to make it clear that he or she finds the Speaker's train of thought comprehensible. Participants working by cassette are denied all such levels of support. In a collaborative journal that we kept, both JB and LI reported difficulties in this respect.

> *LI:* I feel very uncomfortable doing this.
> *JB:* It's like speaking into a void.

At the same time though, the very strangeness of the experience provides opportunities for personal growth.

> *JB:* As Understander I really felt I was being pushed to develop new skills in terms of how I talk to people. I had to pick my words so carefully to convey exactly what I wanted to say.

Being Listened To

In time, the participants became skilled at Attending, and LI felt able to comment:

> *LI:* I felt I was attended to. You were very thoughtful about your response. There were no negative vibes. You with-

held being judgmental or evaluating. . . . I also noticed that your comments helped me Focus.

In the era of E-mail and digital recordings, the use of the cassette might be deemed old-fashioned. As far as Attending is concerned, however, the cassette has a clear advantage because it can so successfully record the human voice, and even with limited and inexpensive equipment, LI and I both felt that hearing the voice of the other participant contributed greatly to the success of the exercise.

Having looked at these two more general issues regarding audio-recorded communication, we can now concentrate on three more specific concerns: delayed response, asynchronous discourse, and outcomes.

Delayed Response

The Speaker is in a position to respond to the Understander's feedback only after receiving the cassette some days after the event. The turnaround time for us of sending a cassette and receiving a reply tended to be about ten days. LI commented in our collaborative journal:

> *LI:* In the time between the recordings and me hearing your reactions a number of things have changed. Firstly, my ideas have changed because I look at things differently now. Secondly, there may have been new developments that cause me to reassess my previous position. The result is, sometimes in the passing of a week, my comments and your responses have become irrelevant to my situation.

However, it would not be fair to judge the effectiveness of the process merely by the speed of the response. In fact, the gap that is created in turnaround time serves the purpose of establishing a critical distance. The loss of immediacy was compensated for by the sense of development, of having moved on, which the tape-recorded data was in a perfect position to capture.

JB: It could be an advantage that we have recorded the fact that ten days ago you had this wide range of ideas and plans and, either through the help of the Understander in Focusing, or just a change in your attitude to your work, you have narrowed that down. I think we can say that's part of the reflective process.

Asynchronous Discourse

The asynchronous nature of the exchanges is clearly the main complication, but this too proved to be beneficial as well as problematic. Of course, the dubbed tape is not a record of interaction; it is itself a contribution to an interaction. Similarly, the Speaker is unable to respond directly to the Understander's Reflecting and Focusing, but can do so at a future stage if he or she wishes. We describe this asynchronous interaction in terms of time frames. They are, in principle, infinite in number, but for practical purposes, we found three usually to be sufficient.

> *Time frame 1:* The Speaker Speaks.
> *Time frame 2:* The Understander Understands selected points.
> *Time frame 3:* The Speaker responds with comment and/or further exploration.
> (*Time frame 4:* The Understander Understands again, etc.)

Significant factors in this asynchronous discourse are the review and pause-button facilities. These enable an unusual pattern of interaction in which the Understander can comb back through the recording and stop at points he or she considers interesting. The demands of face-to-face interaction dictate that exchanges between participants run as smoothly as possible, with silences largely viewed as something to be avoided. By cassette, however, both participants have the luxury of pausing the tape and thinking through clearly what it is they want to say and how to express it. LI and I both found this useful, especially at the beginning of our collaboration when a certain self-consciousness inhibited our performance as Understander.

LI: When somebody speaks you respond at that moment
and you don't have a whole lot of time to think, and you
don't get a second chance, or you can't tell them to stop
the conversation while you think, whereas here, with
the cassette, you have the opportunity to go back over
what the Speaker has said and respond in a thoughtful
manner.

This facility can be compared to Neil Cowie's description earlier in this chapter of his experience with CD by E-mail. Neil
points out that the ability to revisit significant parts of the discourse (and in his case, of course, to copy and paste) provided the
opportunity for a better quality of Reflection.

This procedure, then, enabled the Speaker to maintain a flow
of ideas in real time, which could later be broken down and
treated individually by the Understander in the secondary time
frame. In the following example, JB as Understander is able to mirror with hindsight. By this, I mean he is able to highlight key concepts over an extended period of Speaker talk. This has clear advantages when dealing with the summarizing and Challenging
skills of cooperative development, because a verbatim account of
what the Speaker said can be reviewed, rather than having to rely
on the memory of the Understander.

Extract 2

01	SPEAKER	It seems to me that I'm taking away opportunities
02		for my students to struggle with the language, to
03		think for themselves, which is really against my
04		philosophy. I really believe in participation and
05		unconsciously I feel that I am taking that away from
06		them. That's . . .
07	UNDERSTANDER	Okay, that seems an important point worth
08		mentioning. You see, you see it as taking away
09		opportunities from students, is that right?
10	SPEAKER	There's also the issue of correcting, correcting errors.
11		When I go about correcting, let's say a composition
12		or any type of writing, first of all I make an effort to
13		put checks by the positive things they have done. I

14		like to reward them for what they have done and not
15		just to focus on the errors. Second of all, I don't
16		usually focus on all of the errors. In other words …
17	UNDERSTANDER	Okay, I can understand that you say you want to
18		reward them for positive things. You don't just want
19		a page full of red ink with all the mistakes they've
20		made.
21	SPEAKER	I might pick out some of the most salient errors, or
22		the most important, or if I see a pattern and identify
23		them …

Outcomes

Although CD stresses a need to move to action, the major successes of this experience were found in moments of crystallization and realization: crystallization as the Understander draws together different strands of Speaker talk to help create a coherent whole and realization by the Speaker as a new way of seeing things comes to the surface. It seems reasonable to speculate that one of the effects of delayed response and asynchronous discourse might be that they do not lead easily to Goal setting—the outcomes are found in the exchange itself. For us, it was the ability to make the implicit become explicit that proved so rewarding, both in terms of the intellectual and the emotional.

I think the following series of exchanges is indicative of this point and also typifies the nature of the collaboration across its time frames (TFs).

Extract 3

01	(TF 1)	When I'm doing the explaining for the errors, it
02	SPEAKER	seems that I'm doing most of the talking. When I
03		look at their faces, they don't seem to be very
04		interested. It's kind of "I've completed this and let's
05		move on, it's done!" For them it's done.
06	(TF2)	I can sense some disappointment there from
07	UNDERSTANDER	where you say, "They just look at it and it's done,"
08		and you've obviously put some effort into that
09		marking.

10	(TF3)	Thanks for those comments. We don't have the
11	Speaker	opportunity as teachers to talk openly to other
12		colleagues about our feelings, disappointments,
13		angers and sometimes it's just nice to hear the
14		response of an empathetic listener.

In a situation where teachers find themselves geographically or perhaps ideologically isolated from colleagues but still keen to reflect on their practice with the nonjudgmental help of others, a version of cooperative development by cassette, similar to the above, may prove viable.

Refreshing the Hearts That Other Approaches Don't Reach

Andy Barfield

Setting

In Japanese, the characters for *busy* mean *dead heart*. How are we to remain fresh and unjaded in what we do as teachers? It was this question that my colleague Bill Plain and I decided to address in 1995 by experimenting with cooperative development. Our shared dilemma was a sense of routinization: we felt rushed for time; we had little space for reflecting openly and honestly on our teaching; information overload was bearing down; and there was no organized discussion of learning and teaching at our workplace at that time. We felt locked into unshakable routines of work and teaching. We began to focus on our need to break through this sense of routinization.

The approach that I will describe is directly derived from the model of cooperative development explained elsewhere in this volume. While Bill and I were aware of Julian's model, we also wished to explore what would happen if we followed the two roles of Understander and Speaker with a minimum of other conditions set. In turn, this flexibility allowed us to interpret the same overall process in different terms and from different perspectives.

Procedures

In the initial session, we agreed on roles and format. Bill and I agreed to meet once a week for an hour as often as our schedules would allow. In the first half hour, one of us would play the role of Understander and the other the role of Speaker. The Understander role was seen by us as the more critical part: it required both discipline and practice. We saw this role as being based on:

- not agreeing or disagreeing but listening in order to Reflect back what the Speaker was trying to say;
- mirroring the body language of the speaker and following attentively and with respect;
- encouraging the Speaker to clarify his thoughts; and
- Reflecting back, at an appropriate juncture, the Speaker's key ideas, using cues such as, *"So, let me just reflect back what you're saying ... "*

We would then reverse roles and continue for another half hour.

The one-hour sessions were audio-recorded by each of us, and each week before the next meeting, we would individually listen to the previous meeting and review where we were going.

Starting Phase: Orientation, Negotiation, and Adaptation

Collaboration requires negotiation. We found that there was an initial phase when we established common ground, articulated our individual areas of interest, and clarified our roles. We were fortunate in that we both trusted and respected each other, and we felt willing to open up to each other about our teaching. This helped us to proceed quickly and, to some extent, to shorten this initial phase.

Extract 1

SPEAKER

To a large extent, this factor of choosing what you want to learn is very fundamental. It is not always that you choose that you want to learn what you are doing at present. Sometimes you are given something to do in which you find your own interest and curiosity and therefore it becomes light learning, not heavy. But the moment the imposition is felt as an imposition, then it does produce this sort of counterreaction or force which wells up from within the individual and itself opposes the act of learning ...

The whole process has become darkened by the process of internalization of the fact that learning is something which comes from outside and it is directed from outside.

UNDERSTANDER	So, key words there are *conflict, choice, imposition,* and *from the outside.* You seemed to emphasize when you were speaking that it is a conflict, but it is an unclear conflict. It is buried deep inside the adult student . . .
SPEAKER	Precisely. This comes to one back through, I think, the ideas of Krishnamurti and his concept of freedom as a way of developing the self but also as a way of learning . . .
	Realizing that while I try to do this with university students where the majority are not able to benefit from the fact of being given freedom in the classroom, it is an enormous problem trying to let the student be aware that he is in a position of freedom and that that freedom gives him the possibility of doing something for himself. Most seem to shy away from the situation.

In these exchanges, the Understander helps the Speaker develop his line of thinking. The Understander refrains from intervening with his own opinion or evaluation of the Speaker's stance. Instead, the Understander highlights the key points of what the Speaker is saying.

This requires a great deal of concentration at the beginning, because it is a quite different mode of interaction from usual styles of conversation, discussion, or debate. In time, too, the Understander would begin to probe what the Speaker said (*"When you say . . . what do you mean exactly?"*) and to encourage the Speaker to articulate concrete actions (*"So from this, what are you intending to do with this class?"*), all the while seeking to help the Speaker become clearer about what he was conceptualizing and beginning to rethink. This, in a nutshell, is the effort after deroutinization that we set out to make.

Secondary Phase: Perception of Inner and Outer Processes

In this secondary phase, we discovered a process of deblocking in what we later came to call the inner and outer processes. By *outer process,* we refer to the routines that the person has established in the classroom as a teacher and a sustained critical examination of them. The *inner process* refers to an increased awareness of one's own mental and emotional routines and defences and to internalized models as an evaluative standard of one's own perceived and unattained goals as a person or teacher. Within the inner process, questions of irritation with one's students or oneself; moments of rebellion, surprise, and disbelief; a sense of dissatisfaction; or questions of authority and trust may come up as each person notices the patterned routines of how he or she behaves and responds.

At the same time, through reference to external models, the Speaker begins to become aware of other goals and possibilities and begins to visualize change in broad detail. As this is happening, within the outer process, the Speaker starts to question his or her conventional understandings and images of the classroom, to set new classroom goals, and simultaneously to begin to break through his or her established teaching methods and routines by taking risks and trying something new. Trying something new here does not necessarily mean a new type of exercise, but rather it refers to a substantial change in one's conceptual framework for teaching.

Extract 2

UNDERSTANDER	So you are trying to give the students control over some aspects of their learning?
SPEAKER	Of their style of learning. . . . I think the important thing is the setting of the goal rather than reviewing the goal. To review the goal is important. I have often done diaries at the end of the lesson. I hadn't done diaries at the beginning of the lesson to help them sort of reflect or think about what they are about to do. I think this is a key part, maybe. I think also the key part is giving them space to plan. I am not sure how I am going to do this with the low-level class but I think a reflectiveness about what they are going to do is a good thing to aim for.

Third Phase: Dynamic of Experimentation

This third phase is where the development begins to take off. We noticed that we began to try out a new range of options in the classroom, to adopt a different teaching role, and to ask our learners also to move beyond their established learning routines. Here we started to perceive more keenly our own development and to become more deeply reflective about the processes of classroom learning/teaching. Simultaneously, we became more engaged in the teacher-development process itself. As a result, we started to reevaluate our roles in both the inner and outer processes. This is to some extent where, after the difficulty of the second phase, the payoff for investing effort in one's development as a teacher begins to take shape and where one's own personal and professional motivation are enhanced.

Extract 3

SPEAKER   People work within a paradigm and stay within a paradigm because of the time and often the money invested and personal involvement invested in creating that way of doing things—often at a theoretical level it becomes a whole approach, a whole philosophy, a whole way of doing something and therefore a total paradigm. And to let change occur you have to be willing to lose the time that you spent on creating what you have already created.

This dynamic opened the door wider toward future experimentation.

Fourth Phase: Increased Awareness

This fourth phase was characterized by a steeper gradient of change and a more finely focused development. We began to set ourselves new and unexpected questions in the inner process and to express unformed ideas to each other. Meanwhile, in the outer process, we started to resee with different eyes. We set different interpretations on classroom events that would previously have gone unnoticed or have been merely ascribed a routine meaning. We also perceived the classroom with an increased power of observation and sense of experimentation; we began to adopt a more inquiring, hypothesizing stance toward how our learners were acting and learning.

Fifth Phase: Cyclical Growth

It is from this phase onward that we felt ready to research in more concrete terms what we and our learners did in the classroom. I am concerned that the growth and change in awareness described in the preceding four phases may seem abstract and remote to the reader. The experience is difficult to communicate, but it is similar to the awareness-driven progression from unconscious incompetence to unconscious competence that Underhill discusses (1992, 76), drawing on original work by Howell (1982).

Outcomes

With hindsight, I would characterize the process that Bill and I explored as being at one step removed from classroom realities, in that it dealt with our own reflections on classroom events and processes rather than directly with classroom data, as action research, for example, might. This may be seen as a limitation, or it may be seen as one possible stage in a wider process of deroutinization. I believe it is helpful to see growth spurts and learning plateaus as part of a process of development. Growth spurts may come in quick succession at the start of such a period, but plateaus of development will tend to last longer as the process continues, with changes in awareness becoming finer (Braham 1995). As Braham notes, "The challenge is to learn to love the plateau since that is where you spend the major part of your life" (Braham 1995, 68).

We both benefited from our exploration of cooperative development and continued with teacher development in different forms and modes (e.g., Barfield and Kotori 1997; Barfield 1999; Smith and Barfield 1999). Cooperative development was an important foundation for that: it refreshed our hearts as teachers and broke many of our entrenched routines.

Interchange

Anne McCabe

Setting

Four of us at St. Louis University's Madrid campus decided to use a variant of the cooperative development interaction framework in order to work out a problem in course design. The specific course was English 150, the first course in the set of what is known in U.S. American universities as freshman composition. Its purpose is to prepare students for writing assignments at the university level, and it involves them in writing several compositions during the course of a semester. It also involves intensive reading, along with analysis and discussion of the reading.

We all taught the course, and we found that at previous departmental meetings, each teacher would present his or her point of view but that we would never come to a consensus on what should be included in the course and how it should be assessed. We felt that this may have been because when one person was speaking, the others were clinging to their own points of view, while perhaps also thinking of how they would respond in a way that would allow them to present their views as preferable.

We decided to attempt a nonjudgmental approach in order to make a serious attempt to understand the others' points of view and then to incorporate as many views as possible into a common approach to the course. We gave our meetings in this mode the name, *interchange.*

Procedure and Outcomes

After an initial discussion of the CD framework, we held our first interchange meeting. We decided that each of us would be Speaker for fifteen minutes, during which time the others would try to Understand. In presenting two extracts from our work, I want to highlight first the extreme helpfulness of being Understood when it happens. Second, I look at the very basic difficulty that we had in keeping to an Understander role, before we came to see that what we were doing suited our purposes very well. I use pseudonyms throughout.

In the first extract, Angela is the Speaker. She is trying to explain how she chooses texts for students to read in the 150 course.

Extract 1

01	ANGELA	But you know where people disagree with me,
02		where I've often gotten into, um, struggles with
03		people is taking in a boring scientific text . . . Not
04		boring, Okay, I mean I wouldn't take in . . .
05	MARY	Dry . . .
06	ANGELA	Yeah, but it's text that would . . .
07	MARY	Technical . . .
08	ANGELA	Yeah, technical or dry, because I think that there are
09		a lot of different ways that you can look at a text
10		that don't necessarily, um . . .
11	MARY	I agree entirely with that, I think, oh!
12	ANGELA	Yeah! (general laughter) . . . that don't necessarily
13		have to engage the reader totally in their content,
14		because, um, one thing, that's something that they
15		have to do constantly . . .
16	MARY	Is what you're saying that in fact that the text itself
17		can be approached in many different ways?
18	ANGELA	Right!
19	MARY	And that a lot of it is the way in which you approach
20		it and you encourage the students to approach it?
21	ANGELA	Exa- yes, exactly! (general laughter)
22	MARY	Let's get this technique down!
23	ANGELA	Yeah, you are, I mean you've learned it better than
24		anybody! (general laughter) Yeah, yeah, that's what I
25		think.

There are two interesting perspectives on this extract: the meta-comments on the discourse itself and the experience of the process.

The metacomments in the "oh!" (11) and the "Yeah!" (12) signal Mary's realization that she is being evaluative and Angela's corroboration of this. What is then interesting is the discourse work that Mary does (16-17, 19-20) in order to Reflect nonevaluatively what she Understands Angela to be saying. Angela expresses her delight at this in her "Right!" (18) and "exactly!" (21), and the whole group (12, 21, 24) joins in the recognition and enjoyment of what has happened. Mary (22) and Angela (23-25) express this appreciation explicitly.

To comment on the experience, I have to refer forward to some work that the group has been doing in the form of workshops in Spain to introduce our approach to other people. At one such workshop involving analysis of the above extract, one of the participants said that she thought that what Angela was saying here was very clear, so that in fact it was easy for Mary to Reflect it back to her. This comment surprised Angela, who responded:

> I remember feeling not very clear on it at all once it was out there in the air. Maybe even wanting to take it back. So Mary's encapsulation made me feel good about it and able to explore it further.

Angela said afterward that she was amazed that someone took what she was saying as clear, when she still remembered the frustration of a lack of clarity, of direction, on this point.

Through experiences such as this, then, we learned the power and usefulness of this new discourse discipline. But things were not always like that, as we shall see in Extract 2.

Here, Mary is the Speaker. She has been Speaking about a group of U.S. Americans who seemed to dominate her class. She has suggested a separate class for them, as they already understood such concepts as thesis statement and topic sentence. She also goes on to say that they are very vocal in class discussions centered on assigned readings. Up to this point, the Understanders have mainly been clarifying what Mary has been saying, but then Roger makes a different move.

Extract 2

01	ROGER	I find that as well with the Americans in my, uh …
02	ANGELA	You can't do that, you're violating the rules.
03	ROGER	I am?
04	ANGELA	It's Mary's turn.
05	ROGER	I thought I was … I was going to put it in the form
06		of a question, though.
07	ANGELA	Oh, Okay.
08	ROGER	But first I was going to give the necessary
09		information to understand the question (general
10		laughter). I have a few Americans in my 150 class as
11		well …
12	CARL	You have seven seconds! (general laughter)
13	ROGER	… and, uh, I guess what I wonder is, um, I know of
14		people who taught the 150 class in America as well,
15		sort of introduce the uh thesis statement uh concept
16		via paragraph formula and that sort of thing and
17		then sort of move on from it pretty quickly, so that
18		most of the class really involves uh more discussion
19		of the readings and uh the different types of writing
20		styles. So what I'm wondering is, if you think that
21		maybe as you have already explained the thesis
22		statement, topic sentences uh and that, now you'll
23		be moving on and the rest of the class moving away
24		from that type of teaching more towards probably
25		readings that have to do with the particular writing
26		styles, whether you think the problems with the
27		Americans might just sort of work itself out?

As things turned out, Roger's extended move (13–27) allowed Mary to explore a possible different future for the class, rather than dwell on the problem as she was seeing it at that time. From a strictly CD-oriented perspective, however, we would want to say that dwelling on the problem was what Mary needed to do if she was going to find her own way forward. What happened here was that Roger brought into the exchange his own knowledge and experience of a similar situation (13–20) and used this to suggest to Mary how it might be useful for her to see things (20–27). As in the first extract, there are metacomments signaling the unacceptability of Roger's initial move (02, 04), but here (as he signals in lines 05–06) the discourse work that Roger does is to turn his suggestion into the *form* of a question. The form, however, does not address the issues of respect, empathy, and sincerity as they are defined in nonevaluative discourse, anymore than it makes the function of the utterance any less of a suggestion.

Outcomes

In retrospect, one way to describe our interchange work on the 150 class would be to say that it stayed in this kind of in-between mode. I think it would be more accurate, however, to say that the change in our discourse that we brought about for the interchange sessions represents very well the purpose with which we set out. These sessions were not essentially dedicated to the self-development of the individual members of the group; they represented primarily a problem-solving approach to a shared issue. They also led to the development of the group itself via the mutual development of its members. What I want to emphasize is that this process had very positive outcomes for us.

We feel at the end of the sessions on this topic that, precisely because we made an extra effort to put aside our own beliefs in order to Understand the Speaker, each of us now has a greater understanding of what the purpose and the objectives of the course are, and we converge on those. At the same time, rather than feeling that we should all follow a uniformly set way of teaching the course, we now feel that we each bring our own strengths to it, which provides a wide pool of valuable resources that we can all draw from in deciding on course content.

We have learned a great deal about what empathic listening is, and we have gained in respect for each other. After an early session, Mary exclaimed, *"This approach really lets you see the good in people!"* As a direct outcome of the experience of being well listened to, we have each also found that we are more open to the suggestions that colleagues make exactly because these suggestions are based on an Understanding of what we have said and not on a dismissal of it.

In interchange, we do not always practice purist CD Understanding, but we do take the time and make the effort to listen to each other carefully, and that has made a huge difference.

Postscript

Date: Sat, 30 Sep 2000 18:32:17 +0200
From: Anne McCabe
To: Julian Edge <J.Edge@aston.ac.uk>
(edited)

Hey!
I had the four 2-hour sessions this past week at the Colegio de Doctores y Licenciados (held at the Complutense). I think I might have told you that I entitled the whole workshop, "A Profession of Growth: Teacher Development through Cooperation, Inquiry and Reflection."

The first 2 evenings we did CD. My colleagues, "Mary," "Carl" and "Roger," helped out for those. The first evening we showed our use of it—in terms of group development and problem solving. The participants were really insightful in looking at the transcripts, but you could feel some resistance to it.

The second evening we went over a more "fundamentalist" approach and Carl and Roger CD'd me. That was powerful because it was so real. I wanted to talk out my research fragmentation, my wanting to go in so many directions and not really going anywhere. I'm interested in teacher development, teaching writing, and "doing linguistics" in the way that I did in the Ph.D. Some very interesting things came out of me . . . related to professional envy, wanting to emulate others. So once I got past that, I got to a place where I started to talk about what I find unique to me. That was exciting—you could feel the participants following the train of all of this thought—they were hanging on to it as if it were some kind of action film. Afterward, two of the participants came up to me and said they were "shocked"—but in a good way. They were really amazed that I allowed myself to identify and remove through talking the block in my pathway to development. It really did open up people's eyes to the power of a true-blue CD exchange—my eyes included.

It was good, too, because in the discussion later, we talked about how safe we feel behind our blocks—life's scary out there beyond it! Then it was their turn—they had had a taste of it the first day, but here we were hoping for more engagement, and I think we got it. Not from everyone . . . there are some real sceptics out there! But those that did really got into it. Good discussion, too—about the difficulty of staying away from suggestion, and one pair found it really difficult not to offer comfort to the other! I asked if they didn't find the active listening itself comforting, but it wasn't that the Speaker wanted to be comforted—the Understander wanted to comfort. Very rich input for the discussion.

So, cool all around—'specially since I learned so much! One thing I really liked is that I discovered some threads running through the three sections that I hadn't seen when I decided on the title. In the literature on all three, there are mentions of things like "illuminating what we do" and "moving away from the isolation of the classroom." So it was a very seamless workshop, and there was a good group feeling at the end.

And the icing on the cake is that I went into this workshop feeling fragmented about my future research direction—knowing that I was going to have the CD session on my research fragmentation, but having no idea where that would lead me—and I've come out with the realization that I can bring together my different research areas in a way that is right for me. What a week! (All of that on top of a regular teaching load!!)

Un abrazo,
Anne

A Counseling-Learning Perspective

Bob Oprandy

Setting

My decades of experience in Counseling-Learning (Rardin et al. 1988; Counseling-Learning is registered as a trademark) and of working elements of this tradition into my professional life (Gebhard and Oprandy 1999) provide a privileged perspective from which to compare and contrast the nature of speaker-listener discourse in C-L and CD. When I worked with Julian at St. Michael's College, Vermont, in 1996, we discovered a number of similarities in the way we work with fellow teachers and with pre- and in-service teachers in our respective teacher-education programs. Since then, we have taken any opportunities that arise to collaborate and learn from each other. In this piece, I am drawing on a workshop that we conducted at my workplace, the Monterey Institute of International Studies, in 1997. The workshop included two ten-minute sessions in which Julian and I modeled the kind of discourse we both have found so helpful in our teacher-development work. What follows are transcribed excerpts from one of those sessions interspersed with reflections on the nature of the discourse. I am the Speaker.

Data and Interpretation

Extract 1		
01	BOB	It's very strange because here we are a year later
02		doing this (laughs), and it's not the same as having a
03		continuing conversation. At that point people were
04		part of a very intensive experience there in Vermont
05		for about six weeks, and they knew where we were
06		coming from. Here it's even more artificial in some
07		ways; I just wanted to say that.
08	JULIAN	There's this nervousness about it.
09	BOB	Yeah.

10	JULIAN	And there's also this sort of angst because we're in a
11		less familiar environment . . .
12	BOB	Right, right. And I have no idea where this is going.
13		This is real; I just want people [in the audience] to
14		know that I'm hanging out with Julian. This is real,
15		and it's very much spontaneous.

Julia catches my nervousness (08) in modeling this kind of Understanding in front of a group with little or no knowledge of it. In our work, we have found that naming an emotion, if it is labeled accurately, can be incredibly relieving for the Speaker. That another human being is in tune with such feelings is extremely *convalidating*, to use Curran's (1972) word. It opens the space for so much more to emerge. Being Understood about my nervousness frees me to make a further confession (12): I have little idea of what I am about to discuss. From my past experience of being delicately Understood by my fellow C-L associates as well as by Julian, I trust that the process will again work, as it almost always does. That is, I know experientially that the listener will give me the space, the Understanding, to begin with an unformed idea, open it up, and see where it takes me.

Extract 2

01	BOB	The thought that came to mind was something that
02		you said yesterday: "This is our time." Here we are in
03		our late forties and we have things that we want to
04		put out in the world; and it's time to *put* them out
05		into the world. And I feel that my work has been a
06		bit scattered, you know, in terms of a bit of methods,
07		of materials, and I'm very interested in listening and
08		some of the ideas of humanistic education, and so
09		on. But I'm really feeling at this point now I want to
10		get deeper.
11	JULIAN	Yeah.
12	BOB	You know, the breadth has been fine, and I'm sure
13		I'll continue to be broad, but I want to get deeper
14		now.
15	JULIAN	It's not that you're unhappy about covering a lot of
16		ground.

17	BOB	No.
18	JULIAN	But now it's time to—find a focus?
19	BOB	Yes, yes.

From my nonverbal communication, tone of voice, and the words I use, Julian Understands that I am happy to be a generalist—*and* that I want to develop a fuller expertise in one area. My double affirmation (19) is a sign that he is with me. In what follows, I talk for a while about the importance of listening in my work, and then we come to a key moment.

Extract 3

01	BOB	And as you were just talking [to the audience] about
02		the power of listening, I realized that . . . listening is
03		one of the areas that I really want to explore much
04		more . . . And even though I . . . bring it into my
05		teaching, I want to see what I want to write about
06		listening, so that's one of the areas . . .
07	JULIAN	When you mentioned listening just a couple of
08		minutes ago, I got the idea that you had more or less
09		decided this was the focus, and then right on the
10		end of that, you said, "So this is one of the areas."
11	BOB	Uh huh! (laughs) Yeah, there are still other areas too
12		that I'm exploring, and I feel that listening has to be
13		the one that's at the core of what I do. I'm sure it's
14		going to spill over into other areas that I still want to
15		explore.

I am struck by how well Julian connects something I mentioned a bit earlier in the discourse with what I say later (07–08). By paraphrasing my statements that on the one hand I want to focus on listening and on the other that listening "is one of the areas" I want to explore further, he holds up to me what seems to be a contradiction. Do I really want to gain depth at the expense of breadth or not? The dilemma I began with is now straight up against me, and I am forced to confront it. What seems a contradiction is left unlabeled and is merely held up by Julian as two points I expressed. He does not judge me, but I do experience a contradiction of my own making. In resolving it, I see more clearly that I can keep listening as a core interest and spin off from that into other areas of interest that are connected to it.

Extract 4

01	JULIAN	Now with this piece of work that you are doing, I
02		know you've identified listening as a core area for
03		you to work in, and right now we're moving on to
04		other possibilities. Do you want to talk about a range
05		of possibilities, or do you want to focus on listening?
06	BOB	(laughs and touches Julian's arm) Very good! Yeah,
07		that's been sort of the problem—is that I *do* want to
08		see the connections, and maybe part of looking at
09		this thing in more depth is also seeing the
10		connections of listening to other areas. And that can
11		be done.

The either/or choice (04-05) pushes me to consider what is most important to me. What emerges (07-11) is that the connections to listening *are* important in terms of achieving the depth for which I am searching. The realization that that can be done is freeing. I am being pushed a bit by a choice *I* am struggling with and not one that Julian comes up with on his own. He hears my struggle and places it before me in the form of a questing question, not a questioning one.

Julian's either/or question also provides a contrast to what I would normally do as a listener. If the roles were reversed, I may have said, *"You're saying two things: that you want listening to be your chief area of interest and that you also want to discover connections between listening and other closely connected topics of interest."*

Julian's response and the one I might have offered both derive from a profound desire to Understand the Speaker's message. His sets up a frame in the form of two pathways and leaves me to decide which one to travel. Mine would not coax the Speaker to choose a direction. It would merely reflect back to him or her the two messages he or she communicated. The difference between the two Understanding responses is obviously quite subtle, and one to which we shall return. But for the time being, I am talking about listening.

Extract 5

01	BOB	Yeah. Right, right . . . I think still as much play as it's
02		gotten in the last [twenty years], I feel that when
03		you go into classrooms, it's still, I don't see listening
04		worked on as well as I think it can be. I think it's a
05		really critical skill for language students as well as for
06		professionals doing this kind of professional
07		development work together.
08	JULIAN	When you've talked about listening so far, I guess
09		I've been thinking of listening as one of "the four
10		skills" . . . Is that what you were talking about in
11		terms of language teaching? Were you talking about
12		that or were you talking about . . . listening-
13		understanding?
14	BOB	Yeah, it's really . . . listening-understanding, and I
15		think that that kind of listening also can play a very
16		significant role in language classrooms.

Julian's question (08–13) functions to clarify, both for him and myself, which kind of listening I am referring to. I become clearer (14–16) that "listening-understanding" rather than the usual kind of listening tasks for language learners is what I want my focus to be.

Extract 6

01	BOB	And I want to continue exploring with you and
02		other people that I've worked with on teacher-
03		training workshops, how listening plays—this kind
04		of active Understanding more than just listening
05		the kind of role that plays with teachers working
06		with one another and really going on a journey
07		together and exploring each other's teaching.
08	JULIAN	Okay, so it's that kind of listening-understanding,
09		developmental listening, that you see as a central

10		area you stand in, and you'll be looking from that to
11		find connections.
12	BOB	Yeah, classroom connections and teacher
13		development connections.

I want to be sure Julian hears that classroom connections are also part of the equation. My need to repeat that (12) may have sprung from not hearing him Reflect that back to me, but I am satisfied that he understands that "listening-understanding" will be my focus. I've often seen that if an Understander misses an important enough piece of the Speaker's puzzle, such as "classroom connections" in this case, the Speaker will invariably mention it again.

Extract 7

01	JULIAN	And a while back you mentioned writing, let's say
02		your writing. You talked about it in terms of what
03		you want to write about. Is that, anything you want
04		to work around that?
05	BOB	Right. Yeah, I've got these two writing projects right
06		now . . . and there are pieces of this kind of
07		Understanding that will fit into the one book with
08		Cambridge on teacher development. But the other
09		one is not connected at all. That's actually
10		connecting architecture and city planning with what
11		we do in classrooms. So that's not really connected.
12		Except that it is in a way, in that the person I'm
13		writing about, Jane Jacobs, who wrote *The Death*
14		*and Life of Great American Cities,* talks about really
15		understanding who the people of the cities are and
16		what their needs are. And I'm gonna try to find
17		connections between what she says about city
18		planning and what we do in teaching. So, maybe
19		there is some connection, yeah.

Julian reaches back (01) to something I threw out many turns earlier that fits within my discussion of what I want to explore and contribute to our field. If I were the Understander here, I might have stayed with what the Speaker was talking about at the moment, letting the Speaker direct his or her own course, which perhaps would eventually cycle back to writing goals. This, it seems, is one of the distinctions between my focus on what Julian calls *reflection* and the wider repertoire of strategies highlighted in CD. Julian's skillful weaving of the writing goal back into our discussion (01–04) pushes me to think about my writing in relation to my overall professional goals (05–19), rather than risk losing that thread of the conversation.

Whether there is a connection or not between Jane Jacobs's work and my core interest in "listening-understanding" (08–19) is not of importance in terms of our discussion here. However, the fact that I have the space with Julian as listener to brainstorm possible connections is noteworthy. A kernel of something that I actually *did* develop later on in the published version of that chapter (Oprandy 1999) may very well have germinated into consciousness at this moment. By trusting the kind of relationship we have developed in doing CD or C-L work, or the combination of the two, we are no longer surprised by the number of creative flashes that mark our work together.

Extract 8

01	JULIAN	As we are about to come to the end of this
02		particular exchange, would you like to say anything
03		more about the other possibilities, or would you like
04		to say anything about this particular goal orientation
05		to move in a straight line with this idea of working
06		on listening?

Here's another point where I feel a difference between C-L Understanding responses and CD strategies. I might say, *"We have about one more minute,"* leaving it up to the Speaker to determine how to bring our session to closure. Instead, Julian again provides a frame around the two paths I have taken to see if there's anything more I need to say about them. By reigning me in a bit, he keeps my focus on those two threads. He does so with a gentle, open-ended invitation of *"would you like to say anything"* more about them. This invitation helps me collect my thoughts and reiterate where I went with them, as you can see in my next turn.

This is the subtle difference between the approach I'm familiar with and what I've referred to in playful conversations with Julian as the *pushier* side of CD. In C-L the Speaker is always in complete control of the conversation, using the paddles provided by the Understanding responses of the listener to move the canoe in whatever direction the rower chooses to take it. The expectation is that when the rower is ready to move in a particular direction or with more power or speed, he or she will do so. In CD, the Understander seems to provide more frames to move the Speaker forward in a goal-oriented direction. There are more points at which the Understander indicates the doors that might be opened, gently allowing the Speaker to determine which one(s) to go through, thus promoting development in a more obvious way.

While there are such subtle differences in the way the Understander works, both approaches are essentially the same in terms of the relationship between the Speaker and Understander. In both C-L and CD, the underlying goal is to listen actively and empathetically with all one has to what the Speaker is saying in an effort to uncover his or her perspective on the topic(s) without adding to the mix one's own worldview, opinions, questioning questions, or advice. Understanding others in a way that allows them to hear (or rehear) what they are saying not only acknowledges the importance of what they think but also, and more importantly, what they *feel* about things that concern them. Time and again, those we have worked with and we ourselves have marveled at the clarity of thought and feeling that usually emerges from such discourse. And when there is not clarity, the extent of how muddled our thoughts and feelings are can also be powerfully realized. In any case, Speakers know that they are in a safe space in which to explore anything they want to during the time period in which they have agreed to follow the rules of this particular kind of discourse.

The frame Julian set for me in his prior turn allows me to voice a conclusion to this discussion.

Extract 9

01	BOB	Yeah, what I'm hearing myself say, I think, is that I
02		want to go into depth with . . . one thing I want to
03		put out into the world, into the language-teaching
04		world, and that might be enough for a while—just
05		seeing what the subtle connections might be to the
06		other areas of interest I have, but always knowing
07		there's a core that I'm coming from and that I want
08		to put out there. Yeah, because I think now *is* the
09		time.

Julian uses this opportunity to synthesize my conclusion into one final Understanding response, one that affirms he has heard my final and central point.

Extract 10

01	JULIAN	So it would be fair to say that you don't want to lose
02		the breadth, but you do want it to be coming out of
03		a particular focus. And from that focus point there's a
04		statement you really want to make.
05	BOB	Yeah, it's kind of like in yoga when you come back
06		to your center and you get centered . . . Good. Thank
07		you. I think that's it. Yeah.

I am satisfied with my newer, deeper understanding of what I want to put out into the world, of where my center is, and the yoga analogy helps me establish a further sensation of what I will be striving for in my return to the listening-understanding core.

Outcomes

One important, specific outcome of the session is explicit in my closing interpretation above. There was also a further deepening of my working relationship with Julian, as well as a range of individual outcomes for the participants in the workshop. I hope there will be further outcomes for readers and users of this book. For my part, I am grateful to Julian for asking me to work on this piece because it allowed me to get back to the listening-understanding core of my professional work that I became so much clearer about as a result of his skillful listening to me. This analysis of excerpts from our work in Monterey is evidence of a step in that direction.

La lucha continua.

Part 4
Looking Back and Looking Ahead

Chapter 12 allows me to acknowledge the sources on which I have drawn in the writing of this book and in the formulation of the ideas and actions that it represents. In some cases, I pursue further the ideas arising from these sources. While I also comment in this way on some of the tasks in chapters 4 to 8, there is in no case anything like a suggested answer or outcome to those tasks, which are meant to be open-ended. I recommend, furthermore, that the tasks should always be done before reading my notes about them in this chapter. Only in that sequence does the reader have a chance of learning from a comparison between the experience and the reading.

At this point, I have made my attempt to communicate what I know about continuing cooperative development, its sources and some current adaptations. In the spirit of CCD, however, I believe that this episode of the story can only come to its necessarily interim conclusion by looking ahead.

Chapter 13 seeks an end and finds three. First, I take readers out to the ragged edge of my own thinking on a topic that motivates me. Second, I return to the first group development meeting, from which this book began, and show how another significant moment from that session still has a life of its own. Third, I sketch a big-picture goal toward which the book will attempt to make its own small contribution.

Chapter 12   Sources

People

First of all, as far as my sources are concerned, I want to acknowledge all those colleagues who have been engaged in various forms of cooperative development, group development, and related activities over the years, including the visiting Speakers to our development forum. As far as the data used in this book is concerned, I have adopted a policy of anonymity and pseudonyms with regard to Speakers and Understanders, but in addition to those who appear here under their own names in chapter 11, I particularly want to thank: Khaled Abd al Rabbo, David Block, Michael Boshell, Henny Burke, Gudrun Çomu, Chris Gallagher, Michael Hoey, Susan Hunston, Shazreh Hussein, Liisa Ioannidou, Debbie Jagaraki, Argyro Kantara, Yuko Kataoka, Cathie Lacey, Paul Lawrence, Azra Malik, Nikolaos Michelioudakis, Tom Morton, Paulo Oliveira, Heather Oxley, Mary Reid, Keith Richards, Peter Roe, Jane Sunderland, Helen Todd, Anne Walker, Mike Wallace, Sue Wharton, and Jane Willis.

Readings

In this section, I go back through the book on a chapter-by-chapter basis, acknowledging key texts that have been influential for me and that I hope might be of use to those who wish to read further in these areas.

Chapter 1

The essential function of chapter 1 is to place cooperative development in a historical professional context and to associate it with the traditions of *reflective practice* and *action research*. The key source text in terms of reflective practice is Schön 1983. Whitehead 1993 is inspirational in terms of setting individual practice at the heart of the growth of educational knowledge, and Moon 1999 locates reflection at the center of professional development. The appearance of the journal *Reflective Practice* in February 2000 might be seen as giving this movement a new kind of presence and even legitimacy in the discourse of professional self-development. We might make a similar point about action research with regard to the 1993 appearance of the journal *Educational Action Research*. Altrichter, Posch, and Somekh 1993 provides a thought-provoking as well as eminently reliable field manual, and Reason 1994 (38) writes compellingly on the centrality of participation and cooperation to action research:

> *cooperation is not merely an actual or potential attribute of human nature, but constitutes human nature; we are not human without extended socialization and the mother-child relationship.*

Unless one wants to discuss the differences between them, I see no real need to regard the action research and reflective practice movements as separate phenomena, and both have been influential in the field of TESOL for some years, as the following references make clear: Nunan 1989, 1992; Allwright and Bailey 1991; Wallace 1991, 1998; Fanselow 1992; Edge and Richards 1993; Bailey and Nunan 1996; Nunan and Lamb 1996; Field et al. 1997; Freeman 1998; Head 1998; Richards 1998; Burns 1999; Gebhard and Oprandy 1999; Johnson 1999; De Decker et al. 1999; and Edge 2001. Just before this book went to press, I received a copy of Bailey, Curtis, and Nunan 2001, which will clearly be another landmark addition to the above tradition. It is in this context that the book you are holding sets out to facilitate further entry into the domains on which these authors report.

Chapter 2

Standing usually in the shadow of scientific progress over the last few hundred years of what we might loosely refer to as a Western culture, there is a philosophical tradition of emphasizing kinds of knowing other than the purely intellectual. The eighteenth-century Italian Giambattista Vico wrote about the importance of knowing ourselves differently than we can know nature, because human society is our own construction (Burke 1985). The nineteenth-century German philosopher Dilthey was concerned with grounding an approach to the human sciences that would parallel the physical sciences, and it is his three-part terminology of *erleben, verstehen,* and *ausdrücken* that I have adopted in my use of *experiential understanding, intellectual comprehension,* and *articulation* (Dilthey 1976; Rickman 1988). In my earlier book, I used the term *expression* for the last of these, and I still miss the affective elements of that word. My shift to *articulation* has certainly been influenced by my reading of Charles Taylor. As well as the 1985 book I refer to in chapter 2, I find his 1991 *The Ethics of Authenticity* a compelling and illuminating text regarding the search for personal, values-based coherence, a theme that is related directly to teacher development by the papers in Grimmet and Neufeld 1994. Perhaps I overemphasize the importance of terminology, but what we decide to call something carries an important informational load in terms of what we communicate by that naming. I can, for example, balance the attractions of Taylor's *articulation* with the way in which Reason and Hawkins (1988, 79, 81) develop their use of the term *expression* as:

> *the mode of allowing the meaning of experience to become manifest. It requires the inquirer to partake deeply of experience, rather than stand back in order to analyze ... We are arguing that the expression of experience, and thus inquiry into meaning, is an important aspect of research which has been almost ignored by orthodox science.*

Short of inventing a new term, I swing between the use of these two, the more cerebral *articulation* and the more passionate *expression.* I am led to doubt that it is a coincidence that we do not have a term to bridge this unfortunate dualism. Not that dualisms are always bad for us. As well as his insightful discussion of empathy that I refer to in chapter 2, Elbow 1986 (300) uses the two poles of what Elbow calls *methodological doubt* and *methodological belief* to construct a compelling argument for augmenting our ways of learning along lines that are very sympathetic to what we are trying to achieve with CD:

> *I have tried to suggest a larger, more inclusive conception of rationality by adding to the traditional emphasis on critical thinking an emphasis on what has traditionally been felt as primitive and irrational: believing everything or swallowing anything. But this powerful mental activity is not primitive, irrational or dangerous when it is given the discipline we learned in developing methodological doubt.*

Still on the topic of ways of learning, Kolb 1984 is a classic source text not only for psychological perspectives on learning as "the process whereby knowledge is created throughout the transformation of experience" but also for a philosophical stance that sees human survival as depending on "the emergence of a cooperative human community that cherishes and utilizes individual uniqueness" (62).

Similarly impressive in its detailed specificity and its overarching range of vision, Heron 1996 ties in the emotional to the rational and the interpersonal to the political in a characterization of what the author calls *co-operative inquiry:*

> *Recent work on emotional intelligence (Goleman 1995) shows that effective choice is rooted in emotional values. (17)*

> *There are two complementary kinds of participation involved in co-operative inquiry. There is* epistemic *participation to do with the relation between the knower and the known. . . . And there is* political *participation to do with the relation between people in the inquiry and the decisions which affect them. (20)*

The main reference for this chapter, however, and for the whole book is the work of Carl Rogers (1961, 1973), most recently updated for educational purposes in Rogers and Freiberg 1994.

This work is rooted in the involvement of the complete person in learning.

Significant learning combines the logical and the intuitive, the intellect and the feelings, the concept and the experience, the idea and the meaning. When we learn in that way, we are whole: we use all our masculine and feminine capacities. (Rogers and Freiberg 1994, 37)

But beyond this, Rogers's works is also the source for the whole approach to what I have called cooperative development, most especially in terms of the underlying attitudes of respect, empathy, and sincerity. Once again, the terminology is open to debate. I have shifted over the years from *honesty* to *sincerity* as the final term, because the latter seems to make it more clear that this third concept does not introduce a new aspect of the interpersonal relationship but relates to the quality of the respect and empathy that are offered. I feel that I have still not properly integrated Rogers's concept of *congruence,* which to me appears to be the overall effect in the Understander of behaving in such a way as to demonstrate the authentic achievement of sincere respect and empathy. But then, I am merely nibbling at one application of Rogers's work, and there remains a great deal that I do not fully understand! The interactive moves that I use to structure the Speaker/Understander relationship in cooperative development are adapted from the work of Egan (1986).

Having acknowledged Rogers and Egan, I want to make a point that I consider essential to my own work, to what I am calling cooperative development. I very deliberately do not use the term *counseling,* and this decision/omission needs to be commented on. Cooperative development is not counseling in either of the two ways in which the term is usually understood.

Firstly, cooperative development is not counseling in the social or clinical sense of the term. There is no sense in which teachers involved in cooperative development should be categorized as "having problems"; they are committed to developing according to their own purposes.

Nor should cooperative development mean becoming involved

in the personal problems or traumas of a colleague. That is to say, teachers should not take on such responsibilities any more than they would otherwise do in their relationship with a colleague. Most importantly, the techniques we have learned here should not be misused in areas for which we are not qualified. In cooperative development, there is no counselor/client relationship. People who believe in the desirability of counseling as a form of therapy or personal development should inform themselves of where properly qualified counselors are available. If friends or colleagues are interested in or in need of such services, they can then be put in touch with qualified people. For those who want to read more about counseling, a very accessible and authoritative introduction to the field is Nelson-Jones 2000.

It is precisely because the word *counseling* carries with it for many people the psychological associations of therapy and trauma that I avoid using it. I realize that I may be accused of thus perpetuating an overcrude understanding of the term, but I find that preferable to confusing a useful mode of cooperation among teachers and researchers with a form of psychotherapeutic treatment in which the unqualified should not dabble.

Secondly, cooperative development is not counseling in the sense that this term is most often met in the educational literature (e.g., Stones 1984; Handal and Lauvas 1987). This use of the term regularly refers to a style of teacher supervision or mentoring that is based on some variant of a trainer/trainee, apprentice/master relationship. I have absolutely no wish to attack either this usage or the style of work involved, which I believe is responsible for much of the best work currently being done in teacher training and education. Once again, however, the fundamental relationship is not the one we are working with in cooperative development, where the peer relationship is central.

This issue of counseling runs me into some trouble when I acknowledge my debts to the work of Charles Curran (1968, 1972, 1976) and of his associates (Rardin et al. 1988) in Counseling-Learning. I can best deal with this in terms of a personal narrative. Like many people involved in TEFL/TESOL, I first came across Counseling-Learning via the work of Earl Stevick (1976,

1980) and as a form of language teaching: community language learning. It was some years later that I started to formulate what I have called cooperative development on a Rogerian basis, initially out of a desire to work more effectively as a teacher-educator giving feedback to teachers. At this point, I had quite simply integrated what I had learned from Stevick into my practice and thinking to such an extent that I had forgotten the debt that I owed. I say this with some embarrassment. It was only later, through personal contact with Mark Clarke, John Fanselowe, and Stevick himself, that the connections became clearer to me, further cemented by Stevick's later publication (1990) and then by the chance to work with Bob Oprandy and to talk with Jenny Rardin. Curran was himself, of course, a student of Rogers, and his work is more directly related to our general field. I see now how I had followed two paths that for me led to very adjacent spots on the mountain. I recount this brief narrative here in order to acknowledge the debts that I owe to the thinkers and educators mentioned earlier. None of this makes me think that it would be a good idea to use the term *counseling* in relation to cooperative development.

These, then, are the most important sources that I need to acknowledge for the first part of the book. In part 2, the references I give arise from the activities that are featured in chapters 4 to 8.

Chapter 4

Task 4.5. I learned this exercise, which highlights links among physical posture, emotion, and thought, at a workshop on neurolinguistic programming (NLP), for which the basic source text is Bandler and Grinder (1979). NLP has spread in many directions since then, but I am not familiar enough with any TESOL-specific references to make any recommendations.

Task 4.6. It is very easy to slip into overgeneralizations when it comes to body language. I suggest that it is also very easy to assume that one's individuality makes one so different from everyone else that no generalizations could possibly have any truth to them. Pease (1981, 60) tells the following anecdote.

During a recent lecture tour in the United States, I opened one particular meeting by deliberately defaming the characters of several highly respected men who were well known to the seminar audience and who were attending the conference. Immediately following this verbal attack, the members of the audience were asked to hold the positions and gestures they had taken. They were all quite amused when I pointed out that about 90% of them had taken the folded arms position immediately after my verbal attack began.

A useful experience for me was when I read in Pease that someone sitting with their legs crossed as in the photograph here is displaying a potentially aggressive attitude.

"This is obvious nonsense," I thought. "I always sit like that. I can't cross my legs any other way and be comfortable." This is true. But I then have to ask myself why it is that I have grown to be comfortable with my legs crossed in this way. One explanation is that there is a lot of aggression in my personality. I have come around to believing this to be true.

Here are some comments for you to consider on the photographs shown in task 4.3.

> **Photo 1** shows what I take to be an open, receptive posture, with the slight inclination of the head signaling interest.
> In **Photo 2,** the slight turning away of the head, with the hand to the face and the index finger extended toward the temple, seems to suggest that the Understander is doing an amount of thinking "on his own account," as it were.

In **Photo 3,** when the fingers, or fingers and thumb move around the chin, there is a suggestion that the Understander is evaluating what he hears, rather than putting all his energy into Understanding it.

Photo 4 shows the mouth being partially covered, which can imply that the Understander would have things to add at this point but is holding them back.

In **Photo 5,** the hand has slipped round under the chin and appears to be supporting it. A possible inference is that the Understander is getting bored.

Photo 6, with its crossed arms and lowered chin, may suggest disapproval.

In **Photo 7,** belying the smile, we may have the physical evidence of where the expression, "a pain in the neck" comes from.

Photo 8 shows a hand formation referred to as *steepling,* which can be read as signaling a feeling of superiority in the person using the gesture.

Photo 9 illustrates a position that can be inferred to indicate the attitude: "If only you were as clever as I am!"

With regard to the last of these. I fondly remember a workshop participant objecting, *"Oh, I can't go along with that one! Our Head of Department always sits like that!"* There was a brief silence, and then no one laughed louder than she did.

If you want to follow up more seriously in this area, a recent treatment of body language in workplace communication is Furnham 1999.

Chapter 5

Task 5.4. I have adapted this task from Weeks, Pedersen, and Brislin n.d., which contains many useful exercises for cross-cultural awareness raising. Of all the tasks and activities I have been engaged in during this work, this is, for me, the one that takes us there. If the ability to Reflect is the essential skill to acquire, then this task is a key experience. I have seen each character ranked first and each character ranked fifth, and I have an indelible memory of an Arab male almost bursting with the effort to respect a southern African female's evaluation of the father's actions. As artificial as the activity may seem, it can act as a vehicle for a deeply authentic learning experience.

Task 5.5. This task, along with Task 6.4, arises from my work with Bill Johnston (Edge and Johnston 1999). Johnston 1997 reports on research into the extent to which EFL teachers (in Poland) have a sense of a coherent career in the field. He finds that his interviewees speak rather of accidental entry into teaching English, of chance movements, of other professional identities (possibly more important to them), and of aspirations in other directions. The identity of each individual is then best seen as something constructed in the telling, arising from the meeting point of these *competing discourses,* to use the terminology of Bakhtin (e.g., 1981), which informs Johnston's analysis and interpretation.

The inspiration for Johnston and myself to combine our interests came from Teich 1992, which brings together the whole-person approach of Rogers with the work of Bakhtin in the following terms (11):

> *The "whole-person" of humanistic psychology signifies the recognition that such attributes as affective and cognitive, or rational and intuitive, comprise a self of multiple parts— or, as we might now say, multiple selves in the various conditions and situations of one's existence.*

These ideas were brought home to me in the most direct terms possible in 1998 when I was invited to teach at a U.S. American university for a semester. I very much wanted to accept that invitation. However, my daughter was thirteen years old at the time, and I knew that she would hate to be taken out of her British school for half a year. Were I to decide to go alone, I also wondered how many more springtimes she would want to spend hanging out with her dad. I found the idea of myself as a construct of competing discourses very helpful at this point. I no longer had to agonize about which was, so to speak, the real me, parent or teacher.

I felt that two of my identities needed to dialogue. In fact, I had a better opportunity open to me than dialogue alone. I worked to Understand each Speaker inside me as fully as I could. Living by this metaphor, I did not feel that a part of me was somehow being suppressed or thwarted. When I made my decision, it was not difficult, and the "whole me" was satisfied.

Chapter 6

Task 6.2. I learned the form of this exercise from John Morgan in 1987, and I came to think about it more following a conversation with Adrian Underhill as to whether different activities have different potentials for the quality of experience that they make available or whether the difference turns on the quality of self that one brings to each activity. I continue to believe that, say, walking up a mountain and seeing a bald eagle soar overhead is an experience with more "quality potential" than washing the dishes. But I cannot dispute that I engage more of myself in it. I am attracted by the proposition that the closer I can come to a high quality of engagement with *whatever* I am doing, the higher quality of experience I can find in my life. Although I find Czikszent-mihalyi's (1990) concept of "flow" a little difficult to hold on to at times, I am convinced that this area of investigation is of great importance in our search for meaningful experience.

Task 6.4. Please see my notes on Task 5.5. The idea of development arising from identifying a lack of congruence between our actions and our underlying values is again borrowed from Johnston and his work based on Bakhtin's theories of internal dialogue.

Task 6.5. This task is based on the use of mandalas in Zdenek 1985 to stimulate right-brain activity. Differential hemispheric control of holistic/creative processes (right brain) and analytical/logical processes (left brain) is no longer thought to be as clear-cut as it was, but I include this task because I have found the results of even one such brief exercise to be interesting enough, often enough, for a sufficient number of people. While the first list of words tends toward the critical and intellectual, the second sometimes reveals more affective aspects of a person's self-image, even elements of their vulnerability. As I say in chapter 3 regarding all these exercises, their function is not to provide answers but to encourage us to think about ourselves.

Chapter 7

Task 7.2. This activity is based on an exercise I learned in a journaling course (Progoff 1975).

   Task 7.3. This task is adapted from Brandes and Ginnis 1986.

   Task 7.4. This task is a simplification of the idea of *mind-mapping* developed by Buzan (Buzan and Buzan 1996). Mann 1997 first brought focusing circles and mind-maps together as alternative ways of getting started on an action research project.

Chapter 8

Task 8.2. This task tries to open up the interlocking possibilities of action research as they reach out from the specifically pedagogic to the institutional and social, as well as from the professional to the personal. I have a few more things to say about this myself elsewhere (Edge 2001), and the texts referred to in chapter 1 also apply here. With regard to institutional change, Fullan (1993, 1999) is insightful and challenging. Prabhu 1990, Clarke 1994, and Edge and Richards 1998a deal with theory/practice relationships in TESOL, while Stevick 1998 relates pedagogy to social values, a connection also attempted in Edge 1996. Goodson and Hargreaves 1996 contains some excellent papers on teachers' professional lives. If you want to push out the possibilities of interconnectivity in your thinking into more abstract areas, then my own recommendations would include Capra 1982, Capra 1997, Zohar 1991, and Zohar and Marshall 1993 on the relevance of new visions of science to human society; and Wilson 1999 on sociobiology and the search for common explanations for diverse phenomena.

   Task 8.4. This task is based on an analysis of decision making in Everard and Morris 1985.

   Task 8.5. This task is my own extension of criteria suggested in Altrichter, Posch, and Somekh 1993 (40–41).

   Task 8.6. The arguments over differing research paradigms

and about how research outcomes can be evaluated outside a scheme of before-and-after testing have also generated a sizeable literature of their own (e.g., Denzin and Lincoln 1994; Denzin 1997). Much as the area fascinates me (Edge and Richards 1998b), I do not feel that we need to pursue these arguments here. It *is* important that we monitor our work, think about how it affects others, and maintain an openness to feedback that will help us grow in a healthy relationship with our environment, but this is not the same thing as feeling that if we cannot always devise explicit proofs of demonstrable success in specific projects, then the game is not worth the candle. I am content to leave the final word on this topic to Reason (1988, 231):

> *Finally, what is important is that human inquiry is a process of human experience and human judgement. There are no procedures that will guarantee valid knowing, or accuracy, or truth. There are simply human beings in a certain place or time, working away more or less honestly, more or less systematically, more or less collaboratively, more or less self-awarely to seize the opportunities of their lives, solve the problems which beset them, and to understand the things that intrigue them. It is on the basis of this that they should be judged.*

In **Part 3** of the book, I am dealing in one sense with the language of my workplace, and this field has a literature of its own (e.g., Gunnarsson, Linell, and Nordberg 1997; Sarangi and Roberts 1999). This is, however, a literature of the description and analysis of language as it is. Where a pedagogic motivation or an interest in bringing about change arises (Roberts and Sarangi 1999; Pierre 2001), it is based on an awareness-raising approach to that language use rather than on the type of direct intervention that I am describing here. My colleagues and I set ourselves new goals and deliberately learned a style of language use—a *genre* (Swales 1990), we might want to say—that allowed us to realize these goals as individuals and as a group. So I shall not go further down the road of referencing the literature of workplace discourse.

Nor, of course, do I have any intention of trying to reference the astonishing range of topics, allusions, and insights that arose during the work of our group development meetings and the development forum. Each group will have its own.

The only issues that I do feel it necessary to return to now are those of multiple identities and differentiated understanding in chapter 9, the zone of proximal development in chapter 10, and Counseling-Learning in chapter 11.

Chapter 9

The issue reported on here of a whole person being the discoursal meeting place of multiple identities arose directly from reference to Teich's (1992) work and, via this, to Bakhtin's, as I have sketched these matters with reference to Task 5.5. The desire to help locate the "whole person" in the "postmodern" remains a powerful motivation.

I return to differentiated understanding, because I think that this requires one more reference to Bakhtin 1981, this time to his concept of *heteroglossia.* That is to say that the words that we use have been used and heard many times before by the people who are listening to us as we speak, and all of these meaning potentials drench the communications that we attempt. In Bakhtin's own words (1981, 293):

> *Each word tastes of the context and contexts in which it has lived its socially charged life . . . .Language, for the individual consciousness, lies on the borderline between oneself and the other. The word in language is half someone else's.*

I find this a tremendously powerful formulation and one that illuminates the difficulties of Understanding that we attempt as a group (which are discussed further by Steve Mann in chapter 11) and the demands on empathy that these make.

Chapter 10

I promised further comment on the methodological decisions that I made regarding the anonymity of Speakers and Understanders in our visiting Speaker sessions. I found these decisions on representation difficult, but decisions had to be made.

It is quite normal to conceal the identity of real people with pseudonyms. I decided that it was legitimate to take the extra step of using gender to preserve anonymity because I have not found, in twelve years of this work, that gender is a significant issue with regard to the people who choose to become involved. This is not to dispute what I take to be the broadly accurate generalization that, across swathes of human society in mixed-gender groups, men talk and women are assumed to be listening. For the purposes of this book, therefore, I maintain that gender is not an issue. This is a pretty bald assertion and, as such, lends itself to testing and potential falsification by anyone who cares to do the research.

The decision not to identify the different Understanders in the group was even more difficult. In the end, I was constrained by my main motivation in choosing the extracts that I did in order to represent the sessions: the desire to demonstrate and illustrate the developmental process as it was facilitated by nonjudgmental Understanding. In choosing the extracts that best represented the process in linguistically explicit, concise, and coherent terms, I misrepresent the nature and extent of the involvement of the various members of the group. Authentically to represent the individual group members in their interactions would have involved the presentation of a quantity of data that would have been unacceptable even to a reasonably enthusiastic reader. As it is the process that most interests me and that I most wish to communicate, and as it is the relationship between the Speaker and the Understanding group that is central to that process, I came to my decision about how to represent what happened.

I am still not altogether satisfied. However, let us return to matters of content.

Vygotsky's (1978, 1986) work represents the nature of thought and language as interdependent developmental processes, grounded in social interaction, in the context of the growing human child. This vision, centrally featuring the concept of the zone of proximal development (ZPD), has also proved attractive to theorists in other areas, not least that of second-language acquisition (SLA). Van Lier (1996, 4) claims it as fundamental to his work, and Lantolf and Appel 1994 brings together a number of SLA researchers who operate on Vygotskian principles. There are times, I feel, when the attraction of an image can lead a concept to be transferred in a metaphorical sense away from the field in which it had its actual conceptual validity. The metaphor itself may be very useful in its own right (as I think it is in Rebecca's usage here), but it is also necessary to remember that it is now only a metaphor. If, for example, you come across the expression ZPD used with regard to teacher education or development, you may wonder what this has to do with the predictable, developmental stages of infancy mapped out in such generic detail by, among others, Vygotsky, Piaget (1959), and Bruner (1983).

As I reread my closing thoughts in this chapter on the relationship between personal and professional development, I am struck by the echoes, once again, of previous statements by Stevick. For years, I have passed on to teachers his advice (1982, 201), and now I find myself struggling toward an articulation of a perception similar to the one from which his advice must have arisen.

> *Teaching language is only one kind of teaching, and teaching and learning are only two limited aspects of being human. I therefore hope, first of all, that you will take time to sit down and read again whatever philosophical or religious writings you have found most nourishing to you.*

In his statement I hear encouragement. My own feels more like a warning.

Chapter 11

It is very helpful to me that Bob picks out the "pushy" nature of CD in comparison to his own C-L approach. In an oblique way, this corroborates my intuition that the skills of Reflecting are at the heart of what we are both about, even though it leaves me slightly concerned about the influence on my work of my own personal preferences for having things sorted out or *planned,* as Bill defines that term in chapter 9. In his commentary, Bob uses some C-L–specific terms that, although more or less self-explanatory, perhaps deserve a comment. I understand *convalidation* to be what we offer someone when we succeed in communicating to them our empathic acceptance of what they are saying, based not on agreement but in respect. The description of a question as being *questing* rather than *questioning* characterizes it as being sincerely dedicated to the Understander's commitment to travel with the Speaker rather than intended to call the Speaker's position into question. I enjoy the way in which a person comfortable with his or her own terminology can use it in ways that let its meaning unfold, as Bob does here. Curran's own work has quite a large amount of specialized terminology, which some might find off-putting. Rardin et al. 1988 provides a very readable and terminology-light introduction that nevertheless illuminates the educational significance and social relevance of the approach. Stevick 1990 (chap. 5) takes on the conceptualization and terminology in serious depth. Further information can be gotten from Dr. J. Rardin, The Counseling Learning Institutes, 1450 Palisade Avenue, #2A Fort Lee, N.J. 07024, USA.

I believe that I am back up to date. It is almost time to stop.

Chapter 13 Stopping

Out on the Edge

To finish writing a book is to come face-to-face with all the things you have not said, all the promises to your text that you have not kept. There is an inevitability about this, because to write a book is anyway to be engaged in the development, via articulation, of the ideas with which you started out. Because my topic is development, I should be inured to this problem. For the same reason, perhaps because the book deals with working on ideas out at the edge of a person's current thinking, I find it particularly difficult to break away from the ideas that are there just beyond the page, waiting to be articulated, wanting to be expressed. Most of them are signaled somewhere in the book by a certain choice of word or phrase, with its significance then compressed into the references of the last chapter.

When talking about the power of reflection in chapter 5 (p. 62), for example, I write:

> It keeps the Speaker's ideas available for being worked on for much longer than usual. The ideas are held in a state of unfinished perturbation, as it were—not yet finalized, not yet demanding the Speaker's full commitment. They can be taken back, revised, improved.

The half-reference here is to the work of the physical chemist and Nobel laureate, Ilya Priogine (Priogine 1980; Priogine and Stengers 1984), which I know of only very partially and through secondary sources. I understand something of the concept of a self-organizing system or open system, a system that is both stable and utterly dynamic. Like the human body, it functions by taking in disparate elements from its environment and processing them to serve its own patterns. It maintains its own integrity (or stability) by being always in a state of process (or change). Priogine's work was to identify similar processes in organic and inorganic chemistry, in which what he termed *dissipative structures* also "maintain and develop structure by breaking down other structures in the process of metabolism" (Capra 1982, 292). Heron 1996 (168) refers to this process as one "in which new order is created by perturbation" in the sense of "the self-organizing dynamic of a complex system that gets itself to the edge of chaos and then emerges at a higher level of complexity." Zohar and Marshall 1993 (116) extends this concept in the following direction:

> *Self-organizing systems take chaos from the surrounding environment and pull it into a dynamic, ordered pattern. . . . In the case of the conscious mind, the chaos is the plethora of information that bombards the brain at every moment. Mind takes the chaotic information and draws it into a pattern—if this is cultural information, into a "world view" or a lifestyle.*

One source of excitement for me is the view that emerges here of a common thread of description running from the inorganic world through the organic and on into human consciousness and social behavior.

More specifically, I am excited by the connection between these ideas and the status of the Speaker in cooperative development. For this is where the Speaker stands, facing the potential chaos of information out beyond what he or she understands and having the courage and determination to draw it into a pattern—the stable but dynamic coherence of the Speaker, in which all things may change (as the cheese sandwich in the stomach changes into energy and waste, as all the cells except brain cells in our body are replaced over a few years) but a sense of coherence and integrity continues.

I feel a similar excitement, also intimately connected to a desire to experience our deep relationship to our large-scale environment in the everyday activity of our professional lives, when I read Zohar 1991 (183):

> *It is this capacity of the quantum self to pluck reality from multiple possibility, the capacity to make experimental worlds, some of which will be improvements on the last, and our ability to articulate (through self-reflection) what made them so, which essentially links our freedom and our creativity.*

Here again, we have an image of the Speaker that sets him or her in a worldview that spans the inorganic, the organic, the conscious and the social. Furthermore, these insights and discoveries that Speakers achieve as they articulate their experimental worlds do not come as a smooth flow, but as sometimes unexpected leaps in unpredictable directions. As I suggested in chapter 5 (p. 57), we can see the work of the Understander as contributing the increased energy that makes these quantum leaps possible. In order to make this contribution, the Understander must work to accept the Speaker both as a single person and as a set of relationships or, in Zohar's terms extrapolated from quantum physics, both as a particle and a wave. When I subtitled this book, "for Individuals as Colleagues," I was seeking to express something similar.

Moreover, without the Understander, there is no Speaker. Let us return briefly to Reason and Hawkin's 1988 (81) exposition of *expression*—what it is, what it is not, and how it is achieved:

> *To make meaning manifest through expression requires the use of a creative medium through which the meaning can take form. This is not to be confused with a conceptual grid which divides up experience, it is rather the creation of an "empty space," a Lichtung, or clearing, as Heidegger de-*

scribes it, which becomes a vessel in which meaning can take shape.

Reason and Hawkin's concern here is with the creative medium of storytelling as a form of inquiry, but mine is with the empty space in which meaning can take shape. The construction of this is in great part the responsibility of the Understander or Understanders. And as Understanding creates the space, differentiated Understanding is what gives each group Understanding its contributory shaping effect on the meanings that the Speaker can make.

I pause. I hesitate. I have learned that Rogers himself (1980, 130–32) suggested linkages of the kind that I am exploring here, although, in my own mind, I made these connections for myself. I had meant to be further on. It was my firm intention before writing this section to have read the Priogine, to have read the Heidegger. I am forcefully reminded of our visiting Speaker David's admission, quoted in chapter 10 (p. 177):

> *I am, to be honest, I think quite naturally, worried that if I tell you what I don't understand, then you'll think less of me.*

But this is where the Speaker has to dare to go, and I thought it only fair that I should go there once with you. Perhaps my dabbling in secondary sources is merely harmless New Age waffling. More seriously, it may be self-deluding intellectual imposture (Sokal and Bricmont 1998) based on terminological coincidence and metaphorical cleverness. That is the risk I am currently taking. Through it I have learned a little more of Heidegger, if only at two removes (cited with the following emphasis in Reason and Rowan 1981, xvii, from Friedman 1964):

> *The student is forced out into the uncertainty of all things, upon which the necessity for commitment then bases itself. **Study must again mean taking a risk . . .***

Ends, Beginnings, and Interactions

Date: Fri, 1 Dec 2000
To: "Harry"
From: Julian
Subject: Writers

Hey,
Read this one when you can take a few minutes (!) out (!!!).

3rd February 1998 was our first GD session "proper"—when we tried the format of Speaker and Understanders, with a slot for what we did not yet call Resonances. I was Speaker, and my topic was, or came to be, "renewing CD." In the section where Understanders gave their own individual responses, you said, in a way that I think was humorous but essentially serious (?), rather than serious but essentially humorous (?):

"In hearing you talk, it's made me realize that I am not a writer. Or, that I am a writer in a very different sense. Not that I have ever thought of myself as a writer, though I have always written lots . . . What it opened up for me quite genuinely, I know it's humorous, is this realization that just the term writer and what it means to us are—the two are very different. For you it's thinking about the book, it's really wanting to say something, and for me, it's a task that you fill with words."

I'd be truly grateful for your comments on:

1. what you remember meaning then;
2. what that Resonance means to you now;
3. how you view that description of yourself now;
4. any connection that you see between that Resonance and now.

Best,
Julian

(It seems best to stay that brief and elliptical for now.)

Hi,

Thanks for the chance to follow that one up—lots of fun looking back at it and thinking about it. Can't vouch for the quality of the response, though. Here goes:

>1. what you remember meaning then;

I think I wanted to say that up to then I'd just thought of writing as being, well, more or less a process of producing a certain kind of text and something we have to do as part of our job—I'd never thought in terms of "being a writer." But hearing you speak, I realized I was hearing someone talking about "being a writer" in the sense of really wanting to say something that had to be said as a writer (i.e., not in a conference or as part of teaching). So I was drawing a distinction between a writer who writes because they have something they want to say and a writer who writes because they are expected to say something.

>2. what that Resonance means to you now;

More or less that. I think "humorous" is problematic, though. What I really should have said was that I wanted to draw a serious distinction which was new to me (at a conscious level), even though one part of the distinction might be expressed in a rather funny (= odd—"humorous" was wrong) way: "a task that you fill with words". What I would want to point out now is that this was an important insight for me because I'd never realized that I saw my writing in quite such an instrumental light. It actually started me thinking about what academic writing for me is—and what I might want it to be.

>3. how you view that description of yourself now;

Part fits, part doesn't. I rattled off a 4,000-word cobbled-together paper for a web collection in a couple of hours last week after someone out of the blue asked me for a write-up of a conference paper I delivered almost a year ago. Definitely a task filled with words. And I have another conference paper for publication to write after Christmas which will fall more or less in the same category, though it won't be cobbled together and will take a lot longer than a couple of hours. BUT in that there will be an idea or two that I will play down because they ARE things I want to say and want to say well. They'll be put in a different paper—when I feel ready to write it. And of course there's the book that I've recently got down to, which is something I want to say and want to do well. So I now operate in two conscious modes: "I will write this because it's a task I've agreed to take on," and "I will write this because I want to take people with me along this road to understanding." In the original Resonance I treated these as belonging to two different types of writer. Now I see myself as many types of writer, but these two still stand out.

>4. any connection that you see between that Resonance and now.

You're right to be elliptical in asking questions, but those on the receiving end always put their own interpretation on what you're "getting at," so I'll come up with mine. I think that amongst other things you may be interested in whether the Resonances have Reverberations (see how I've capitalized)— where they might have led, what long-term changes they might have contributed to. And since that's what I'm thinking, that's how I'm going to answer this question. Only last night (at 5:43 exactly, as I crossed over the last road before the station) I was thinking about my writing and what I wanted it to be, and I was feeling happy that I'd decided it would be done in my own time and in my own way because at rock bottom that's important to me. It's a part of the balance I think I've now just about got right between my work and the rest of my life. What sparked these thoughts was something I'd read in John Swales's latest book about how he started out his academic life aiming to write an article a year and when he made it to professor found that he was aiming at five a year. That for me (but obviously not for him) would be "tasks filled with words," and though I might do it I couldn't get to care about it. This is tied in (I reflected—not the first time—on my walk to the station) with the fact that almost all of what "academics" write is hot air that they use to warm one another; very little amounts to anything. So I'm still happy to puff where I have to, but in some things—the things that matter—I'll write because I care and because I want to share. I don't think I would have thought about all this in quite that way without the Resonance.

Hope that helps.
Have a good weekend.
Cheers,
"Harry"

Taking a Deep Breath

The previous two sections are aimed to show, respectively, me as Speaker, out on the crumbling edge of what I know about a topic that interests me, and Harry, after Understanding, drawing his own significance from the group development session that opens chapter 9, in which his Reflection was so significant for me.

Now it really is time to take a deep breath and let go, let the book go out into the world and see if it can make a contribution by itself. I don't mean that to sound either naïve or hubristic. I am not alone in seeing a need, even if we were to disagree about the required response.

I refer in chapter 2 (pp. 23–24) to Tannen 1998, for example, which deals at book length with what Tannen calls our *argument culture.* As she analyzes the pervasiveness of argument in our quotidian discourse, it is clear that behind the arguments portrayed is less the cool logic of rational thought than the power-related moves of influence and domination. On a crowded planet, with our well-established species history of violence at all levels of human interaction, we do need to try to do better. Tannen (1998, 298) sums up her conclusions like this:

> *We need to use our imaginations and ingenuity to find different ways to seek truth and gain knowledge, and add them to our arsenal—or, I should say, to the ingredients for our stew. It will take creativity to find ways to blunt the most dangerous blades of the argument culture. It's a challenge we must undertake, because our public and private lives are at stake.*

I am convinced that approaches to communication and inquiry based on the aware acquisition and use of nonjudgmental discourse do have the potential to make a meaningful contribution. Not that I have any illusions about the world in which we live, which I think has moved only relentlessly onward in terms of the description offered with a kind of prescience by Corder 1985,

31), at a time when I had only recently bought my very first word processor:

> *The world wants the quick memo, the rapid-fire electronic mail service; the world wants speed, efficiency and economy of motion, all goals that, when reached, have given the world less than it wanted or needed. We must teach the world to want otherwise, to want time for care.*

As I said at the outset, I have written this book for people who teach.

References

Allwright, D., and K. Bailey. 1991. *Focus on the language classroom: An intro-duction to classroom research for language teachers.* Cambridge: Cambridge University Press.

Altrichter, H., P. Posch, and B. Somekh. 1993. *Teachers investigate their work: An introduction to the methods of action research.* London: Routledge.

Bailey, K., and D. Nuna, eds. 1996. *Voices from the language classroom: Quali-tative research in second language education.* Cambridge: Cambridge University Press.

Bailey, K., A. Curtis, and D. Nunan. 2001. *Pursuing professional development: The self as source.* Boston: Heinle and Heinle.

Bakhtin, M. 1981. *The dialogic imagination.* Trans. C. Emerson and M. Holquist. Austin: University of Texas Press.

Bakhtin, M. 1986. *Speech genres and other late essays.* Trans. V. McGee. Austin: University of Texas Press.

Bandler, R., and J. Grinder. 1979. *Frogs into princes: Neurolinguistic program-ming.* Moab, Utah: Real People Press.

Barfield, A. W. 1999. Teaching, administration and research: Understanding insti-tutional constraints on teacher development. In *The web of English cur-riculum development.* Japan: University of Tsukuba, Foreign Language Center.

Barfield, A. W., and C. Kotori. 1997. A reader's perspective on giving a writer feedback over e-mail. *Explorations in Teacher Education* 5 (2): 17–23.

Boshell, M. In press. What I learnt from giving quiet children space. In *Teachers' narrative inquiry as professional development,* ed. K. Johnson and P. Golembek. Cambridge: Cambridge University Press.

Brandes, D., and P. Ginnis. 1986. *A guide to student-centred learning.* Oxford: Blackwell.

Brock, M., B. Yu, and M. Wong. 1992. "Journalling" together: Collaborative diary-keeping and teacher development. In *Perspectives on second language teacher education,* ed. J. Flowerdew, M. Brock, and S. Hsia. Hong Kong: City Polytechnic.

Bruner, J. 1983. *Child's talk: Learning to use language.* New York: Norton.

Burke, P. 1985. *Vico.* Oxford: Oxford University Press.

Burns, A. 1999. *Collaborative action research for English language teachers.* Cambridge: Cambridge University Press.

Buzan, B., and B. Buzan. 1996. *The mind map book.* London: Plume.

Capra, F. 1982. *The turning point.* London: Flamingo.

Capra, F. 1997. *The web of life: A new synthesis of mind and matter.* London: Flamingo.

Clarke, M. 1994. The dysfunctions of the theory/practice discourse. *TESOL Quarterly* 28(1): 9-26.

Corder, J. 1985. Argument as emergence, rhetoric as love. *Rhetoric Review* 4(1): 16-32.

Curran, C. 1968. *Counseling and psychotherapy.* New York: Sheed and Ward.

Curran, C. 1972. *Counseling-Learning: A whole-person model for education.* Apple River, Ill.: Apple River Press.

Curran, C. 1976. *Counseling-Learning in second languages.* Apple River, Ill.: Apple River Press.

Czikszentmihalyi, M. 1990. *Flow: The psychology of happiness.* London: Rider.

De Decker, B., Van Thielen, B., and M. Vanderheiden, eds. 1999. *TDTR4: Teachers develop teachers research.* CD-ROM available from *Marleen.Vanderheiden@clt.kuleuven.ac.be.*

Denzin, N. 1997. *Interpretive ethnography: Ethnographic practices for the 21st century.* Thousand Oaks, Calif.: Sage.

Denzin, N., and Y. Lincoln, eds. 1994. *Handbook of qualitative research.* Thousand Oaks, Calif.: Sage.

Dilthey, W. 1976. *Selected writings.* Ed. and trans. H. Rickman. Cambridge: Cambridge University Press.

Edge, J. 1992. *Cooperative development: Professional self-development through cooperation with colleagues.* London: Longman.

Edge, J. 1996. Cross-cultural paradoxes in a profession of values. *TESOL Quarterly* 30(1): 9-30.

Edge, J., ed. 2001. *Action research.* Alexandria, Va.: TESOL Inc.

Edge, J., and B. Johnston. 1999. Exploring interaction in teacher development. Workshop at TESOL Convention, New York.

Edge, J., and K. Richards. 1998a. May I see your warrant, please? Justifying claims in qualitative research. *Applied Linguistics* 19 (3): 334-56.

Edge, J., and K. Richards. 1998b. Why best practice isn't good enough. *TESOL Quarterly* 32(3): 569-76.

Edge, J., and K. Richards, eds. 1993. *Teachers develop teachers research.* Oxford: Heinemann.

Egan, R. 1986. *The skilled helper.* 3d ed. Belmont, Calif.: Wadsworth.

Elbow, P. 1986. *Embracing contraries: Explorations in learning and teaching.* New York: Oxford University Press.

Everard, K., and G. Morris. 1985. *Effective school management.* London: Harper Education Series.

Fanselow, J. 1992. *Contrasting conversations.* White Plains, N.Y.: Longman.

Field, J., A. Graham, E. Griffiths, and K. Head, eds. 1997. *TDTR2: Teachers develop teachers research.* Whitstable, U.K.: IATEFL.

Freeman, D. 1998. *Doing teacher research: From inquiry to understanding.* Boston: Heinle and Heinle.

Friedman, M., ed. 1964. *The worlds of existentialism: A critical reader.* New York: Random House.

Fullan, M. 1993. *Change forces: Probing the depths of educational reform.* London: Falmer Press.

Furnham, A. 1999. *Body language at work.* London: Institute of Personnel and Development.

Gebhard, G., and R. Oprandy. 1999. *Language teaching awareness: A guide to exploring beliefs and practices.* Cambridge: Cambridge University Press.

Goleman, D. 1995. *Emotional intelligence: Why it can matter more than IQ.* London: Bloomsbury.

Goodson, I., and A. Hargreaves, eds. 1996. *Teachers' professional lives.* London: Falmer Press.

Grimmet, P., and J. Neufeld, eds. 1994. *Teacher development and the struggle for authenticity.* New York: Teachers College Press.

Guba, E., and Y. Lincoln. 1994. Competing paradigms in qualitative research. In *Handbook of qualitative research,* ed. N. Denzin and Y. Lincoln. Thousand Oaks, Calif.: Sage.

Gunnarson, B., P. Linell, and B. Nordberg, eds. 1997. *The construction of professional discourse.* London: Longman.

Halliday, M. 1978. *Language as social semiotic.* London: Edward Arnold.

Handal, G., and P. Lauvas. 1987. *Promoting Reflective Teaching.* Milton Keynes, U.K.: Open University Press.

Head, K., ed. 1998. *TDTR3: Teachers develop teachers research.* Whitstable, U.K.: IATEFL.

Heron, J. 1996. *Co-operative inquiry: Research into the human condition.* London: Sage.

Huberman, M. 1993. *The lives of teachers.* London: Cassell.

Johnson, K. 1999. *Understanding language teaching: Reason in action.* Boston: Heinle and Heinle.

Johnston, B. 1997. Do EFL teachers have careers? *TESOL Quarterly* 31(4): 681–712.

Johnston, B. 1999. Putting critical pedagogy in its place: A personal account. *TESOL Quarterly,* 33, 557–65.

Kolb, D. A. 1984. *Experiential learning: Experience as the source of learning and development.* Englewood Cliffs, N.J.: Prentice-Hall.

Krishnamurti, R., ed. 1964. *Think of these things.* New York: Harper Perennial.

Lantolf, J., and G. Appel. 1994. *Vygotskian approaches to second language research.* Norwood, N.J.: Ablex.

van Lier, L. 1996. *Interaction in the language curriculum: Awareness, autonomy and authenticity.* Harlow, U.K.: Longman.

Mann, S. 1997. Focusing circles and mind-mapping. *IATEFL Newsletter* 136:18–19.

Marley, B. 1980. Redemption song. *Uprising.* Island Records ILPS 9596. Lyric © Rondor Music Ltd, London.

Mattinger, J. and DeCarrico, J. 1992. *Lexical phrases and language teaching.* Oxford: Oxford University Press.

Moon, J. 1999. *Reflection in learning and professional development, theory and practice.* London: Kogan Page.

Nelson-Jones, R. 2000. *Introduction to counselling skills.* London: Sage.

Nunan, D. 1989. *Understanding language classrooms: A guide for teacher-initiated action.* London: Prentice-Hall.

Nunan, D., ed. 1992. *Collaborative language learning and teaching.* Cambridge: Cambridge University Press.

Nunan, D., and C. Lamb. 1996. *The self-directed teacher: Managing the learning process.* Cambridge: Cambridge University Press.

Oprandy, R. 1999. Jane Jacobs: Eyes on the city. In *Expanding our vision: Insights for language teachers,* ed. D. J. Mendelsohn. Toronto: Oxford University Press.

Pease, A. 1981. *Body language.* London: Sheldon Press.

Piaget, J. 1959. *The language and thought of the child.* London: Routledge and Kegan Paul.

Pierre, L. 2001. Going global: Communication at (the) stake. In *Action research,* ed. J. Edge. Alexandria, Va.: TESOL Inc.

Prabhu, N. 1990. There is no best method.—Why? *TESOL Quarterly* 24(1): 161–76.

Priogine, I. 1980. *From being to becoming.* San Francisco: Freeman.

Priogine, I., and I. Stengers. 1984. *Order out of chaos.* New York: Bantam Books.

Progoff, I. 1975. *At a journal workshop.* New York: Dialogue House.

Rardin, J., D. Tranel, P. Tirone, and B. Green. 1988. *Education in a new dimension: The Counseling-Learning approach to community language learning.* East Dubuque, Ill.: Counseling-Learning Publications.

Reason, P. 1988. Reflections. In *Human inquiry in action,* ed. P. Reason, 221–31. London: Sage.

Reason, P., ed. 1994. *Participation in human inquiry.* London: Sage.

Reason, P., and P. Hawkins. 1988. Storytelling as inquiry. In *Human inquiry in action,* ed. P. Reason, 79–101. London: Sage.

Reason, P., and H. Bradbury, eds. 2001. *The handbook of action research, participative inquiry and practice.* London: Sage.

Reason, P., and P. Rowan, eds. 1981. *Human inquiry: A sourcebook for new paradigm research.* Chichester, U.K.: Wiley.

Richards, J., ed. 1998. Teaching in action: Case studies from second language classrooms. Alexandria, Va.: TESOL Inc.

Rickman, H. 1988. *Dilthey today: A critical appraisal of the contemporary relevance of his work.* London: Greenwood.

Roberts, C., and S. Sarangi. 1999. Hybridity in gatekeeping discourse: Issues of practical relevance for the researcher. In *Talk, work, and institutional order,* ed. S. Sarangi and C. Roberts, 473–503. Berlin: Mouton de Gruyter.

Rogers, C. 1961. *On becoming a person.* London: Constable.

Rogers, C. 1973. *Encounter groups.* Harmondsworth, U.K.: Penguin.

Rogers, C. 1980. *A way of being.* Boston: Houghton Mifflin.

Rogers, C. 1992. Communication: Its blocking and its facilitation. In *Rogerian perspectives: Collaborative rhetoric for oral and written communication,* ed. N. Teich. Norwood, N.J.: Ablex.

Rogers, C., and H. Freiberg. 1994. *Freedom to learn.* 3d. ed. New York: Macmillan College Publishing.

Sarangi, S., and C. Roberts, eds. 1999. *Talk, work and institutional order: Dis-*

course in medical, mediation and management settings. Berlin: Mouton de Gruyter.

Schön, D. 1983. *The reflective practitioner: How professionals think in action.* London: Temple Smith.

Smith, R. C., and A. W. Barfield. 1999. Teacher-learner autonomy: Ideas for conference and workshop design. In *TDTR4: Teachers develop teachers research,* ed. B. De Decker, B. Van Thielen, and M. Vanderheiden. CD-ROM available from *Marleen.Vanderheiden@clt.kuleuven.ac.be.*

Sokal, A., and J. Bricmont. 1998. *Intellectual impostures.* London: Profile Books.

Stevick, E. 1976. *Memory, meaning and method.* Rowley, Mass.: Newbury House.

Stevick, E. 1980. *Teaching Languages: A way and ways.* Rowley, Mass.: Newbury House.

Stevick, E. 1982. *Teaching and learning languages.* Cambridge: Cambridge University Press.

Stevick, E. 1990. *Humanism in language teaching.* Oxford: Oxford University Press.

Stevick E. 1998. *Working with teaching methods: What's at stake.* Boston: Heinle and Heinle.

Stones, E. 1984. *Supervision in teacher education.* London: Methuen.

Swales, J. 1990. *Genre analysis.* Oxford: Oxford University Press.

Tannen, D. 1998. *The argument culture.* London: Virago.

Taylor, C. 1985. *Human agency and language.* Cambridge: Cambridge University Press.

Taylor, C. 1991. *The ethics of authenticity.* Cambridge: Harvard University Press.

Teich, N., ed. 1992. *Rogerian perspectives: Collaborative rhetoric for oral and written communication.* Norwood, N.J.: Ablex.

Underhill, A. 1992. The role of groups in developing teacher self-awareness. *ELT Journal,* 46(1): 71–80.

Vygotsky, L. 1978. *Mind in society: The development of higher psychological processes.* Cambridge: Harvard University Press.

Vygotsky, L. 1986. *Thought and language.* Cambridge, Mass.: MIT.

Wallace, M. 1991. *Training foreign language teachers: A reflective approach.* Cambridge: Cambridge University Press.

Wallace, M. 1998. *Action research for language teachers.* Cambridge: Cambridge University Press.

Weeks, W., P. Pedersen, and R. Brislin. (n.d.) *A manual of structured experiences for cross-cultural learning.* Yarmouth, Maine: Intercultural Press.

Whitehead, J. 1993. *The growth of educational knowledge: Creating your own living educational theories.* Bournemuth, U.K.: Hyde.

Wilson, E. 1999. *Consilience.* London: Abacus.

Zdenek, M. 1985. *The right-brain experience.* London: Corgi.

Zeichner, K., and B. Tabachnich. 1991. Reflections on reflective teaching. In *Issues and practices in inquiry-oriented teacher education,* ed. B. Tabachnich and R. Zeichner. London: Falmer Press.

Zohar, D. 1991. *The quantum self.* London: Flamingo.

Zohar, D., and I. Marshall. 1993. *The quantum society: Mind, physics and a new social vision.* London: Flamingo.